THE EXPERIENCE O

Implications for Teaching and Stu

THE EXPERIENCE OF LEARNING

Implications for Teaching and Studying in Higher Education

Second Edition

EDITED BY

FERENCE MARTON
DAI HOUNSELL
NOEL ENTWISTLE

FOREWORD BY

WILBERT J. McKEACHIE

SCOTTISH ACADEMIC PRESS
EDINBURGH

First published in Great Britain, 1984
Second Edition, 1997
by Scottish Academic Press Limited,
56 Hanover Street, Edinburgh EH2 2DX

ISBN 0 7073 0749 X

Typeset by Trinity Typesetting, Edinburgh and
printed by J. W. Arrowsmith Ltd, Bristol

Contents

Foreword

WILBERT J. MCKEACHIE

Professor Emeritus, University of Michigan

We Americans are terribly provincial on our views of psychology. As contrasted with the pre-World War II period when every psychologist read German and French and knew that familiarity with European journals was essential to being an effective scholar in Psychology, we have now come to read only our own journals, (if any), and to purchase only American books. Our provincialism has had the potentially good consequence of establishing a single language in psychology, English, but it should not excuse Americans from our lack of knowledge of other languages and does not excuse lack of familiarity with scholarly contributions in English not written by Americans. Thus, I want to represent strongly to my fellow countrymen that they will be missing an important contribution to the understanding of teaching and learning if they miss this book written by British and Swedish psychologists.

It would not be fair to the authors if this foreword were to attempt to summarize all of the rich conceptualization found in this volume. Nonetheless, it is important for Americans to realize what this book contains. The authors deal with problems of learning in real educational settings. They bring to bear on these problems both a sophisticated methodology and theoretical positions fully informed by modern cognitive psychology. Their approach offers ways of looking at the phenomena of learning that complement American studies. Unlike many edited books, this book has a focus — research on student learning in higher education. Also, unlike most writing in this area, it involves learning in two different cultures. The common focus of the research methodology and conceptual framework provides insights which ring true not only for Great Britain and Sweden but for North America and other countries as well. In fact, both those concerned about applications of cognitive psychology to education and those concerned about basic understanding of cognition will find useful and interesting ideas in these chapters.

The research approach used is what Marton calls *phenomenography*. Essentially this is a sort of hard nosed phenomenology in which intensive interviews of learners are systematically collected and analyzed. These may then be followed by experiments testing the understanding gained from interviews. The results are not only useful for theory building because their intrinsic relationship to actual experiences of students also offer compelling insights for teachers. Moreover, the book is written in a readable and interesting style that holds the attention both of the expert and of the university teacher who is not an expert in cognitive science. In fact, since the book is about learning from the student's point of view, I would expect that many university students would benefit from the book.

Modern cognitive psychology has stimulated university teachers to give greater attention to the importance of understanding and meaning as contrasted with recognition and reproduction as a goal of learning and higher education. This book gives us not only a great deal of research evidence with respect to the ways in which students achieve understanding but also has clear implications for methods of teaching and testing which help students find meaning — meaning which can be retrieved and used as a basis for further learning and problem solving. Faculty members uniformly think of their courses as contributing to the development of thinking that is more analytic or critical. Yet in practice we often teach in ways that direct our students to rote memorization, and then blame the students for the fact that they have not achieved our objectives.

I have often said in lectures that professors frequently confuse difficulty of a test with high standards of educational value, and that it is easy to make a test difficult without making it a more effective measure of achievement. This book has helped me to see what I was fuzzily describing. It attacks the 'building blocks' conception of knowledge—that knowledge involves knowing more and more details of a particular discipline, such as more historical dates or more historical figures. Test questions are made more difficult as they become more and more peripheral to the phenomenon or as they become narrower in scope, encompassing "very specific details of an event or minor part of a phenomenon". Such a conception of knowledge is frequently portrayed in our short answer and objective test items. Higher education, on the other hand, is generally concerned with introducing conceptions of knowledge involving greater understanding and analytic ability.

At the heart of this book is the notion that students' approaches to learning are affected by their intentions — "students who did not get 'the point' failed to do so simply because they were not looking for it". In short, some students focused on the test in itself — the pages, the words, the reproduction of the textbook, while other students focused upon the author's intentions, the main points, and the conclusions to be drawn. This finding illustrates the value of the methods used by these authors. Our typical input-output models would simply determine that some students had learned the material, and other students had not, but we would not know how these differences in achievement were related to differences in the students' purposes and strategies of learning. "It is the intention to learn from the text which makes people misunderstand it."

Qualitative methods are applied not only to learning from textbooks but also to the experiences of lectures, to essay writing in history and psychology courses, and to analysis of the process used by students in carrying out assigned problem solving tasks. Finally, the approach is applied to the total educational orientation of students toward university life.

As contrasted with my own and other books on teaching and learning, this book is not prescriptive; nonetheless, it is helpful. What the authors do is to illustrate ways in which learning occurs and how learning has been facilitated by teachers. Readers are then left to work out for themselves how the insights may be applied to their own situations. In short, the range and depth of the book represent a major contribution to our understanding of university teaching and learning.

Preface

The scope of this book is both broad and narrow. It is about learning, and contains ideas of fundamental importance to all those who are interested in how people learn. The book has a narrow focus insofar as it presents the results of research from a series of related studies into the way students learn in higher education. Its claim to generality, however, stems from the radical nature of both the research methodology and the emerging conceptual frameworks. It provides a way of understanding student learning which has very direct implications for teachers and students in colleges and universities, and also for psychologists interested in the phenomenon of human learning in an academic context.

The similarities in the types of learning demanded of students attending universities and colleges in different countries make the findings of this research relevant across most educational systems. Or, at least, the effects of any major differences in the systems can be readily inferred from the variety of educational situations described by the authors. Their experiences cover both Swedish and British universities, and both conventional institutions and the Open University with its emphasis on distance learning. The main teaching methods — lectures, tutorials, practical work and comments on returned assignments — will be found throughout tertiary education. The theme of this book is thus of relevance and potential interest to educators in different countries and in different kinds of institution.

The research drew its momentum from ideas developed by Ference Marton and his colleagues Lars-Owe Dahlgren, Lennart Svenssen, and Roger Säljö in the University of Gothenburg which challenged established views both of learning and of research methodology. Those ideas were taken up in Britain by research groups at Lancaster University, Surrey University, Edinburgh University and the Open University and led to a series of projects both funded and as doctoral research, all with a common focus of interest on student learning and with similar use of interviews to collect data and an approach to research later described as phenomenography.

The evidence presented in the book derives mainly from these interviews. Thus there is little in the way of complex statistics which would be off-putting to readers who are not familiar with social science research. Rather the findings are built up through the systematic presentation of representative extracts from interview transcripts, so the learners are speaking directly to the reader about their experiences. Of course, there are conceptual frameworks derived from the data, and these bring in technical terminology. But the new terms are carefully explained, and are often self-explanatory. The book is therefore a research report — it justifies its conclusions carefully on the basis of data which has been systematically collected and analysed — but it is also intended to be accessible to the non-specialist.

Although the structure of the book follows the design for a research monograph or symposium — a general introduction followed by chapters by researchers talking about their own research findings, with more integrative chapters to present an initial framework and a concluding analysis to pull the findings together — the level of writing and the amount of detail presented is intended to make the ideas accessible to a wider audience. There has also been a considerable effort put into creating overall coherence in the monograph. Coherence was easier than usual to obtain because similar theoretical perspectives and research approaches had been adopted by all the contributors. But in addition it was possible to bring the contributors together on two occasions, thanks to financial support from both the Swedish and the British Social Science Research Councils, first to discuss the structure of the book and then to have lengthy and detailed discussions of the draft chapters. The result is a research monograph with a difference: we hope that difference shows.

Since the first edition of this book was published, one of the main ideas it contained has had a substantial influence on both the direction of research into student learning and staff development in higher education. That idea is the distinction between a *deep approach* to learning, through which the student seeks personal understanding, and a *surface approach* where the student is content simply to try to reproduce the information presented during the course. Although deceptively simple, this dichotomy has had a marked impact on the way many academic staff have come to think about their teaching. They have come to realise that the way they teach and assess, directly affects not just how much students learn, but also the quality of that learning. To departments in many parts of the world which are having to demonstrate the quality of their teaching, these research findings convey an important message by inviting them to consider higher education from the student's perspective.

The original research studies were carried out in the 1970s and early 1980s, but their findings are still relevant to the situation in higher education today. For this Second Edition, the introductory chapter has been substantially expanded to provide an overview of the concepts to be introduced in the subsequent chapters, while a more theoretical and technical chapter discussing the inter-relationships between concepts and research methods has been omitted. Most of the authors have taken the opportunity to update or amend their chapters, and four additional chapters have been specially written for this new edition.

When the first edition of the book was published, interest in research on teaching and learning in higher education was still very limited among academic staff in higher education. Since then, the increasing emphasis on quality assurance and quality assessment of teaching has begun to change attitudes. Now the terms 'deep' and 'surface' will be heard not just in staff development workshops, but also in everyday discussions among staff. This book provides the background necessary fully to understand these key concepts, and so be able to use them in thinking about how best to provide more effective teaching which directly supports students in their learning.

The Editors wish to thank Dorothy Entwistle for undertaking the substantial work involved in copy editing this Second Edition.

Contributors

CHARLES ANDERSON is a Lecturer at the Institute for the Study of Education and Society, University of Edinburgh.

LIZ BEATY is Principal Lecturer in the Teaching and Learning Unit, University of Brighton.

LARS-OWE DAHLGREN is Professor of Education at the University of Linköping, Sweden.

ABIGAIL ENTWISTLE is currently working with Fauna and Flora International in Cambridge.

NOEL ENTWISTLE is Bell Professor of Education at the Institute for the Study of Education and Society, University of Edinburgh.

GRAHAM GIBBS is Director of The Oxford Centre for Staff Development at Oxford Brookes University.

VIVIEN HODGSON lectures at the Management School at Lancaster University.

DAI HOUNSELL is Director of the Centre for Teaching, Learning and Assessment at the University of Edinburgh.

DIANA LAURILLARD is Professor of Educational Technology and Pro Vice-Chancellor at the Open University.

FERENCE MARTON is Professor of Education at the University of Gothenburg, Sweden.

ALISTAIR MORGAN is a Senior Lecturer in the Institute of Educational Technology at the Open University

PAUL RAMSDEN is Professor of Higher Education at Griffith University, Brisbane, Australia.

LENNART SVENSSON is Professor of Education at the University of Lund, Sweden.

ROGER SÄLJÖ is Professor of Communication Studies at the University of Linköping, Sweden.

Most of the work reported in the first edition of this book had its origins in three research groups — in Gothenburg (Marton, Dahlgren, Svensson and Säljö), in Lancaster (Entwistle, Hounsell and Ramsden), and at the Open University (Beaty, Gibbs and Morgan), although some of the reports also derive from doctoral research at the University of Surrey (Beaty, Hodgson and Laurillard).

Part I

Background and Basic Concepts

CHAPTER ONE

Contrasting Perspectives on Learning

NOEL ENTWISTLE

Introduction

This book is about the experience of learning as seen from the student's point of view. But in this chapter that experience is examined first from perspectives adopted by other groups — lecturers, psychologists, and educational researchers in an attempt to explore the meaning of learning as it is understood by these different interested groups. The student's perspective will be used in subsequent chapters as a way of developing a new conceptualisation of learning, but always it will be important to recognise the continuing existence of alternative frameworks for understanding learning in higher education.

Each group and, ultimately, each individual, has an interpretation of reality which is in some sense unique. And yet effective communication depends on shared assumptions, definitions, and understanding. Out of this paradox both teachers and researchers struggle to make sense of the contrasting experiences of learning reported by those involved in the process of education. While earlier research tended to use ready-made concepts from psychology and sociology to explain differences in student attainment, the new research reported here develops a set of concepts altogether more accessible to teachers and students and firmly rooted in their common experiences. These concepts provide a radically different perspective on learning which should bring about a better, shared, understanding of learning processes which are currently interpreted very differently by these two groups.

The research focus of this book is higher education. Almost all the detailed evidence in subsequent chapters is drawn from that particular setting, and yet implications, in a general way at least, can be seen more broadly. In every educational system one of the prime considerations of administrators, teachers, and students alike, at each age level, is what we call the outcome of learning — what students can demonstrate of their increases in knowledge and changes in understanding as a result of their experiences in school or college. This book explores what students learn and how that learning takes place.

Educational research can be seen as careful, systematic attempts at achieving a better understanding of the educational process, with the aim of improving its effectiveness. Our task is thus to describe more clearly how learning takes place in higher education, and to point out how teaching and assessment affect the quality of that learning. From these descriptions, teachers should be able to draw their own conclusions about how to facilitate their students' learning.

All the evidence presented in the main body of the book comes from studies carried out either in Sweden or Britain, and yet the similarities in the forms of teaching and learning in higher education across the world suggest that our main message should strike home to lecturers and students in every country. The message, in its simplest form, is that as educators we need to think carefully about the quality of learning in higher education. Much of our current teaching and assessment seems to induce a passive, reproductive form of learning which is contrary to the aims of the teachers themselves. That message, and its elaborations, can be followed throughout the book. It is introduced here as an assertion, but later an impressive array of research evidence, with both logical and empirical analyses will be used to justify it.

Lecturers' Perceptions of Student Learning

If we are interested in the outcome of learning, a sensible starting point is the aims of higher education. We should then examine what is actually achieved in relation to what is intended. What are students expected to learn? Clearly the answer will differ in detail from subject area to subject area, but is there any general consensus? A study at Lancaster University sought to examine educational objectives in higher education by interviewing lecturers. Rather than asking general questions which attract vague answers, the interviewer, Keith Percy, concentrated on the everyday concerns of lecturers and asked about specific course objectives — what differences they found between 'good' and 'poor' students; how they graded examination answers; and how they decided whether their own courses had been successful or not. Out of their comments (Entwistle *et al*, 1971) came an indication of the lecturers' intentions and expectations, and an assessment of how well their students were living up to those expectations.

Most lecturers saw university as having general effects on the quality of students' learning and thinking, and their own specialism as making a distinctive contribution to this educational process. It was considered that university forces students to make

> a great attempt to get to grips with conceptual problems…, (it seeks) to make them think about explanations, … [making] them a bit more self-conscious about their categories … At 'A' level (18 + examination) they learn too much detail — they've no time for thinking.

An economist argued that the study of economics involves a characteristic way of thinking;

> More recently I've come round to the view that economists have acquired a way of looking at the world which is indelible, and even though they may not find themselves in a position where they can use their analytical techniques very consciously, in fact their whole way of treating questions is affected by this kind of training.

Similarly, a philosopher outlined a 'philosophical approach'

> which should bring out and develop the ability to approach questions analytically, … distinguishing very clearly such different questions as the empirical, the evaluative, the historical, and the psychological.

A scientific mode of thinking was described by a psychologist as being concerned with the nature of evidence on which you base argument, a sort of perpetual quest to set forward an argument, and then see what information will support the argument.

Of course, many lecturers stressed the importance of acquiring skills and detailed knowledge. For example, a lecturer in physics had a clear idea of what he and his colleagues were trying to achieve with their students.

We want to develop certain skills in the laboratory ... the ability to design the apparatus necessary to carry out the particular experiments, to get the answers that you wanted to get at and not any other answers, to interpret the numbers that come out of the experiment and analyse them. Secondly, we want to develop mathematical and deductive skills, to allow them to analyse their experiments ... or any other problem. Thirdly, we want — perhaps too much — to cover the entire ground of classical and modern physics so that they have a fairly comprehensive idea of what the entire corpus of knowledge is in the subject — with a fair amount of emphasis on the latest developments so that they can get out into a job knowing what physics is like today.

Other lecturers were more critical of the value of knowledge. They saw background knowledge as an essential prerequisite for thinking critically and imaginatively about their subject, but were often apprehensive about over-emphasising factual knowledge and binding the student too firmly within currently accepted theoretical frameworks.

Most of one's time one is enslaving (the student) to certain techniques and disciplines in order that he shall be accepted as an exponent of that sort of discipline... One must also liberate him from them, enabling him to stand back from them and see that they are a rather arbitrary historical collection of techniques which are not the end of the story... Very few students will actually do this ... (but) one would be doing an injustice to them in not making it clear to them that their path of duty lay not in accepting, but in changing, the subject.

The unifying theme of lecturers' views about the main purposes of university education can be summarised by the term critical thinking — indeed, more than that — what Ashby (1973) has described as post-conventional thinking.

The student moves from the uncritical acceptance of orthodoxy to creative dissent... (In higher education) there must be opportunities for the intellect to be stretched to its capacity, the critical faculty sharpened to the point at which it can change ideas (pp. 147–9).

The thinking and actions indicated by the comments of lecturers can be seen as implying broad, generic skills used in most disciplines and areas of study, although exemplified in rather different ways and with differing emphases in each discipline or subject area. This set of generic skills is, however, no longer considered to be fully adequate for the education of graduates. The Enterprise in Higher Education Initiative in Britain, for example, has identified additional 'personal transferable skills' which are increasingly valued by employers (see

Tate, 1993). These include problem-solving, communication skills, and working effectively with others. These additional skills are required to allow knowledge and understanding to be used appropriately and effectively at work, and in collaboration with others.

In the interviews with lecturers in the 1970s, of course, these additional skills were not mentioned. But there was substantial consensus about the importance of critical thinking, although it was far from clear how this was expected to be achieved through the predominant teaching methods of lectures, tutorials, and practical classes. It was also far from clear that methods of assessment contained the same emphasis on 'critical thinking' that ran through the lecturer's comments on their expectations. In fact, the predominant impression from the descriptions of methods of teaching and assessment was that there was a profound contradiction between lecturers' intentions and what the students achieved. It seemed that lecturers looked for critical thinking, yet taught and assessed conformity in ideas and the acquisition of detailed factual knowledge (Entwistle & Percy, 1974). There may thus be only a tenuous connection between the 'teaching objectives' (what lecturers say they want to do) and their 'teaching activity' (what they actually do) — a lack of relationship between "intention and performance" (Entwistle, Percy & Nisbet, 1971, Vol. 2, Cht. 13, p. 12).

This unrecognised contrast between intent and the effects of teaching is often expressed as a distinction between the formal and the 'hidden' curriculum. Snyder (1971) at MIT pointed out that the formal curriculum, as defined by the staff, demanded originality, problem-solving, independence of thought, and analytic skills. In contrast, the hidden curriculum — the message received implicitly but strongly by students — depended on the teaching methods and assessment procedures, and these encouraged question-spotting and rote memorisation of facts and theories considered important by the teachers. The Lancaster lecturers were, on the whole, not aware of the wide divergence between intent and teaching procedures. Although they were aware that many students showed a disappointingly low level of understanding after three years at university, they also had ready explanations for such disappointing outcomes — explanations which were based on the inadequacies of students.

> There are two kinds of (weak students) really: the downright indolent (or those who put efforts into other than academic work) and ... some who don't understand... (Again there is the student who) is not very well motivated; he takes the courses largely because he likes other courses even less. He may be doing his degree on that basis ... only attending university because there's nothing else more intelligent occurred to him to do.

Out of a depressingly uniform set of comments berating students for their inadequacies of intellect or motivation, only one lecturer pointed out a difficulty in accepting such simple explanations of poor performance.

> The main trouble is unwillingness to get down to work, but having said this, there is no doubt a paradox ... in that at some time in the past, in order for a person to have got here, presumably he had been willing, and something is going on which diminishes this willingness.

The resolution of this paradox will become clear as soon as we look at this situation from the student's viewpoint. But for the moment let us look instead at two other sets of contrasting perspectives. Both the psychologist and the educational researcher have a professional interest in learning, but they have looked at the phenomenon in quite different ways, and made use of a variety of research methodologies. The different questions raised and methods followed produce characterisations of learning which have rather little in common.

Psychological Research on Learning

Research into memory and learning

Teachers look to psychologists for explanations of fundamental principles of learning. It used to be accepted that an understanding of underlying brain mechanisms and functions would have direct implications for the teacher. Now the 'direct' links seem less clear, as we shall see. But much of the early work in experimental psychology involved attempts to uncover general principles of learning, and followed as closely as possible the well-tried research procedures in the physical sciences. To investigate memory, for example, psychologists such as Ebbinghaus tried to avoid the 'distorting' effects of previous knowledge. Scientifically, it was much sounder to see how well people remembered new material. And what better way could there be to ensure that it would be new to every experimental subject than to present nonsense syllables? Thus a whole tradition of memory research was built out of nonsense, but was only much later recognised as such.

The teacher, at least, is intent on helping pupils to build meaning. Early in the development of psychological ideas about learning, William James had argued intuitively for the importance of associations in determining what is remembered. The early experimentalists were able to confirm these introspective impressions of the effects on memory of contiguity (remembering ideas or facts closely associated with each other) and of exercise (repetition). It was also noted that we tend to repeat behaviour which leads to satisfying consequences (law of effect). It was, of course, an age-old principle that behaviour could be controlled by reward and punishment, but Skinner was able to demonstrate how complex sequences of behaviour could be built up in pigeons by systematic linking of behaviours with positive reinforcement (food pellets). Out of the behavioural 'shaping' of pigeons and rats grew a research industry, and a whole educational technology (programmed learning), which put impressive weight behind the importance of immediate reinforcement (through knowledge of results) and of the presentation of increments of knowledge arranged in small sequential steps. Knowledge could thus be efficiently assembled, like a brick wall, out of its component blocks.

Yet the extrapolation from experimental results on the behaviour of animals to general principles of learning in the classroom stretches credibility more than a little. Skinner may have felt justified in the generality of his principles of learning by noting important similarities between learning in animals and humans. But subsequent generations of students and teachers have found this view a wholly inadequate description of teaching and learning. Many have resented the image of the teacher as a 'manipulator of learning', criticised the view of learning as solely the acquisition of information, and found the principles of programmed learning to be of limited value in the classroom.

Intelligence and individual differences

Another important thread in the psychological study of learning has grown out of the early attempts of Spearman and Pearson to investigate individual differences in the speed and efficiency of learning. In common parlance, people who learn fast and well are considered to be 'intelligent'. Intelligence is a hypothetical construct — an inferred concept which can be used as a way of explaining observed differences in intellectual performances. Spearman was able to show that there was, in school children, a general factor 'g' which described a tendency for pupils to show similar levels of performance in different school subjects. In France, Binet had been able to distinguish between normal children and those who were considered to be ineducable, by means of a set of graded intellectual tasks involving memory, knowledge, and reasoning. Allying Pearson's statistical findings to Binet's development of graded sequences of intellectual tasks produced what came to be known as intelligence tests, and from them the IQ or intelligence quotient which provided a ready sorting device to determine the educational futures of generations of children.

Again both a technology and an industry were born and, above all, out of the short-term consistency in IQ scores came beliefs both about its resistance to change and its general validity as an indicator of educational potential. The idea that a single set of tasks could provide a good indicator of 'general intelligence' has been difficult to shift. Its simplicity is appealing. But even the early work of Thurstone on students showed that up to seven 'primary abilities' could be identified — perceptual speed, memory, verbal meaning, spatial ability, numerical ability, inductive reasoning, and verbal fluency. These dimensions emerged from the statistical analysis of psychological tests, but subsequently Gardner (1984) argued for a broader definition of intelligence to include 'multiple intelligences' derived from a whole range of human competencies. He has suggested that we should recognise at least seven distinct intelligences, including linguistic, musical, logical-mathematical, spatial, and bodily-kinaesthetic. His list also includes two forms of personal intelligence, 'intrapersonal' which depends on a 'sense of self' and 'interpersonal' which involves the capacity to 'read' other people's intentions and feelings in a social setting.

Intelligence, it seems, can be viewed as a global or summary variable, containing elements of many subsidiary skills. It is also modifiable, at least within limits. It is largely stable, but importantly variable. Education and home environment can, and do, affect the levels of measured intelligence. And people exhibit more intelligent behaviour in some aspects of their life than in others.

Besides intelligence, other traits have been used to describe relatively stable characteristics of individuals which may affect the speed or efficiency with which they learn. The term motivation has been used to describe the motive power which creates the 'movement' of learning. Unfortunately this crude mechanical analogy implies that the natural state of the human body and brain is at rest. This contradicts experience: differentiated activity and fluctuating awareness is the waking norm of human behaviour. Nevertheless it is still useful to ask about the motive or goal of a person's behaviour, and to question the causes of the particular level and direction of a person's current activities.

In the subsequent psychological literature, several distinct forms of motivation have been described (Entwistle, 1987). Competence motivation describes the positive orientation towards learning created by the repeated experience of successful learning activities. Extrinsic motivation describes the seeking after external reinforcement for learning, from school marks, grades, or qualifications. Intrinsic motivation takes two forms, one in which learning is explained by interest and perceived relevance, and another generally described as achievement motivation, relies on a striving for success which feeds on perceived success and boosted self-confidence.

These forms of motivation are describing learning in terms of traits which are the habitual forms of satisfaction derived by different people from their experiences of learning (see Kozeki, 1984). But they also have negative poles. It is salutary to consider what form of (de)motivation is built up by the repeated experience of failure and humiliation, and to ponder the educational consequence of 'incompetence demotivation' or of having no achievable or satisfying goal in learning. Of course, the occasional experiences of low marks or failure may increase determination, and some anxious people seem to go through their education driven more by a fear of failure than by a hope for success. In other research, fear of failure has been shown to influence the extent to which students are prepared to seek their own personal understanding of what they have been asked to learn (Entwistle, 1988a).

Cognitive structure and processes

Research into human memory has tried to describe how information is processed, coded, and stored. A simple information processing model envisages a short-term, working memory (STM) which sorts out incoming perceptions and relates them to previous knowledge, and a long-term memory (LTM) in which experiences and conceptual knowledge are stored. Psychologists such as Lindsay and Norman (1972) have described how conceptual hierarchies are developed. Their models present the memory as involving logically ordered sets of concepts, stored in terms of increasing generality. But this emphasis on the logical properties of concepts applies mainly to everyday objects whose defining features are readily deduced. Abstract concepts, or those which have no agreed formal definitions, cannot be stored in this way. They are built up from sets of experiences which are only partially shared with others.

Learning thus becomes a matter of the individual construction meaning, and this view of learning (constructivism) has recently become widely accepted within education.

Central to the vision of constructivism is the notion of the organism as 'active' — not just responding to stimuli, as in the behaviourist rubric, but engaging, grappling, and seeking to make sense of things. In particular, learners do not just take in and store up given information. They make tentative interpretations of experience and go on to elaborate and test those interpretations (Perkins, 1992, p.49).

New information has to be interpreted in terms of prior knowledge and concepts which contain shared, but also unique, shades of meaning. And the meaning may also depend on the situation and on shared social conventions. What a student learns can only be what is taught, when the content is limited to facts or formally defined concepts. Otherwise, the student will develop an interpretation of knowledge which contains personal and social 'auras' of meaning which extend beyond what the teacher had in mind. It will be that meaning which the student subsequently will try to communicate in any assessment task.

In much of the writing on educational psychology, a clear distinction is made between rote learning (memorisation) and meaningful learning (Ausubel *et al.*, 1978). Ausubel and his colleagues suggest that students develop learning 'sets' which predispose them to utilise either rote or meaningful learning in tackling academic tasks. But much learning in education takes the form of 'meaningful reception learning' which is of an intermediate form. It is not strictly memorisation, but it seems not to involve the learner in interacting with the information presented.

Learning as personal development

The more recent ideas about constructing personal understanding can be seen to link with earlier ideas described by Carl Rogers (1969). He described human learning out of his own experiences of working with people as both a psychotherapist and a university teacher. He came to believe that significant learning is possible only when the individual has self-confidence in his ability to learn and feels that the experience of learning will be personally rewarding and meaningful. Freedom of self-expression and the teacher's unqualified regard for the student were the linchpins of Rogers' views on education. In his influential book *Freedom to Learn*, he was strongly critical of traditional approaches to teaching which foster competition and provide experiences of failure for many students. He condemned didactic or expository methods, unless they formed part of an entirely different approach to education. Rogers wanted knowledge to be made subsidiary to the process of learning how to learn, because to-day's new ideas become to-morrow's outdated information. And above all he wanted to set the learner free from the type of experiences which crush both curiosity and self-confidence. He also believed that students and teachers should recognise that emotions are an essential part of learning — that is of 'significant, existential' learning, learning which develops personality as well as the intellect.

Not the lifeless, sterile, futile, quickly forgotten stuff which is crammed into the minds of the poor helpless individual tied into his seat by ironclad bonds of conformity. I am talking about LEARNING — the insatiable curiosity which drives the adolescent boy to absorb everything he can see or read about gasoline engines in order to improve the efficiency and speed of his 'hot-rod'... We frequently fail to recognise that much of the material presented to students in the classroom has, for the student, the same perplexing, meaningless quality that the list of nonsense syllables has for us... Thus education becomes the futile attempt to learn material which has no personal meaning. (pp. 3–4).

In contrast Rogers wanted to establish a 'community of learners', free to pursue those ideas which excite them, ideas which have intense personal meaning. He wants, above all,

to free curiosity; to permit individuals to go charging off in new directions dictated by their own interests; to unleash a sense of inquiry; to open everything to questioning and exploration; to recognise that everything is in process of change... [And] the facilitation of (such) significant learning rests upon certain attitudinal qualities which exist in the personal relationship between the facilitator and the learner (pp.105–6).

For Rogers these qualities are 'realness' (the teacher shows authentic feelings such as boredom, interest, anger, or sympathy), 'prizing, acceptance, trust' (of the student's personal and intellectual qualities), and 'empathetic understanding' (the ability to feel how learning seems to the student).

This view of learning has a richness, and immediacy of impact, which is lacking from the mainstream psychological research in learning. It also seems to be more closely related to the aims of higher education as indicated by the lecturers' comments on what types of learning they expected of students. But the distinction between learning as the acquisition of discrete packages of information, and as a change in the student's conceptions of himself and the world around him, recurs in the research literature and throughout this book. Both views of learning are strongly felt and vigorously defended.

Educational research on student learning

With the exception of the work reported in the last section, psychological research on learning has been carried out in a laboratory setting or has made use of artificial or over-simple learning materials. Even Rogers' ideas derive mainly from a clinical setting. Attempts at applying the theories derived from this research directly to classroom situations have not been particularly successful. It is now recognised that psychological theories must have 'ecological validity' — that is, the theories must be derived from the settings to which they are to be applied. Otherwise there can be little confidence placed in the utility of the theory. Educational research workers have also approached student learning using contrasting perspectives and methodologies. Here, the clearest distinction is between studies which have sought to predict subsequent academic performance and those which have attempted to describe students' experiences of higher education. In moving from one focus to the other there is also an important shift in research paradigm which is of particular significance in understanding the studies reported in subsequent chapters. This paradigm shift is thus presented as a separate section.

Selection and prediction studies

Educational research has provided a great deal of evidence about the factors associated with student learning. In the 1960's and early 1970's the main research interest was in selection and prediction. Was it possible to improve the accuracy of selection for higher education by using head-teachers' ratings or tests of academic aptitude? To what extent could degree class be predicted from measurements made during the first year of studying? In the United States the Scholastic Aptitude Test had proved effective as a way of selecting students for universities and colleges. Substantial correlations between test scores and college marks have regularly been reported (e.g. Scannell, 1960). However, attempts to use a similar test in Britain proved unsuccessful, with scores on aptitude tests adding little to the accuracy of selection based on entry qualifications alone (Choppin et al., 1973). Head-teachers' ratings of pupils showed somewhat higher correlations with degree class, but Nisbet and Welsh (1966) found that teachers' ratings failed to discriminate among the crucial group of students with minimum entry qualifications where they might have been most useful.

The search for other determinants of academic performance led other researchers to look towards the different forms of motivation described earlier. Entwistle and Wilson (1977) reported the use of cluster analysis to demonstrate the existence of groups of students with contrasting forms of motivation. Two main clusters were described as having 'fear of failure', and 'self-confident, hope for success'; other types of students were described as 'radical and extraverted', and 'idle and unmotivated'. The first three groups all achieved above average degree results, while the last group did very badly indeed.

Wankowski (Raaheim & Wankowski, 1981) has argued that students who come to university for clearly defined reasons and with distinct vocational goals, are more likely to be successful than students with diffuse, unarticulated goals. Wankowski is describing a form of extrinsic motivation, while attempts at measuring students' motivation have more commonly concentrated on the competitive form of motivation described as academic achievement motivation. Although correlations with degree success have still been quite low, motivation scales do seem to supplement prediction from academic aptitude tests (Entwistle & Wilson, 1977).

Perhaps the best-known early inventory of study habits and attitudes was devised by Brown and Holtzman (1966) who reported encouraging correlations with grade-point average. Work on study habits indicates, above all, that organised study methods and promptness in completing assigned work are associated with high grades. More recent research has associated organised study with both a strategic approach to studying and to achievement motivation, and it is again found to correlate with academic achievement (Entwistle, 1988a).

In an Australian study, Pond (1964) compared the comments made by contrasting groups of students. The 'high-achievers' reported that they organised their studying and time allocations, worked during free periods, decided on priorities and tried to improve their study techniques. The 'low-achievers' did not consider organised study to be important. Their comments suggested a transfer of blame for their poor performance. They tended to be critical of facilities, mentioning too much chatter, over-crowding, or scarcity of books. Presumably better-organised students modify their study strategies to overcome any defects in the academic environment and so maintain a more positive attitude to their studies.

Although such studies have demonstrated relationships with academic achievement, this whole line of research has been criticised for failing to suggest how the underlying traits lead to the learning outcomes described. As a result, there is little indication of what might be done to improve the situation. There is also a tendency to use a deficiency model of student behaviour, in which the blame for inadequate academic performance is attributed wholly to the student. It has taken an entirely different research paradigm to present the situation more fairly, as an interaction between the characteristics of the student and the experiences provided by the institution. The changed methodology involves looking at the situation from the student's perspective using interviews and observations and qualitative, interpretative analysis.

An alternative research paradigm

The research which has grown out of prediction studies and that derived from students' experiences differ not just in the methodology used: there is a more fundamental philosophical division (Entwistle, 1974). Quantitative methods imply reductionism and tend to produce formal or mechanical models which embody assumptions about fixed paths of causality. In contrast, the alternative qualitative paradigm involves approaches to research rooted in phenomenology which derive from a direct exploration of students' experiences of learning. The traditional research paradigm involves explaining student behaviour from the outside, as a detached, objective observer. The alternative approach seeks an empathetic understanding of what is involved in student learning derived from students' descriptions of what learning means to them. It involves a shift not just of methodology, but of perspective.

Returning to one of the comments made by lecturers about students' lack of achievement, this switch of perspective can be illustrated quite dramatically. Remember, the lecturer had seemed puzzled by the apparent lack of motivation.

> The main trouble is unwillingness to get down to work, but having said this, there is no doubt a paradox ... in that at some time in the past, in order for a person to have got here, presumably he had been willing, and something is going on which diminishes this willingness.

When students were interviewed (Entwistle, 1975), they saw no paradox. A reversal of perspective provides an immediate, if uncomfortable, insight for the lecturer.

> So often are students bored by uninspired teaching or disenchanted by badly taught material. While university lecturers are undoubtedly knowledgeable, they are totally untrained and unexamined in the art of communication... The completely incorrect assumption is that anyone with a good degree will automatically be able to impart this knowledge to others.

As already suggested, the quantitative tradition involves an attribution of responsibility, at least by implication. It assigns blame for a poor academic performance solely to the student without asking how the student came to lose motivation or interest. Finally, it ignores the responsibilities of the institution and the teacher for the outcomes of learning. The new research paradigm switches perspective and so provides insights for the teacher which are not only firmly rooted in real-life situations in higher education, but are also more illuminating. They present a description of student learning from an unusual perspective — that of the student — and yet lead to important implications for teaching as well as for studying.

This new approach to educational research was introduced into the British literature in an influential paper by Parlett and Hamilton (1972). Educational research was criticised for following too slavishly a paradigm which had proved successful in the physical sciences — the hypothetico-deductive method. It was argued that the success of this paradigm with inanimate matter, or with plants and animals, was not a good reason to believe it would be equally applicable to human behaviour — which is essentially purposeful. Parlett and Hamilton criticised what they termed the 'agricultural-botanical' experimental paradigm in educational research, in which research designs incorporated a belief that students react to contrasting educational treatments as consistently as plants react to fertilisers. They contrasted the traditional research paradigm with the procedures used by social anthropologists, who observe and question people in different cultures in an attempt empathetically to understand their customs and beliefs. They subsequently used the term 'illuminative evaluation' to apply to research designs which sought to evaluate educational innovations from within. The more general approach — investigating a variety of educational situations from within — is the alternative paradigm which is used almost exclusively in the studies reported in the following chapters.

Research into students' experiences of higher education

The specific research methodologies adopted in our studies vary to some extent, depending on the different problems tackled. But they have important similarities which will be introduced in the next section. They also have an affinity to two well-known studies carried out in the United States by Howard Becker and his colleagues (1968) and by William Perry (1970). In *Making the Grade*, Becker entered as fully as possible into the students' experiences of learning through participant observation, attending classes and becoming involved in the students' social life. Their approach was very much that of the social anthropologist who takes detailed field-notes of the information provided and observations made. Their main finding, as the title of the book suggests, was that students' academic life was dominated by assessment demands. Students' activities could be seen largely as coping ploys designed to achieve the grades necessary to make progress through the university system.

One problem with Becker's study was that its focus was broad — on the totality of students' social and academic life, with little concern for the content of what was being studied. William Perry, working as a student counsellor at Harvard, had a different focus of concern. He was interested specifically in students' intellectual and ethical development. In particular, he was struck by a qualitative change in students' thinking during their years at college — a change from dualistic thinking to contextual relativistic reasoning. Students seemed to move from a belief that all questions have simple answers which are either right or wrong, to a gradual recognition that few problems, particularly in real life, have simple solutions. Even where facts are agreed, personal interpretations lead to differing conclusions, making relativism the rule rather than the exception. And the strength to make a commitment to a personal interpretation derived from relevant evidence became the final stage of the development scheme (Perry, 1970, 1981).

Although Perry's students did discuss their experiences on specific courses, the general tenor of the discussions and the interest of the researcher led to categories being identified which described general intellectual development. A study in Edinburgh came closer to the focus of the research reported in this monograph. Miller and Parlett (1974) applied the principles of illuminative evaluation to an investigation of students' reactions to the assessment procedures in a small number of departments, carefully chosen to cover the range of different practices then in use. These researchers followed Becker's procedures in part, using participant observation, but also made use of semi-structured interviews and questionnaires. Analysis of the interviews involved coding their transcripts into themes or content areas which were analysed separately. The researchers' interpretations of the emerging themes were cross checked against the impressions of a small panel of independent judges, but even so Miller and Parlett were conscious of criticisms which might be made by researchers unfamiliar with this paradigm.

> Some will argue — even with this degree of methodological circumspection — that what we did falls short of the highest standards of rigour in social science, being dependent — as it certainly is — on personal interpretation of data, much of which cannot be made public. Our answer is two-fold. First, one must recognise that many of the supposed ills of 'subjectivity' are not confined to research of the type described here: even the most rigorous statistical survey study requires constant exercise of human judgement — e.g. in what questionnaire items to include; in what statistical comparisons will be made and how; and, most of all, in what light the findings are presented or summarised for others. This is not always acknowledged... Finally, there is, of course, one powerful check on the study's validity—arguably the most powerful of all. Does the study present a 'recognisable reality' to those who read it?" (Parlett and Hamilton, 1972, p. 12).

Miller and Parlett focused their analysis mainly on students' experiences of the assessment procedures, and differentiated students' comments on the basis of 'cue-consciousness'—the extent to which students recognised or actively sought out 'cues' from staff to help them guide their attempts to play the assessment game. Cue-seekers

> button-holed staff about the exam questions; sought them out over coffee; made a point of discovering who their oral examiner was, what his

interests were and, most of all, deliberately tried to make a good impression on staff (p. 52).

Cue-conscious students were aware that there were cues and that these were important, but made no attempt to approach staff directly. The final category was 'cue-deaf' — a group of students who did not believe that marks were affected by the impressions made on staff. They saw the assessment system as essentially objective and not open, in any way, to being influenced by extraneous factors.

Miller and Parlett's approach to research comes close, in methodology and 'spirit', to the research to be discussed in this book. Our data have been derived mainly from fairly open interviews with students discussing their experiences of learning. Some of the learning has been in experimental settings, but using realistically complex learning materials. These are termed 'naturalistic' settings — they resemble normal studying in important respects, but retain elements of experimental control and manipulation. Other studies have been carried out in 'natural settings' in which students have been asked questions about their everyday experiences in general or about particular pieces of academic work they are tackling at that time. This latter set of studies follows closely the procedure outlined by Miller and Parlett, and shows a similar concern with the context of learning.

It is important, in this alternative approach to research, to keep in mind the implications of the change in perspective which shifts attention from the teacher's or the researcher's view to that of the student. This shift is crucial in ensuring that the explanations of student learning not only have ecological validity within the real university or college context, but also to enable the researcher to make an interpretation of the findings which does justice to the totality of the students' own experiences. To reach this empathetic understanding, the alternative research paradigm has become essential. Its advantages should become clear from the 'recognisable reality' which is portrayed in each of the subsequent chapters.

Concepts and Categories Describing Learning and Studying

The chapters which follow report a series of research studies on differing aspects of learning and studying in higher education which together help to portray *The Experience of Learning* from the student's perspective. Although all academic staff have experienced this type of learning, it is surprising how rapidly that experience seems to fade once the role of teacher is taken on. There are thus substantial advantages in reminding staff about this perspective, which leads to the important implications for teaching discussed in the final chapter. In seeking to describe the differing aspects of learning and studying, the previous chapters all introduce categories and concepts. Although there are a substantial number of these, they can be seen together as a coherent set. They are therefore introduced here as a way of suggesting connections between the various chapters.

The concepts can be seen as varying in their breadth. Some of them are of considerable generality, while others refer more specifically to one or other study task or teaching method. The two most general concepts have been labelled *learning orientations* and *conceptions of learning*. Students coming into higher education differ in their reasons for doing so — their learning orientation (Chapter 5). Some have a mainly *vocational* orientation; for others the orientation may be more *academic, personal,* or *social*. Although all students have mixed motives, it has proved helpful to describe the balance between these motives, and the extent to which students have an extrinsic or intrinsic interest in the content of the courses they are taking. These different types of interest in the course affect ways of studying.

Students also come into higher education with differing conceptions of learning (Chapter 3). From their previous educational experiences, students may see learning as mainly a matter of acquiring information and *reproducing* it accurately as required by the teacher. Alternatively they may believe that learning depends on *transforming* information in the process of reaching personal understanding. With this conception of learning, assessment involves the necessity of thorough explanation.

The conception of learning seems to have a strong developmental component. Students fresh from school often see learning in narrow reproductive terms, but going through higher education their conception broadens as they recognise the importance of developing their own understanding of course material. This developmental aspect is brought out clearly in the case studies reported in Chapter 14, where it is seen also in terms of growing self-confidence. Such self-confidence often seems to depend on the quality of the relationship with a tutor (Chapter 12) and so draws attention to crucial emotional and social components of learning.

The term 'conception' also has been used to describe a general understanding of the discipline or subject area — acquiring, for example, a conception of history — and as general way of thinking about how to write essays by showing differences in the ways in which students organise them as, for example, *argument, viewpoint,* or *arrangement* (Chapter 7). The importance of the way in which students organise their ways of thinking about academic material is also seen in relation to the nature of study skill (Chapter 4), and revision (Chapter 9). Finally, the term 'conception' has been used even more narrowly to describe the way in which a student comes to understand a particular topic within the syllabus — for example, a conception of force in Newtonian mechanics.

The broad distinction between conceptions of learning as involving reproducing as opposed to transforming can also be seen clearly when it comes to looking at specific tasks. The original work which inspired most of the work described in this book was carried out by a research group in Gothenburg led by Ference Marton. He decided to investigate one of the commonest academic tasks — reading academic articles — using a naturalistic experiment in which students were asked to read an article in their own time and to be ready to answer questions on it afterwards. The analysis looked, first, at the levels of understanding that students had reached after reading the article, and then sought to account for the qualitative differences in understanding that they found in terms of the way in which the task had been tackled.

The researchers also described different categories of learning outcome (understandings of the article) which had distinct relationships among each other. This apparent structure in the variety of individual learning outcomes was called the *outcome space* (Chapter 2). These qualitative variations in understanding were subsequently explained in terms of a combination of the intention that the student had in starting the task and the process used to carry it out. Some students read the text by concentrating on trying to learn discrete bits of information in an *atomistic* fashion, while others were more concerned in a *holistic* manner to make sense of the article as whole (Chapter 4). What proved crucial, however, was the intention. As Marton and Säljö concluded from analysing the transcripts of interviews (Chapter 3),

> all our readings and rereadings, our iterations and reiterations, our comparisons and groupings, finally turned into an astonishingly simple picture. We had been looking for the answer to the question of why the students had arrived at those qualitatively different ways of understanding the text as a whole. What we found was that *the students who did not get 'the point' failed to do so simply because they were not looking for it.* The main difference we found in the process of learning concerned whether the students *focused on the text itself or on what the text was about: the authors intention, the main point, the conclusion to be drawn* (original emphasis).

Originally, this distinction was described in terms of differing 'levels of processing', but recognising that it was the distinctive intention which led to these differing processes, the term *approach to learning* was subsequently adopted. The crucial distinction in the ways students tackled the reading task was captured in the terms *deep* and *surface* approaches to learning. And later research showed how the approach depended on the student's purpose in reading and on conceptions of everyday knowledge (Chapter 6).

In these experiments, students had expected questions on the article after reading it, but they had no idea what kinds of question they would be. In that situation, some students concentrated on surface 'question spotting', while others looked below the surface for the author's meaning. In another series of naturalistic experiments, Gordon Pask and his colleagues investigated how students went about learning when they were required to understand. In that situation, a deep approach was obligatory, and yet Pask found that students still differed in the ways they tackled the task. Some students, right from the start, tried to see how the task fitted into a more global, overall picture, while others preferred to build up their understanding step by step through concentrating, first, on procedures and details. Pask saw these as contrasting *styles of learning* — *comprehension learning* which involved the broad overview and using a 'holist' learning strategy, and *operation learning* which depended on a narrower focus and a 'serialist' strategy. Full understanding, or the effective solution of problems, would often depend on an alternation between comprehension and operation learning (Chapter 8), and where that alternation was carried out flexibly and appropriately, students were said to have a *versatile* learning style, which is essentially equivalent to a fully deep process of learning.

TABLE 1.1
Defining features of approaches to learning

Deep Approach   *Transforming*
Intention — to understand ideas for yourself   **by**

Relating ideas to previous knowledge and experience
Looking for patterns and underlying principles

Checking evidence and relating it to conclusions
Examining logic and argument cautiously and critically

Becoming actively interested in the course content

Surface Approach   *Reproducing*
Intention — to cope with course requirements   **by**

Studying without reflecting on either purpose or strategy
Treating the course as unrelated bits of knowledge
Memorising facts and procedures routinely

Finding difficulty in making sense of new ideas presented
Feeling undue pressure and worry about work

Strategic Approach   *Organising*
Intention — to achieve the highest possible grades   **by**

Putting consistent effort into studying

Finding the right conditions and materials for studying
Managing time and effort effectively

Being alert to assessment requirements and criteria
Gearing work to the perceived preferences of lecturers

The distinction between deep and surface approaches to learning was found in a naturalistic experiment in which the outcome of learning did not 'count' for assessment. Subsequent research looked at learning within its natural setting, and there the quality of studying depended crucially on both teaching and assessment. Students have their own *study contract* (Chapter 5) which decides how much effort they will put into different aspects of their studying, and the influence of assessment led to a third category of approach — *strategic* — in which the intention was to achieve the highest possible grades, while the process depended on cue seeking, well organised study methods, and effective time management (Chapter 13). Table 1.1, above, lists the defining features of the three approaches to learning and studying that have emerged from the studies making up this book, and from other research. These approaches have become central to subsequent research on studying and the development of more effective teaching (see Gibbs, 1992, 1994a).

Different types of assessment seem also to encourage either deep or surface approaches, with essay questions or problems encouraging a deep approach, but only if the questions set demand the demonstration of personal understanding. Some students seem satisfied with a *form of understanding* which is heavily dependent on structures provided in lectures, while other students concentrate on constructing their own individual, tightly organised *knowledge objects* or understandings experienced in a quasi-sensory way (Chapter 9).

The quality of teaching also influences the approach to learning. Some lecturers seem to be able to provide students with a *vicarious experience of relevance*, which evokes a deeper approach to the course (Chapter 10). Recently, there has been considerable discussion of the ways in which the new information technology can be used to support a deep approach to learning (Chapter 11). And, similarly, tutors can provide through tutorial discussion groups the right balance between *encouragement* and *challenge* which both socialises the student into the ways of thinking characteristic of the discipline and also encourages the development of personal understanding (Chapter 12). The context of learning (Chapter 13) describes the effects of certain aspects of teaching and assessment on the approaches to learning adopted by students in a particular course or department. These contrasting approaches then affect the level of understanding which students reach and also the extent to which they develop the personal transferable skills increasingly demanded by employers. Overall, the research findings provide a holistic view of how skill in learning and conceptions of learning develop (Chapters 4 and 14). They also show how the learning environment can be managed so as to encourage the deep approach which is an essential prerequisite for high quality learning (Chapter 15).

The Research Methods

As there is considerable similarity in the methods of collecting and analysing data used in the following chapters, a general description of the approach is given here. Almost all the studies have used interviews with students to explore particular aspects of learning and studying. These interviews are based on what might loosely be called a semi-structured interview schedule. But that description would imply a greater degree of researcher control than was typically involved. A list of issues to cover the main areas of interest was always prepared in advance, but the studies differed in the extent to which a fairly strict order and form of questions was used. In interviews with students, it is often better to follow the line the interview is taking and bring in questions as they become appropriate, rather than following a predetermined sequence. The style of interviewing may also be rather different from the research interview as usually recommended. There is great advantage to be gained in interviewing students by allowing the interview to develop as a natural conversation and a discussion, although guided by a pre-determined framework. Introducing set questions often inhibits the development of ideas, and seems to encourage short, unelaborated answers. Where the interviewer contributes to the effort to explore the student's interpretation of experiences, much fuller descriptions are provided. Of course, the interviewer has to act as a neutral foil to the developing explanations and not present ideas or opinions, but within that constraint a more interactive style does seem to work best for the purposes of this particular type of interview.

With the permission of the students, the interviews are tape recorded and the tapes transcribed in full. Analysis involves repeated reading of both the overall transcripts of individual students and comparable sections from all the students. The structure of the interview schedule will to some extent determine the themes which are found in the transcripts, but with this style of interviewing there are also additional themes brought up by the students themselves. Once the main themes are decided, extracts from individual interviews can be allocated to those themes. Analysis of the extracts leads to the identification of concepts and categories, which are then exemplified and delimited through extracts carefully chosen to bring out the full range and meaning of each category. The categories usually go through substantial modification in an attempt to find the clearest and most parsimonious way of describing the main aspects of the experiences reported by the students. So, the analyses are necessarily iterative, and concepts and categories evolve gradually, as their meanings become clearer. The categories are analytic. They are not used to label individual students; rather they allow similarities and differences between students to be more precisely and uniformly described. Several of the studies have concentrated on both the content of what is learned and the process by which it is learned. The emphasis on content is important, and subsequently became the main focus of a style of research which built on the methodology developed by the Gothenburg research group. Marton has described this approach as *phenomenography* (Marton, 1994) and a wide range of studies has been reported which indicates how different individuals conceptualise academic topics and their experiences of more general phenomena.

It is exceptionally difficult to report findings from this type of research in a fully convincing manner. To provide a full description of the categories identified necessitates the presentation of the whole range of quotations covering the delimiting instances. Only in extensive research reports is this possible (e.g. Svensson, 1976; Laurillard, 1978; Taylor, 1983; Säljö, 1982; Entwistle and Ramsden, 1983; Hounsell, 1984.). In the chapters that follow, readers are generally referred to reports which contain the full range of extracts from the interviews. All that can be provided here are illustrations of typical comments. It should, however, be recognised that these extracts are only selections from the full body of evidence on which the descriptive categories rest.

In Chapter 13, an additional methodology is reported. The description of the three approaches to learning and studying led to the development of an *Approaches to Studying Inventory* — a questionnaire with groupings of similar items which produces scores on a series of scales. These dimensions describing studying were chosen to measure generalised forms of the concepts emerging from the interview studies. Statistical analysis of the students' responses later suggested that several concepts could be linked together into broader groupings described as *study orientations*. A *meaning orientation* brought together deep approach, comprehension learning and intrinsic motivation. *Reproducing orientation* included surface approach, syllabus-boundness and fear of failure, while *achieving orientation* linked strategic approach, organised studying and achievement motivation. This inventory, in one of several forms which have been used (Entwistle & Tait, 1990; Meyer, 1991; Tait & Entwistle, 1996), has been used in a wide range of studies and provides a good indicator at least of the dominant approaches to studying used by individual students within a particular course. Several other inventories have also been developed for this purpose; their effectiveness has recently been critically assessed by Biggs (1993).

The Structure of the Book

This introductory chapter of Part I was intended to provide a historical review of studies on student learning, and to indicate the range of concepts which are to be introduced in subsequent chapters. The remainder of this section focuses on these basic concepts in more detail, with three chapters written by members of the original research team from Gothenburg and a further chapter introducing the concept of learning orientations. Part II looks at four different types of academic task — reading, essay-writing, problem-solving, and revising for examinations, although each chapter also relates these tasks to more general aspects of student learning. Part III looks at different forms of teaching and how these affect the quality of student learning. Starting with specific methods — lectures, multimedia, and discussion groups or tutorials, it moves on to consider the whole context in which teaching, learning and assessment takes place, and students' experiences of this context. The final chapter in this section brings together ideas from the earlier chapters to suggest how staff can reconceptualise teaching in ways which recognise the importance of the whole range of student activities contributing to the quality of understanding students reach. The emphasis is not on innovative *methods,* but on a new way of thinking about how teaching influences learning. Ultimately, teaching methods matter less than how students come to learn, and that theme recurs throughout the chapters.

CHAPTER TWO

Learning Conceptions and Outcomes

LARS-OWE DAHLGREN

The Quantitative Conception of Knowledge

One of the longest-running programmes on Swedish television is a series called *Double or Quits*, which was modelled on similar quiz programmes in the United States and Britain. Below are some examples from one of the programmes:

Which nations were involved in the battle of Lizza in 1866? (from Maritime History).

In Chopin's manuscript of the *Preludes* and in the original German edition, he dedicates them to Joseph Kessler. The first French and English editions however are dedicated to another contemporary of Chopin's. Whom? (from Chopin and his Music).

Questions of this kind are typical of those put to laymen or experts on many radio or television programmes. Since those who take part in the Double or Quits programmes are experts in their chosen subjects, however, the questions asked are ones which the man in the street could not be expected to answer. Yet regardless of their level of difficulty, the questions are all similar in structure in that they demand a brief answer which takes the form of the name of a person or a place, a year when something occurred, a technical term, and so on. Seldom if ever are there questions asking, for example, why something happened.

Conceptions of knowledge form a very important component of what we call the cultural basis of a society. In its purest and most tangible form knowledge is observable in the educational system. The point in presenting the excerpts from the TV-programme, however, was to illustrate that the dominating conception of knowledge is also visible elsewhere. We find signs of an identical conception in informal discussions with adults who lack personal experience of upper-secondary or higher education. When asked, for instance, what they think university students of mathematics or history are engaged in, some will answer in a way that may make professional mathematicians or historians smile, but which nevertheless reveals a conception that is probably very widespread among people in general. Thus it is not uncommon for people to imagine that university students of mathematics are working on immensely difficult calculations, that they are subtracting or multiplying enormously large numbers or unbelievably small fractions. Students of history or professional historians are likewise described as persons who know "a hell of a lot of history", that is, they know not only the year of an important historical event, but also the precise date. Further, a sophisticated historian also has to know not only the prominent historical figures, but also their relatives and the year, date and place of their birth.

As well as appearing ingenuous, these answers tell us something about the way experience of schooling influences our way of apprehending knowledge. It is, however, also self-evident that if one lacks any insight into the qualitative change that the content of studies undergoes at more advanced levels one makes a linear—and horizontal—extrapolation from what is known into the unknown.

A comparison between the questions put in the *Double or Quits* programme and the answers given by people with only a basic education reveals that they are strongly related to each other. None of them indicates a qualitative change in knowledge from trivial to advanced levels. The *Double or Quits* questions are basically of the same kind at the beginning and at the end of the game even though they have become progressively more difficult. The difference that can be observed is that the questions become more and more <u>peripheral</u> to the phenomenon in question, e.g. knowing the name of a person to whom Chopin dedicated a particular composition must be regarded as being of minor interest compared to understanding the structure of the music.

Difficult questions in these contexts are also <u>narrower</u> than "easy" ones, in that they deal with very specific details of an event or minor parts of a phenomenon. This difference between what is trivial and what is advanced is to a great extent preserved when we move into the world of the educational system.

The measurement of knowledge has as long a history as the educational system as a whole. Over the years a number of ways of approaching this problem have been tried, involving both the more technical aspects of educational measurement as well as attempts at more thoroughgoing re-evaluations. Yet if we compare the present state of the art with the past, irrespective of what level of the educational system we refer to, none of the basic characteristics of test items has changed in any dramatic way. There are also very obvious parallels between the demands put on students and on contestants in quiz programmes. These are probably at their most visible in questions representing so-called objective tests, which came into frequent use from the early sixties onwards. Some examples taken from various subjects are given below:

(A) The capital of Albania is:
1. Belgrade
2. Tirana
3. Lisbon
4. Lagos

(B) Relate the following South America countries to the product which is their most important export:

1. Venezuela	a. Copper
2. Chile	b. Coffee
3. Brazil	c. Oil

(C) Complete the sentence below by filling in the missing information:
The Swedish King Gustav II Adolf was killed in the battle of
.... in a long war between Sweden and ....which
ended with the ....peace treaty in the year ....

Many teachers will probably recognise their own way of constructing examination test items in these examples. They will also be aware of the reasons why questions are presented in that form, and to a large extent these reasons are simply pragmatic. Test items should be easy to construct, to answer, and to mark.

A less obvious reason for this form of question is that it is symptomatic of a *conception of knowledge* which has a long tradition in education as well as in quiz programmes. This conception, which was introduced in Chapter 1, can be characterised as *quantitative* and *reproductive*. The degree of difficulty sought is achieved by formulating questions which refer to low-frequency, peripheral and narrow information. Generally speaking, neither understanding nor analytic ability is required of the respondent. That would create problems of judgement for the teacher or the compere of the quiz programme. It is much easier if answers are recognisably right or wrong.

This widely held and culturally deep-rooted view of knowledge is found in the study of Perry (1970) which was described in Chapter 1. Perry found freshmen students generally to have a *dualistic* conception of knowledge indicated by the expectation that higher education would provide an opportunity to learn to discriminate between true and false, between right and wrong. Many of the students had later abandoned this conception in favour of a *relativistic* one. The students had recognised that, to a large extent, phenomena are described and explained in different ways even in academic textbooks or by different teachers. The solution to this pluralistic world of competing explanation lies in a *personal commitment* whereby students take individually distinctive interpretative stances in deciding how to make sense of central phenomena in their field of study.

Our earlier discussion about the quantitative conception of knowledge suggests that the lower stages of the educational system may be, to a large extent, responsible for reinforcing a dualistic conception of learning.

Traditional Psychological Experiments

As we have already seen in Chapter 1, experiments in the psychology of learning have relied extensively on learning materials which have a low degree of meaningfulness. Since the underlying aim has been to arrive at a description of the process of learning in general, this choice has been justified on methodological as well as theoretical grounds. Hence there is seldom any description of the outcome of learning other than in purely quantitative terms, thus reinforcing that reproductive conception of knowledge. We can see this clearly in Hilgard and Bower's *Theories of Learning*, an authoritative textbook which was first published in 1948 and had reached its fifth edition by 1981. A careful examination of the subject index yields few references to *knowledge*. The most significant entry directs us to the following passage:

A strong emphasis within Gagné's analysis is upon the structure of knowledge, an important supplement to principles of learning whenever a practical instructional task is under consideration.

What is explicitly stressed here is the <u>process</u> of learning. Precisely what the subjects are asked to learn is seen as a problem to be considered elsewhere within the separate domain of instruction.

There is an additional reason why so little is said about the outcome of learning in most literature in the field. In accordance with the research tradition which evolved in the natural sciences, it has become the dominant paradigm of the social sciences to reduce the descriptions of complex phenomena to a minimum number of dimensions. 'Intelligence' or 'learning capacity' is one such dimension that is considered to be of great importance in describing human functioning. For reasons primarily of experimental design, however, such a dimension has to be content neutral, which means that the content of a learning task has the status of a series of examples which are of little interest in themselves.

Against the background of this view of learning it is also easier to understand why certain materials came to be widely used in empirical studies of learning. Nonsense syllables or, more recently, narrative or descriptive texts specially written for the experiments are essentially homogeneous. Each segment of the material is of equal value, and so the likelihood that any one segment will be recalled in a subsequent retention test is no greater than that of any other. Take the following example, taken from Thorndike (1977):

> Circle Island is located in the middle of the Atlantic Ocean, north of Ronald Island. The main occupations on the island are farming and ranching. Circle Island has good soil, but few rivers and hence a shortage of water. The island is run democratically. All issues are decided by a majority vote of the islanders. The governing body is a senate, whose job is to carry out the will of the majority. Recently, an island scientist discovered a cheap method of converting salt water into fresh water. As a result, the island farmers wanted to build a canal across the island, so that they could use water from the canal to cultivate the island's central region. Therefore, the farmers formed a "Pro-canal Association" and persuaded a few senators to join. The Pro-canal Association put the construction idea to the vote. All the islanders voted. The majority voted in favour of construction. The senate, however, decided that the farmers' proposed canal was ecologically unsound. The senators agreed to build a smaller canal that was two feet wide and one foot deep. After starting construction on the smaller canal, the islanders discovered that no water would flow into it. Thus the project was abandoned. The farmers were angry because of the failure of the canal project. Civil war appeared inevitable.

The performance of a subject in a learning experiment using this text would be judged in terms of the sum of the various questions which could be derived from the text, such as: Where is Circle Island situated? What are the main occupations? Why was the canal built? and so on. An alternative way of testing retention would be to ask students to recount the story and mark the number of correct statements included. In both cases the result is a measure of the degree to which the precise wording of the text is remembered. Thus the degree of isomorphy between the stimulus (the text) and the response (its retention) has been the chief interest of learning researchers.

If a similar text were to be used in an educational setting, the measurement of the learning outcome would probably be of the same kind. Even if a task such as "Write a short essay about Circle Island" were assigned, the judgement would probably be based on a scrutiny of how many items from the text had been included in the essay. Consider, however, the following excerpts from an undergraduate textbook (Samuelson, 1973 p. 14):

> If all farmers work hard and nature co-operates in producing a bumper crop, total farm income may <u>fall</u>, and probably will.

> Attempts by individuals to save more during a depression may lessen the total of the community's saving.

These two sentences are taken from one of the most widely used university textbooks in Economics. If a group of students were asked to explain why the sentences are correct, even though they appear to be false, the probability of a correct answer would be highly related to whether the students had <u>understood</u> the principles of Economics that could be applied. It is, however, still the case that a typical test question based on these statements would be of the form "Name the principle in Samuelson's first chapter which is exemplified in these two statements". A question of that kind would not enable a teacher to judge which students had really understood the meaning of the examples.

A Qualitative Conception of Learning

It is obvious from this comparison of different kinds of texts — and of different purposes in reading a text — that prose learning is not an homogeneous phenomenon. Psychological research, in its attempt to investigate learning processes in a 'pure' form, has restricted its definition of learning. By using materials with little or no inherent meaning, such experiments describe and explain only how students set about learning when the task has been <u>drained of meaning</u>. Yet most human learning depends on meaning and it is directed towards it. To learn is to strive for meaning, and to have learned something is to have grasped its meaning. In spite of this dominant interest in learning defined as a quantitative phenomenon, since the time of Bartlett (1932) there has also been a concern with learning defined in <u>qualitative</u> terms. Bartlett investigated the ways in which students recounted a story they had read. The differences in the form of these responses led Bartlett to abandon the conception of memory as a reproductive storage mechanism, where every impression with all its specific characteristics is stored in a defined, neural region. Instead Bartlett's conception of the memory depends on the reconstruction of meaning in terms of *schemata* which represent personal reinterpretations of the learning material.

The qualitative approach to research on learning which is reported in this book represents a development of Bartlett's conception. It rejects the description of knowledge as discrete pieces of knowledge passed passively from teacher to learner, and tested in terms of whether or not the student can reproduce verbatim those elements. Instead of concerning itself with "how much is learned", it seeks to investigate "what is learned". Necessarily this qualitative type of research is concerned with the learning of realistically complex passages which contain a description or an explanation of a phenomenon. If students are given such a text and asked to read it carefully in order to be able to answer questions about its content, it is possible to investigate "what is learned" in a naturalistic setting — an experimental situation in which both content and instructions are closely similar to what students normally experience in higher education.

The next step in the research process depends on generating data about how the subjects have understood the content of the text. The need for intensive and deep information places limitations on the choice of methods. The general research strategy has been to use semi-structured or thematic interviews which are tape-recorded. Identical introductory questions on each topic are followed by questions aimed at eliciting answers in more depth. Depending on the structure and comprehensiveness of an initial answer the interviewer may have to ask for clarification, elaboration or examples. The interviewer must, however, avoid giving any clues about the desired direction which the process should lead. The tape recordings are then typed up and the resulting protocols — once they have been checked by the researcher — constitute the data on which analysis is carried out.

The aim of the analysis is to yield *descriptive categories* of the qualitative variation found in the empirical data. The process involves the reduction of unimportant dissimilarities e.g. terminology or other superficial characteristics, and the integration and generalisation of important similarities i.e. a specification of the core elements which make up the content and structure of a given category. Some examples of this kind of analysis will be presented below.

Many of the studies carried out in Gothenburg during the first half of the 1970s took the form of text reading experiments. Thus in one investigation (Marton, 1975b: Marton *et al.*, 1977) forty students of education were asked to read an article from a Swedish newspaper. The article (which was written by Urban Dahllöf, a Swedish professor of education) was a contribution to a debate about a reform in the Swedish system of higher education. The article can be summarised as follows.

By re-analysing the empirical data used in an investigation initiated by the National Board of Universities and Colleges, Dahllöf arrives at a conclusion which differs from that drawn in the original study. In that study the pass rate of students was found to be very low in the faculties of liberal arts and social science. The pass rate was however considerably higher in more vocationally oriented fields such as medicine, civil engineering, etc. It was therefore concluded that the pass rate could be improved if a number of fixed combinations of subject areas was introduced, in order to make schemes of study in the "free" faculties similar to their more vocational counterparts.

In his re-analysis of the data, Dahllöf makes the assumption that many students who enter the system of higher education do so without the intention of graduating, but only to study a particular subject over a number of terms. Dahllöf excludes from the empirical material students older than twenty-five on the assumption that, at that age, they have probably already gone through some kind of post-secondary education and want to complete that education with a few terms of university studies. Although this group of students are officially defined as drop-outs, that definition does not match their own intentions. Further more, Dahllöf splits the data into sub-groups according to university, sex, subject area, and grade point average from upper secondary school. He thus finds that there are large differences between the different sub-groups. Some have a very low pass rate and some have a pass rate which is similar to that found in the medical or engineering faculties. Dahllöf draws the conclusion that if the purpose of the reform is to raise the pass rate in the faculties of humanities and social science, selective rather than general measures should be taken. The grounds on which he therefore challenges the wisdom of the reform are that a closer look at the empirical data shows that the situation is satisfactory as far as many groups of students are concerned, and very problematic in the case of others.

In the learning experiment students were invited, individually, to read Dahllöf's article carefully at their own pace. They were asked to read it in their usual way, but they were told that they would be asked questions about it afterwards. They were then interviewed and asked questions initially about the general meaning of the article — "Try to summarise the article in one or two sentences. In other words what is the author's intention?" Other questions related to specific aspects of the article and to the processes of learning. Here we are concerned only with the analysis of the extent to which the main point of the article could be recounted.

By applying a rigorous qualitative analysis, the students' responses can be grouped into a number of categories, according to the basic underlying structure expressed. This means that the protocols have to be studied with the intention of understanding what the students are expressing, irrespective of what words or examples they may use, which may show a considerable variation even between answers belonging to the same category. Starting with a comparatively large number of categories the researcher will gradually refine these, arriving at a smaller set of categories that may finally be difficult or impossible to collapse further. In the case of the Dahllöf article, the empirical analysis of students' answers yielded four categories of outcome:

A.   Selective measures should be taken.
B.   Differential measures should be taken.
C.   Measures should be taken.
D.   There are differences between different groups of students.

What then differentiates these categories one from another? Clearly there is a hierarchical relationship between A, B and C with regard to their degree of specificity, in that selective measures (A) are a special case of differential measures (B) while the same relation is applicable also for B in relation to C. Category D, on the other hand deviates from the others by expressing only an aspect of the empirical data. Categories A and B both involve the use of evidence in support of *conclusions*, while categories C and D represent *descriptions*. The C-answers may appear conclusion-oriented but the very general conclusion that 'measures should be taken' is not rooted in the empirical data, but is rather a kind of addition to the reported main point about the differences in pass rates. In other studies (Dahlgren, 1975; Säljö, 1975; Marton, 1976a; Svensson, 1976) categories of outcome have been reported which occupy a level below that of description. Instead, there is a reliance merely on *mentioning* elements remembered from the text.

The range of categories of response found in this study (and in other similar investigations) can be described as the *outcome space* for the text concerned. The outcome space provides a kind of analytic map of variations in what has been learned from a given learning task. It is therefore an empirical concept which is not the product of logical or deductive analysis, but instead results from intensive examination of empirical data. Equally important, as used here, the outcome space is content-specific: the set of descriptive categories arrived at has not been determined *a priori*, but depends on the specific content of the learning material. Indeed it should be stressed that, as Entwistle (1976) has observed, "the verb to learn takes the accusative (case)." There is no learning without a content, and thus no phenomenon of learning *per se*.

Structural Aspects of Outcomes of Learning

This does not mean that differences in outcome are wholly content-based. Although the categories which summarise each level of outcome may also preserve (as in the case of the Dahllöf article) a description of the content, more general structural differences can frequently be identified. For example, as we have just seen, outcomes can be categorised as conclusion oriented, descriptive or mentioning, and such differences can also be said to represent distinct levels of outcome. Similarly sets of outcome categories can sometimes be shown to represent hierarchies, where outcomes are related one to another in terms of their degree of specificity, inclusiveness or completeness.

Our next two examples are both to varying extents concerned with the structural properties of differences in outcome. The first is a study by Wenestam (1980). Like many of the Gothenburg studies, it is a text-related analysis of the content of learning. Instead of making use of a single text, however, Wenestam selected four texts which share a common structure; each describes a particular principle which is then illustrated by an example. The texts vary in length from two to six pages, but in each case, the account of the example takes up a substantial proportion of the passage.

One of Wenestam's texts dealt with the scientific work of the physician Ignaz Semmelweis, who is the discoverer of micro-organisms as the origin of the epidemic diseases. Semmelweis's discovery and the thought and experimental work that proceeded from it, is used as an example of the scientific way of hypothesis testing by means of the experimental method. One of Wenestam's questions was:

> Try to summarise the text in a few sentences. In other words, what did the author want to say?

Four categories of answers to this question were identified:

A. The main point of the text (the testing of hypothesis by comparing two conditions where only one factor, the assumed cause, differs) and its relation to the example (the work of Dr. Semmelweis and the mode of action in his investigations) has been understood.
B. The main point of the text has been understood but not its relation to the example.

C. The main point of the text has not been understood but some other main point has been described in a rather general way (e.g. it is about the causes of a phenomenon: or a method for the solution of a problem).

D. The focus is on one or more of the concrete examples (e.g. it describes a doctor at a hospital in Vienna who worked to find the cause of the high mortality rate in childbed fever among women in labour; or the necessity of maintaining a high standard of hygiene).

This result, that is the gradual weakening of the importance of the principle and the successive upgrading of the example from categories A–D, was an important aspect of the variation in the answers on all four texts used by Wenestam. It exemplifies a tendency which we have termed *horizontalisation.* In texts such as these, the intention is to convey a principle. Examples have a subordinate function, which is to illustrate the principle outlined. In horizontalisation, however, this hierarchy is not preserved; no distinction is made between the status of the principle and the status of the example.

It seems probable that horizontalisation is not confined to learning involving a specific kind of text, but is to be found more widely in formal education. Teachers undoubtedly both hope and believe that the examples or metaphors they use to illuminate a given principle will prove less enduring than the principle itself, but how often this actually occurs is open to doubt. The striking concrete example may turn out to be more memorable than the imperfectly understood abstract principle it was meant to illustrate. Yet though horizontalisation seems to reflect a structural difference of a given kind in the quality of learning outcomes, it should be stressed once again that such differences have to be looked for in relation to specific content and depend, moreover, on empirical analyses of outcomes. There have been attempts to establish general taxonomies (Bloom, 1956; Gagné, 1977) through which the content of different learning tasks can be analysed, but such taxonomies are of little relevance here, for they represent logical analyses of the content and processes of learning. They do not derive from studies of the different outcomes arrived at for a given subject-matter.

In this respect, an Australian study by Biggs and Collis (1982) is an evident exception. Their SOLO taxonomy (in which SOLO is an acronym for the Structure of the Observed Learning Outcome) is an attempt at empirical classification of levels of outcome in a form which has wide applicability. The theoretical basis of Biggs and Collis' taxonomy derives in part from the stages in cognitive development described by Piaget and in part from theories of information processing. Breaking away from Piaget's use of stages to describe the developmental level of an individual child, Biggs and Collis seek to describe the range of answers given to a specific question — in our terms the 'outcome space'. They assume that such levels have a general reality, irrespective of content and question form, and describe five categories as follows, with increasing levels of sophistication.

1. *Pre-structural.*   In relationship to the prerequisites given in the question, the answers are denying, tautological, and transductive — bound to specifics.

2. *Uni-structural.*	The answers contain "generalisations" only in terms of one aspect.
3. *Multi-structural.*	The answers reveal generalisations only in terms of a few limited and independent aspects.
4. *Relational.*	Characterised by induction, and generalisations within a given or experienced context using related aspects.
5. *Extended abstract.*	Deduction and induction. Generalisations to situations not experienced or given in the prerequisites of a question.

Biggs and Collis provide several examples from different school subjects showing how the SOLO taxonomy may be applied in analyses of learning outcomes. One of these examples is an analysis of the answers given to a question which asked why the side of a mountain that faces the coast is usually wetter than the side facing the interior. The following responses illustrate the five categories described above.

1. Because it rains more on the coastal side.
2. Because the sea breezes hit the coastal side first.
3. Because the sea breezes contain water vapour and they first strike the coastal side and so it rains on them and after that there's no rain to fall on the other side.
4. Because the prevailing winds are from the sea and they pick up moisture and as they meet the mountain they're forced up and get colder, the moisture condenses, forming rain. By the time the winds cross the mountain they are dry.
5. This is likely to be true only if the prevailing winds are from the sea. When this is so, the water vapour evaporated from the sea is carried to the mountain slopes, where it rises and cools. Cooling causes the water vapour to condense and deposit. Not only is the wind now dryer, it is then carried up the mountain further, is compressed, now warm, and thus is relatively less saturated than before: the effect is similar to the warm climates experienced on the Eastern slopes of the Rockies in Canada in winter. However, all this makes assumptions about the prevailing wind and temperature conditions: if these were altered, then the energy exchanges would differ, resulting in quite a different outcome. (edited from Biggs and Collis, 1982, pp. 4–5)

The authors conclude that,

These responses are increasingly better in quality. The first is not incorrect, but it tells you nothing about the quality of learning: it could have been given by a student who hadn't learned anything from the lesson. The second presents one relevant fact, the third several; neither gives an adequate explanation. The fourth response gives an interconnected and logical explanation, but as the fifth response makes clear, it could be an incorrect overgeneralisation. The fifth response considers all aspects, including some not given in the original lesson. (It introduces general abstract principles that cover both this situation and others; and it considers alternative possibilities to that implied in this question) (ibid., p.5 adapted).

The SOLO taxonomy represents a general structural analysis of the outcome of learning, as a complement to content-oriented analyses of the kind undertaken in the experiment which used the Dahllöf article. However, the great strength of such a taxonomy — its generality of application — is also its weakness. Differences in outcome which are bound up with the specific content of a particular learning task may remain unaccounted for.

In some of our analyses (e.g. Dahlgren and Pramling, 1982) structural differences in outcome similar to those represented in the SOLO taxonomy can be observed, and yet differences dependent on the specific content are repeatedly found. And subsequent analyses (Pollitt et al., 1985) have shown how the form of an examination question affects the outcome space 'available' to the student. Thus although structural similarities may be useful up to a point, they are likely to be more informative in their instructional implications, if they are combined with content-specific characteristics.

Outcomes as Conceptions

The content-specific analysis of outcome is important in another fundamental aspect. In some analyses, the categories of outcome arrived at can be considered as representing qualitatively distinct conceptions of a phenomenon. In other words, each constitutes a particular way of viewing and thinking about an aspect of the surrounding world. This is best illustrated by a study (Dahlgren, 1978) which ranged beyond the confines of a text-based learning experience. In this study, university students of economics were asked the apparently simple question:

Why does a bun cost about one (Swedish) crown?

In this case two categories of outcome accounted for the qualitative variation in the students' answers:

A. The price is dependent on the relationship between the supply of and demand for buns.
B. The price is equal to the (true) value of the bun.

Answers in category A represent a conception of price as system dependent, in that the price of a commodity is unknown until it is subject to a bargaining situation between producers and consumers in the market. Neither the costs of production nor customers' willingness to pay a certain price can alone determine the price. In the long run the price is determined at the point where customers and producers agree that goods or services will be bought and sold.

The category B answers on the other hand reveal a more object oriented conception of price, for these answers state that the price depicts the production costs and reasonable profits on the various constituents, whether they be products or services. In a sense this also means that B-answers give expression to a product-oriented conception of price. The B conception is one which is commonly found in everyday situations. It is often used, for example, by salesmen of luxury goods like oriental rugs or paintings. As a customer you may hear for example that "this beautiful rug used to cost £1000 but we're only going to ask for £800". What is actually said, or what should have been said if we strive for a more correct description from an economic viewpoint, is that "we tried to sell this rug for £1000. It turned out, however, that that was a wrong price on the market we operate in, so now we are making a new attempt at the level of £800".

To sum up, these two categories of outcome are not just variations in what has been learned from textbooks, but represent two distinct and contrasting conceptions of a real-life phenomenon. The earlier examples can be viewed in the same way. In the case of the article by Dahllöf, for example, the variations in outcomes constitute different conceptions of Dahllöf's analysis of the shortcomings of an impending reform measure. What distinguishes the example about the price of a bun from the Dahllöf example, however, is that the phenomenon concerned occupies a relatively wider and more prominent position in everyday life — and thus more obviously draws on our experience and understanding of the surrounding world that is not confined to a particular text or set of learning materials. But in each case, the outcome does not amount to the retention or non-retention of a disembodied fact which has no meaning beyond itself. Instead, the phenomenon is invested with a specific meaning that both reflects and colours how the phenomenon is thought about.

From this same perspective, we can go further and define learning itself as a change in conception. In other words, when learning has occurred, there is a shift from one conception to another which is qualitatively distinct. Thus a student who had held conception B prior to an economics course and who is subsequently shown to display conception A has achieved more than the acquisition of an understanding of the laws of supply and demand. For the student, the phenomenon of price is now looked at in a fundamentally new way. Thus learning, within this perspective, is not a discrete and self-contained entity but one which has the potential of enabling individuals to consider afresh some part or aspect of the world around them.

The Effects of Education on Conceptions

But to what extent do learning experiences in formal education result in changes in conception? In reviewing the findings of the study of the introductory economics course (Dahlgren, 1978), we had concluded on a far from optimistic note. The main change we had observed was in the students' use of the terminology of economics. There was little evidence of qualitative changes in the students' conceptions of phenomena which had had a central place in the content of the course. Clearly, if these particular findings were representative of the effects of education in general, a reappraisal of the form and content of curricula seemed to be called for (Dahlgren, 1978, p. 18). And, indeed, similar findings were obtained in an investigation involving mechanical engineering students by Johansson et al. (1981). By choosing the seemingly trivial but very fundamental physical concept of force, they demonstrated that although it was taken for granted that the students held the Newtonian conception of force (i.e. that a force is only involved in physical events where there is a change in velocity or direction), some of the students were in fact found to hold a different conception.

One of the questions put to the students was:

A car is driven along a motorway in a straight line at a high constant speed. What forces act on the car?

An analysis of the answers yielded two categories of conceptions of a body moving at a constant velocity. A body in this kind of motion was apprehended either as

A.   Having a constant velocity, due to the equilibrium of forces

(When he drives at a constant speed all the forces counterbalance each other); or

B.   Moving, due to a "motive inequilibrium" of forces.

(And then a force that is directed forwards which has to be greater than those... forces directed in the opposite direction, otherwise it wouldn't move forwards).

Of the 22 students who were asked questions about bodies moving at a constant velocity, a total of 7 gave B answers at the first interview (prior to the course in mechanics) and 6 at the second interview (after the course had finished). Although the outcome on other questions (e.g. the case of decelerated motion, illustrated by an ice-hockey puck gliding straight forwards on smooth ice) was more positive, it seems nevertheless remarkable that a significant proportion of the students could preserve an Aristotelian conception of force.

The effects of formal education on conceptions have also been investigated by Hasselgren (1982), in a longitudinal study. His study focused on the structural level of the subjects' conceptions. A group of pre-school student-teachers were asked to describe what they saw in video-tape sequences of children at play. The sessions were repeated three times; at the start of the course, in the middle of the second term, and at the beginning of the third and final term. A group of physiotherapy students constituted a control group. In interviews following the video-tape sequences, the subjects were questioned about what they had seen. The transcripts of the taped interviews were analysed and a set of four categories of outcome were identified (Hasselgren, 1982, pp. 50–52):

A.   *An abstracting description.* In relating the content of the video recordings, what is shown on the screen is not taken for granted, but instead is considered as a concrete illustration of a principle or abstract idea which might be applied to the material.
B.   *A chronological description.* The activities of the group of children are understood as a chain of events, following a temporal sequence.
C.   *A partialistic description.* The account given deals with a part rather than the whole of the video-tape, often by focusing only on the actions of one of the children.

D. *A fragmentary description.* The account is impressionistic and diffuse, lacking an identifiable perspective and only mentioning what is immediately observable. The children, their play, and the setting in which they are playing, are given equal importance.

In Hasselgren's analysis, these four categories are considered as forming a developmental sequence, in which there is progression from either the fragmentary or partialistic description to the chronological description, and hence to the abstracting description. His analysis shows a substantial difference in the patterns of regression, stability and development for the experimental and control groups as shown in Table 2.1. There were only five instances of regression, all confined to the control group, and a very much higher rate of instances of development amongst students in the experimental group. Hasselgren therefore concludes that the formal educational experiences undergone by the experimental group have had an impact on their way of apprehending a phenomenon that is central to pre-school teacher education.

TABLE 2.1

Distribution of changes representing regression, stability or development

(from Hasselgren, 1982, p. 63)

		Category		
Group	*Regression*	*Stability*	*Development*	*N*
Experimental	—	37	19	56
Control	5	23	3	31

An attempt at summarising research evidence on the effects of education, within the qualitative perspective adopted here, leads to the following observations:

- Education does have an impact as far as the acquisition of subject-specific terminology or the mastery of problem-solving algorithms are concerned, and such outcomes may be the most permanent of any effects which can be identified.
- Conceptual changes are undoubtedly more difficult to trace. Such changes do take place but are probably relatively rare, fragile and context-dependent occurrences. (Dahlgren, 1978; Brumby, 1979;Johansson *et al.*, 1981).
- Nonetheless, at a macro-level of analysis, education has demonstrable effects in terms of structural properties of the ways in which phenomena are apprehended.
  (Perry, 1970; Hasselgren, 1982).

The Qualitative Analysis of Learning

Having provided some examples which illuminate the kind of results about learning that a qualitative analysis can yield, we may make an attempt to integrate the conception of learning and knowledge that springs out of that perspective.

The first point to emphasise may seem obvious, but is sometimes ignored: learning is a many-sided phenomenon. Just as there are many different things to learn about, so too are there different processes of learning and different outcomes of learning. In this chapter we have tried to contrast two main categories of learning. On the one hand there is learning from materials that lack an internal order which might permit us to talk about meaningfulness. In such cases the learning process involves pure memorising either by dint of constant repetition or by imposing some kind of meaningfulness, often through the use of mnemonic strategies.

But a substantial proportion of learning depends on understanding material which does have an internal structure that can be grasped. In these cases the process of learning should aim at finding this structure in as deep a sense as possible. This is a qualitatively different kind of learning which will result in a different outcome. The nature of this outcome is that it represents a conception of a phenomenon in the surrounding world. A conception can in principle mean those very superficial characteristics of a phenomenon such as size, shape or colour. Here that conception is taken rather to denote the nature of an object or an event.

To "understand" or "accept" the colour or the size of an object is a process of a totally different kind than to understand its nature. In the latter case, what is pivotal to understanding is the grasp of the relationships between a phenomenon and its context. External or concrete characteristics of a phenomenon do not alone provide a basis for understanding. In this respect everything is always a part of something larger or more inclusive (i.e. it has a meaning beyond itself) and it is this which makes up what we might call the context of understanding. Meaningfulness is thus not an inherent property of nature or culture. It is imposed by human consciousness, which is itself evolving continually. Learning, then, should be regarded as that aspect of human life through which the environment — or man himself — appears with a higher degree of meaningfulness than before. From this perspective — as in some others too (cf. Popper, 1972) — knowledge is nothing but a series of occasional, provisional steps towards what is often described as an unreachable complete knowledge about reality. Similarly a conception, as Marton (1978) describes it,

> often denotes the implicit (tacit) — that which does not need to be expressed or cannot be expressed because it has never been the object of reflection. (p. 20)

This chapter has shown how it is possible to describe what is learned in terms of sets of categories which can often be differentiated in terms of their structural properties. Such structural differences would seem to hold open the possibility of devising empirically derived taxonomies, such as SOLO, which would allow the quality of a wide range of learning outcomes to be systematically analysed. Yet our research has drawn attention to variations in outcome which cannot fully be understood except in relation to the content of learning. Analyses of learning outcomes in relation to content enable us to describe variations in the conceptions students hold about important parts of their course. These analyses also suggest that, at present, formal education is not as successful as it might be in helping students to develop more sophisticated conceptions. When the questions asked of students are at base quantitative or fail to penetrate beyond what can be more or less unreflectively retained in the memory, students' misapprehensions are disguised within spuriously satisfactory answers or cloaked in technical jargon. More searching questions, though framed in a direct and straightforward way, show up fundamental misunderstandings. Thus a study of qualitative differences in outcome has a vitally important role to play in helping to determine — and ultimately improve — the quality of student learning.

CHAPTER THREE

Approaches to Learning

FERENCE MARTON AND ROGER SÄLJÖ

Explaining Differences in Outcome

How can we account for the qualitative differences in the outcome of learning described in the previous chapter? Let us take the first of our own studies as an example. Students were asked to read an article on university reform intended to bring the pass rates of universities more in line with those of polytechnic institutes (see Chapter 2). As there were substantial differences in pass rates between different groups within universities, the author argued that improvement in pass rates at universities, if necessary at all, would depend on taking selective measures, i.e. measures directed towards the groups with low pass rates and not towards those whose results were satisfying. As we have seen, four qualitative different outcomes were identified (Marton, 1974; Marton & Säljö, 1976a):

A. Selective measures should be taken
B. Differential measures should be taken
C. Measures should be taken
D. There are differences between different groups of students

Now, how did these differences in understanding come about? Those whose answer was of the C-variety, for instance, obviously thought that the author was arguing for something which, in reality, he was arguing against (i.e. general measures). This observation could be seen as a reminder of the kinds of problems one finds when analysing in detail how people read texts and how they learn. Those with a D-kind of understanding, furthermore, seem to have totally missed the point that the author was arguing for anything at all. Probably, they assumed that he simply wanted to describe something, to convey information.

The most obvious explanation of why such variations in understanding arise would be to argue that learning depends on prior knowledge. Thus the differing outcomes could be explained in terms of differing levels of knowledge or linguistic skills. Although such an argument may be true in a general way, it cannot explain the results of this experiment. The article here was chosen specifically because the language used was simple (it was an article taken from a daily newspaper), and because the prerequisite knowledge could reasonably be assumed to be available to all the students (it was about a widely debated university reform). After having, at least tentatively, ruled out that explanation, the next one again seems fairly obvious. The students understand the text in different ways because the students themselves differ; above all some are brighter than others. Apart from the fact that the text could hardly be called intellectually demanding, the proposed "explanation" could be no more than a statistical correlation at best. This type of explanation does not illuminate the fundamental question of how the different ways of understanding the text have come about.

If the outcome of learning differs between individuals, then the very process of learning which leads to different outcomes must also have differed between individuals. This is a fundamental assumption underlying the line of reasoning pursued in these studies. The most obvious explanation of the differences in outcome should derive from a description of the differences in the process that led to the different outcomes.

After having reached such a position, we still face a highly important question concerning the strategy of research: What does it take to describe differences in the learning process? Of course, we could have had a theory or a model of processes involved in learning by reading a text. We could have attempted to test that theory or model by *ceteris paribus* varying one factor at a time between one or several experimental and control groups. In fact we did not have any such theory or model to test in an experimental setting. On the contrary, we started from the assumption that the functional background of differences in the outcome of learning in natural study situations was still largely unknown. In consequence we had to try to find out in what way students function differently in such situations. But what sources of information could we find in order to be able to answer this question? Observing students engaged in studying, is really not a very rewarding research method. There is simply not much to observe. We can measure the time spent on reading the text, we can examine the underlinings and notes made, but such data do not provide useful information. External data of this type do not form a pattern systematically related to the outcome of learning (see Svensson, 1976). And, indeed, there are no good reasons why they should.

The Original Experiment

There are, then, basically two alternatives left for collecting data about what the students actually "do" when trying to learn from a text. One is to scrutinise the various qualitative aspects of the students' performance, of the outcome of learning, in order to be able to make inferences of the type "to recall this, or understand that, the student must have proceeded in this or that way". This was one of the methods used by Svensson (1976, 1977) which led him to the conclusions discussed in the next chapter. Here we shall consider results derived from the alternative strategy (Marton, 1974). Students were asked to recount how they had been handling the learning task and how it appeared to them. To ask the students to describe how they had been handling the learning task is to some extent tantamount to asking them how the learning task and the learning situation appeared to them, because it is the only language in which questions about what we do when we try to learn by reading a text can be answered. Answers to such questions are not of an introspective nature; there is just no way in which we can look into ourselves. What we can do instead is to say how the world appears to us and this was exactly what the students did in our experiments.

The basic methodology was introduced in the previous chapter. Students were asked to read the article, knowing they would be asked questions on it afterwards. Besides the questions about what they remembered of its content, students were also asked questions designed to discover how they had tackled this task. They were asked, for example:

Could you describe how you went about reading the text?
Was there anything that you found difficult?
Did you find it interesting or not?
While reading, was there anything that struck you as particularly important?

Each student participated in an individually run session and all the conversation between him or her and the experimenter was recorded and transcribed verbatim subsequently. The transcripts of the students' answers to these and other similar questions made up the data base for our attempt to answer the main question dealt with in this chapter: how did the students arrive at those qualitatively different ways of understanding the text read?

Methods of Analysis

In Chapter 1 the idea of *phenomenography* was introduced as the method which grew out of the approach developed in this study. Here, more detail is provided to show how the forerunner of this method was used in the analysis of the interview data. Of course, the actual term *phenomenography* post-dates the original work reported here.

The first phase of the analysis, which was supposed to lead to the results searched for, was a kind of selection procedure based on criteria of relevance. Comments which seemed in any way relevant to our enquiry were identified and marked. The meaning of a comment could occasionally lie in the words themselves but, in general, the interpretation had to be made in relation to the context within which that comment had been made. Svensson and Theman (1983) offer an illuminating example of the way in which the same utterance may take on different meanings in different contexts. The phenomenon in question ("differences in the learning process accounting for the differences in outcome") was thus *delimited* and interpreted in terms of interview extracts which were selected quotes from the interviews with the students, while the quotes themselves were delimited in terms of the context from which they were taken.

The selection procedure resulted in a collection of comments relevant from the point of view of the phenomenon to be delimited. Extracts were then brought together into groups on the basis of similarity and the groups were delimited from each other in terms of differences. In very concrete terms it meant sorting the quotes into piles, trying to extract a core meaning common to all the quotes in a certain pile, examining the borderline cases and eventually making explicit the criteria attributes defining each group, not the least in contrast to the other groups. In such a way the group of quotes were turned into categories defined in terms of core meaning, on the one hand, and borderline cases, on the other. Each category was exemplified by a selection of appropriate quotes.

An important difference between the way in which phenomenographic analyses are conducted and how traditional content analysis develops is that the categories into which the comments are sorted are predetermined. The analysis is dialectical in the sense that bringing the quotes together develops the meaning of the category, while at the same time the evolving meaning determined which of the categories are included or omitted. This means of course a lengthy and painstaking iterative procedure with continual modifications in which quotes are assembled, and consequently further changes in the precise meaning of each group of quotes take place. There is, however, a decreasing rate of change and eventually the whole system becomes stabilised. Each category is then as homogeneous as possible. The outcome is a hierarchical structure of categories, chiefly related to each other in terms of similarities and differences.

A second important difference in relation to content analysis is the level at which we examine what the students say about their experience of learning.

The next crucial step in this particular analysis was to consider the whole set of quotes selected to delimit the various categories of description. The researcher's attention now shifted from the individual students (the interviews which had lent meanings to the quotes by being their contexts), to the meanings embedded in the quotes regardless of whether these different meanings originated from the same individuals or not. The boundaries between individuals were thus abandoned and interest was focused on the "pool of meanings". In this way, each quote had two contexts in relation to which it had to be interpreted. First it depended on the interview from which it was taken and then on the "pool of meanings" to which it belonged. The interpretation was thus an iterative procedure which went back and forth between the two contexts for each unit of analysis. The first phase of the analysis was thus a selection procedure carried out within each interview (though taking the other interviews into consideration as a background). The second phase was the shift of attention from the individual interview to the "pool of meanings" consisting of the relevant quotes selected. Then came a third phase which involved a decision about the specific level at which the quotes should be seen in relation to each other. It should be noted at this stage, however, that these different phases were not, of course, strictly sequential. There was a good deal of overlap as the iterative procedure progressed. The differences in the outcome of learning referred to in the previous chapter were described at a certain level and if we were to find the differences in the process of learning accounting for those, we would have to aim at a description at the same level, and outcome and process would have to be described in a comparable way.

There are obviously differences at different levels. There are differences in the way people express themselves and there may be differences in their general orientation, but our interest did not focus on either of these two levels. Differences in outcome had been described in terms of the different ways in which the message of the text read had been understood. We were now searching for differences in the process of learning leading to these differences in outcome. We thus had to look for the different ways in which the process leading to these outcomes had been experienced.

When scrutinising "the pool of meanings" at this particular level, a pattern of a hierarchy of similarities and differences in meaning may ultimately emerge.

We do not believe there is any uniform technique which would allow other researchers to go from "the pool of meanings" to the emerging pattern of a hierarchy of similarities and differences. It is essentially a *discovery procedure* which can be justified in terms of results, but not in terms of any specific method. In each study the discovery process will inevitably be different, depending on the specific purpose and the context of the research. Yet, whatever specific method is adopted, the crucial point is that there is what was described in Chapter 1 as 'rigorous qualitative analysis' in identifying and describing the categories of description, and in examining the relationships between them. Only then can the method be described as *phenomenography*.

Levels of Processing

In the specific case we are dealing with here, all our efforts, all our readings and re-readings, our iterations and reiterations, our comparisons and groupings finally turned into an astonishingly simple picture. We had been looking for an answer to the question of why the students had arrived at those qualitatively different ways of understanding the text as a whole. What we found was that *the students who did not get "the point" failed to do so simply because they were not looking for it.*

The main difference we found in the process of learning concerned whether the students *focused on the text in itself or on what the text was about; the author's intention, the main point, the conclusion to be drawn.* Their focal point of attention was on the pages in the first case and beyond them in the second. The first way of setting about the learning task was characterised by a blind, spasmodic effort to memorise the text; these learners seemed, metaphorically speaking, to see themselves as empty vessels, more or less, to be filled with the words on the pages. In the second case, the students tried to understand the message by looking for relations within the text or by looking for relations between the text and phenomena of the real world, or by looking for relations between the text and its underlying structure. These learners seemed to have seen themselves as creators of knowledge who have to use their capabilities to make critical judgements, logical conclusions and come up with their own ideas.

Some quotes will serve to illustrate the first way of experiencing the learning situation:

> ... the only thing I was thinking about was that I'd got to hurry. What happened was that I read a couple of sentences and then I didn't remember what I'd read because I was thinking all the time, "I've got to hurry to get this done"... I kept on thinking that I'd got to remember what I'd just read, but (then I would wonder) "How am I going to remember this now". "I won't remember anything" is what I thought more or less in several places.

> Well I only concentrate on trying to remember as much as possible ...

> You get distracted. You think "I've got to remember this now". And then you think so hard about having to remember it: that's why you don't remember it.

In a later study carried out at Lancaster University, similar extracts were used
to describe equivalent experiences (see Entwistle, 1988b).

> In reading the article, I was looking out mainly for facts and examples. I
> read the article more carefully than I usually would, taking notes, knowing
> that I was to answer questions about it. I thought the questions would be
> about the facts in the article .... This did influence the way I read; I tried to
> memorise names and figures quoted, etc.

> I tried to concentrate — too hard — therefore my attention seemed to be
> on "concentration" rather than on reading, thinking, interpreting and
> remembering — something I find happening all the time I'm reading text-
> books.

These students did not try to understand the text, they tried to memorise it.
Their awareness skated along the surface of the text. Their only aim was to
be in a position to remember it later when they would be asked questions
about it. It should be remembered that the instructions put no time constraints
on the students and yet the quotations show experiences of heavy time
pressure. The intention to memorise the text, however, contains a paradox.
The students often have the feeling that they will not remember, just because
they are trying so hard to remember. And, indeed, this is exactly what happens.
(This most extreme form of concentrating on the surface of the presentation,
characterised by a failure to learn due to over-anxiety to perform well, has
been called *hyperintention*). So we found that many students were not even
trying to understand the message and, so, in consequence, they did not
understand it. On the other hand, they tried hard to remember the text, yet
failed to do so. (This is because the less meaning something has for us the
harder it is to remember it.)

The analysis also allowed us to identify an entirely different way of tackling
the article. Some students were trying to understand the message. They were
not trying to memorise the text and yet they remembered it very well. The
quotes below, when compared to those above, illustrate the fact that the two
groups of students seem to have been engaged in fundamentally different
activities in a situation which, from the point of view of an external observer,
appeared to be the same for both groups.

> ... and what you're thinking about then, it's, sort of, what was the point of
> the article.

> ... or perhaps I stopped and thought about what they were actually saying
> ... if there was something I thought wasn't right, and so on. You also stop
> and then (wonder) if that really follows that, sort of, is it really logical, what
> they've written. That sort of thing is what you stop for.

> Well, it was sort of the whole aim of (the article) — if that is what is meant.
> The whole aim of the article was what I was thinking of, sort of.

Or, from a Lancaster student:

> I read more slowly than usual, knowing I'd have to answer questions, but I

didn't speculate on what sort of questions they'd be. I was looking for the argument and whatever points were used to illustrate it. I could not avoid relating the article to other things I'd read, past experience, and associations, etc. My feelings about the issues raised made me hope he would present a more convincing argument than he did, so that I could formulate and adapt my ideas more closely, according to the reaction I felt to his argument.

In these cases, the text is not considered as an aim in itself (as in the earlier quotes) but rather as a means of grasping something which is beyond or underlying it—the author's intention, what it is all about. (For a more detailed and systematic description of these two modes of learning see Marton, 1982).

The 'depth' dimension which was implicit in the hierarchies of learning outcomes was thus also distinguishable in the case of the student's account of the way in which they went about the learning task. The qualitative differences in the outcome of learning were referred to as levels of outcome and the qualitative differences in the process of learning were, in these initial stages of analysis, called levels of processing. This term was chosen on the basis of a metaphorical, but only metaphorical, resemblance to Craik and Lockhart's (1972) "levels of processing" concept. (They discussed the correlation between the likelihood of the retention of a stimulus material (usually words) and the level at which the learner has attended it, for instance, in terms of shapes, sounds or meanings.) As we shall see, the use of Craik and Lockhart's term was subsequently abandoned, due to the false equivalence otherwise created with a quite different concept.

Relationships between Process and Outcome

Our search for differences in the process of learning was motivated by the intention to find the functional correlates of the qualitative differences in the outcome of learning. To what extent had we succeeded? First of all, it should be said that even though we were able to discern some differences in the student's experience of learning which we believed to be fundamental, it certainly did not imply that we could use these differences to meaningfully classify all the cases. Quite obviously, there are cases, on the one hand, where the information available in the interview transcript is just not sufficient to tell whether the learner had adopted deep or surface level processing, and there are cases, on the other hand, in which signs of both strategies can be found on the same occasion. In spite of these limitations, we were still able to conclude that there was a very close relationship indeed between process and outcome. Svensson (1976, 1977, and also in Chapter 4) has convincingly argued that the main dividing line, as far as levels of outcome are concerned, lies between categories A and B on the one hand and categories C and D, on the other. This is so, Svensson says, because the fact-conclusion structure, on which the whole article is based, is understood in the first case, but not in the second. And, indeed, the figures in Table 3.1 seem to support this point.

TABLE 3.1

Relationship between level of processing and outcome
(from Marton and Säljö, 1976a)

| *Level of outcome* | *Level of processing* | | | |
	Surface	*Not clear*	*Deep*	*Sub-totals*
A	0	0	5	5
B	1	6	4	11
C	8	0	0	8
D	5	1	0	6
Sub-totals	14	7	9	30

One could argue, of course, that the high correlation between process and outcome reflects the way in which the two main categories of levels of processing were found. We had indeed been looking for differences in the students' accounts of their ways of learning which would correspond to the differences found in their understanding of the article read. The close correlation between depth of processing and quality of outcome in learning has, however, during the decade that has passed since the first publication of the first results, been confirmed several times, even in investigations in which process and outcome of learning have been independently assessed (see Watkins, 1983; van Rossum and Schenk, 1984).

Levels of Processing and Approaches to Learning

As was pointed out above, there are two main alternatives for obtaining information about what the students "do" when they are trying to learn from a text. One relies more on the analysis of outcomes; the other identifies processes. So far we have identified two levels of processing on the basis of what the students said about their experience of the learning process. Then, subsequently, process was related to outcome. Svensson (1976) combined these two sources of information in making an independent and simultaneous analysis of the same set of data with the same intention—to explain the differences in outcome. The implications of his findings are discussed fully in the next chapter; here we introduce on this alternative form of analysis. Svensson concentrated first on students' accounts of what they remembered, and from the characteristics of these outcomes, he drew conclusions about the nature of the processes that accounted for what was remembered. The students' own accounts of how they perceived and experienced that process were used only to complement the analysis of performance data. Svensson's analysis again relied on the iterative procedure of rigorous qualitative analysis, but with different "pools of meaning".

In spite of this very different procedure, a similar distinction was reported but with different terminology. Svensson described the main variation in *cognitive approach* to be between *holistic* and *atomistic*. In the holistic approach during reading, students showed indications of a general direction towards understanding the text as a whole — a search for the author's intention, relating the content to a larger context and delimiting the main parts of the text. The indications of an atomistic approach were: focusing on specific comparisons in the text, focusing on the sequence of the text, but not the main parts, memorising details and, in contrast, clear evidence of a lack of an orientation towards the message as a whole (see Svensson, 1976, p. 93).

Svensson and Marton both used the term 'approach' to describe two distinct forms of understanding, but the categories of process were different (deep/surface, holistic/atomistic). The defining features of the two distinctions were very similar, but there was an important difference in emphasis which led to the differing terminology. The first difference was in terms of epistemological assumptions. Svensson, as he explains in the next chapter, was concerned to retain evidence of both outcome and process within his initial analysis. Marton concentrated first on process, before examining relationships with outcome. The differing sets of data yielded by the two distinct research strategies produced one dichotomy (deep/surface) which emphasised *referential* aspects of students' experiences — their search for meaning or not, while the other (holistic/atomistic) concerned *organisational* aspects — the ways in which they organized the informational content of the article in their reading.

The two aspects are normally inextricably mixed. In order to understand a text, we have to integrate, to reorganise, to see the passage as a whole. It was therefore no surprise to find a close empirical relationship between the two sets of categories. In terms of outcome 29 out of 30 cases were categorised in the same way, while there was complete agreement for 25 out of the 30 categorisations of cognitive approach or levels of processing (see Marton, 1976b, p. 17).

Subsequently, the distinction between the surface and deep levels of processing was included in an SSRC research programme at Lancaster directed by Noel Entwistle (Entwistle and Ramsden, 1983, and Chapter 13). Early work there led him to the conclusion that the term "processing" was too narrow in relation to the differences in learning described (Entwistle *et al.*, 1979a). He was concerned that the crucial intentional component was not a part of its connotation, for instance. He preferred to use the term *approach* , based on Svensson's description, but retaining Marton's categories of *deep* and *surface*. This change also fitted the altered theoretical framework of the work of the Gothenburg group, which had become less and less oriented towards the human information processing school of thought. This new terminology was thus accepted, and has since been widely accepted as the most appropriate label for these qualitative differences. To avoid confusion, subsequent sections of this chapter will thus use the term *approaches to learning*.

At about the same time, Laurillard (1978) and Ramsden (1981) started to investigate approaches to learning in normal study situations in various subjects. As we shall see in later chapters, their analyses produced rather different definitions of the deep/surface dichotomy in everyday learning. The instances occasionally came closer to the difference between an atomistic and a holistic approach than to the original distinction from which they arose. Considering this very close conceptual and empirical relatedness and considering the fact that Svensson had been using the term "approach" from the very beginning, it would appear more correct to talk about surface/atomistic and deep/holistic approaches to learning. Still, we believe that the analytic separation of the referential ("what") aspect, which is the heart of the surface/deep dichotomy, and the organisational ("how") aspect, which is the heart of the atomistic/holistic distinction, remains highly meaningful. Only when they are identified separately can the relationship between them be demonstrated. Indeed Roger Säljö, in Chapter 6, has done just this in showing how a certain meaning-orientation leads to a certain way of organising (segmenting, delimiting) the text and parts of it and how that way of organising the text leads to a certain referential meaning being abstracted from it.

Approaches to Learning in Normal Studies

The main investigation discussed in this chapter had been aimed at illuminating important functional differences in how students carry out their studies. This was done by setting up an experimental situation intended to resemble everyday conditions in important respects. Consequently it is a most reasonable question to ask, whether the differences found in learning experiments represent central differences in studying at university.

This question has been answered in the affirmative many times. In interviews about everyday studying Marton (1974) found that the same variation in approaches to learning could be discerned, even if the "flavour" was slightly different.

In everyday learning situations "text" takes on a metaphoric sense. The studies as a whole can be seen as the "text", on which attention is focused, and which is entirely separate from the "real" world. The relationship between surface approach (in this case certainly less intense and immediate, and more spasmodic) and the examination seems to resemble that between the surface approach adopted in the experiment and the retention test in that context:

> *Interviewer*   How did you read these books?
>
> *S:* (Well) I studied in a way that's typical for what you do when you study for an exam. Well, basic knowledge, sort of, to get in as much as possible.

Those adopting a deep approach in their studies seem to believe, on the other hand, that the idea of these studies is to learn something about reality, to change one's way of thinking about it. For instance:

> When you read something, then just afterwards, you're not really not quite sure about ... things. But, after perhaps a day or an hour or so, as a result of experiences, or events which jog your mind, it sort of works its way into a more solid perception in some way, which you stick to. You don't stick to a conception just after you've read it, then you haven't got any clear conception of it and can't defend it afterwards... And other people's comments provide an impetus to get you thinking along different lines. And they help, even if they don't give you the idea directly.

It was found that there was a close association between a deep approach to studying adopted by freshmen and their success in social sciences courses, in spite of the fact that examination results and qualitative differences in learning can hardly be said to be described in an equivalent way. Svensson (1976, 1977) found a similar relationship between holistic approaches and examination results. He concluded, however, that the relation between approach and examination results is indirect. The direct functional relationship was between approach and study habits, (how much one studies, when one studies, etc.). A holistic orientation is not a necessary prerequisite for being successful in all the subjects at university. If students have an atomistic orientation, i.e. if they read the course literature without understanding large parts of it, then studying will be extremely boring. Consequently, students with an atomistic approach tend to acquire bad study habits; in particular they do less work, besides using an inefficient approach, and so do not succeed in their studies. The students who combine an atomistic approach with hard work are just as successful in their studies (at least in certain subjects) as are students with a holistic approach. We are not arguing that the deep/holistic approach is always 'best': only that it is the best, indeed the only, way to *understand* learning materials.

The ways in which students vary in the processes and outcomes of learning has emerged clearly not just in the Gothenburg studies, but also those reported in later chapters (particularly Chapters 9 and 13). The differences between approaches to learning in different subject areas and in contrasting academic contexts will be considered there, and also in the concluding, integrative chapter.

Now that we have found a difference in the way students learn which we believe to be of fundamental importance, and since this difference goes between two approaches to learning, of which one is clearly preferable to the other, should we not try to make the students who tend to adopt the less appealing approach, change to the more highly valued one?

Changing Approaches to Learning

A significant prerequisite for attempting to influence how people act in learning situations is to have a clear grasp of precisely how different people act. In our case, the problem could be phrased as: what is it that a person using a deep approach does differently from a person using a surface approach. Or to use a slightly different terminology; in what sense do these two approaches differ as "cognitive projects" (i.e. what the learner is trying to accomplish)? The picture outlined so far indicates that a significant component of a deep approach is that the reader/learner engages in a more active dialogue with the text. It is as if the learner is constantly asking himself questions of the kind "How do the various parts of the text relate to each other?"; "Is the argument consistent or are there any logical gaps?"; "How does this relate to what I already know?"; and so on. Since one of the problems with a surface approach is the lack of such an active and reflective attitude toward the text, a fairly obvious idea would be to attempt to induce a deep approach through giving people some hints on how to go about learning.

Questions in the text

In a study aimed at testing this idea (Marton, 1976a), 30 students taking a one-year integrated course in political science, economy and sociology served as participants. The learning material used was the first chapter of an introductory text-book in political science that these students were about to read in their normal studies. The participants were randomly assigned to an experimental and a control group.

The procedure adopted for influencing the approach to learning in the experimental group was to have the students answer questions of a particular kind while reading. These questions were of the kind that students who use a deep approach had been found to ask themselves spontaneously during their reading. The questions, which were interspersed between each of the five sections of the chapter, were of the following kind:

What sub-sections do you think there are in this section? (Say where they start and finish).

Can you summarise the content of each of these sub-sections in one or two sentences?

What is the relationship between the various sub-sections?

Can you summarise the content of the whole section in one or two sentences? (ibid. p. 43).

It should also be added that the design of this study included an immediate, as well as a delayed, retention test. The latter session took place on the average more than two months after the first one.

This attempt to induce a deep approach through forcing people to answer questions found to be characteristic of such an approach, yielded interesting but contra-intuitive results. At one level it was obvious that the approach taken was influenced by the treatment to which the experimental group was exposed. However, this influence was not towards a deep approach: instead it seemed to result in a rather extreme form of surface learning.

TABLE 3.2

Number of items correct in retention test

(from Marton, 1976a)

| Retention Test | Group | | | | | | 't'-test |
| | Experimental | | | Control | | | |
	Mean	SD	N	Mean	SD	N	p <
Immediate	34.5	8.8	15	45.7	8.5	15	0.01
Delayed	21.0	5.5	15	30.2	10.5	14	0.01

Note: Sum values for three independent raters.
SD indicates *standard deviation*

The results on both the immediate and delayed retention measurements (which were quantitative measures of knowledge in this case) showed that the control group, which had not been exposed to any attempts at influencing approach, performed significantly better (see Table 3.2).

How can this rather clear difference in performance be accounted for? The explanation, in our view, reveals a fundamental aspect of how students adapt themselves to the demands they are exposed to. What happened was that the participants invented a way of answering the interspersed questions without engaging in the kind of learning that is characteristic of a deep approach. The technique they used was simply to read the text in such a way that they were able to mention (c.f. Säljö, 1975) the contents of various parts of each section in a rather superficial way. Thus, the task is transformed into a rather trivial and mechanical kind of learning, lacking the reflective elements found to signify a deep approach. What allowed the participants to transform the learning in this way, was obviously the predictability of the task. They knew that they would have to answer questions of this particular kind, and this allowed them to go through the text in a way which would make it possible to comply with the demands (i.e. summarising the various parts of the sections, stating the main point in them, dividing them into sub-sections, etc.) without actually going into detail about what was said. As Marton (1976a) concludes, "this process can be seen as a special case of the common human experience of transformation of means into ends" (p. 47). The questions which were intended as means of helping the students to adopt a deep approach, instead became the objective towards which the learning was geared. In this transformation, the attempts to deal with them in an expedient way became detrimental to learning.

The outcome of this study raises interesting questions about the conditions for changing people's approach to learning. The "demand structure" of the learning situation again proved to be an effective means of controlling the way in which people set about the learning task. Actually, it turned out to be too effective. The result was in reality the reverse of the original intention when setting up the experiment. The very predictability of the "demand structure" in our view played the central role in generating the paradoxical outcome. Therefore, in the next study to be described, while again using the learners' expectations of the questions subsequent to the reading as the independent variable, we tried to restrict their expectations, more indirectly, to the kind of questions, instead of to exact questions.

Questions after reading

In the study reported by Säljö (1975; see also Marton and Säljö, 1976b) 40 university students were divided into two groups. The factor varying between the two groups was the nature of the questions that the groups were asked after reading each of several chapters from an education text-book. One set of questions was designed to require a rather precise recollection of what was said in the text. The questions focused on were, for example, enumerations and listings of causes and consequences of certain events, factual information such as names, percentages, terminology, and so on. The idea behind this was, of course, to see if the participants would adopt a surface approach to meet the demands they could predict they would have to face after reading each successive chapter.

In the second group, the questions were directed towards the major lines of reasoning. The demand for remembering exact information of the kind mentioned above was much lower, and instead the participants had to give evidence that they had understood how the conclusions followed from the developing argument, and they also had to provide judgements as to whether the reasoning seemed consistent and correct. In addition, they also had to recall the text and give a short summary of its main points.

After reading a final chapter, both groups were exposed to both kinds of questions and they were also required to recall the text and summarise it in a few sentences. The outcome here thus served as the major dependent variable of the study. The results show that a clear majority of the participants reported that they attempted to adapt their learning to the demands implicit in the questions given after each successive chapter. This could be seen both in students' subjective reports about how they set about learning as they went from one chapter to the next, and in the way the final chapter was recalled and the questions answered.

Was it, then, possible to influence people to use a deep approach in this more indirect way? Unfortunately, the answer to this question cannot be a simple 'yes'. The crucial idea of this study, that people would respond to the demands that they were exposed to, was verified. In the group which was given "factual" questions this could be clearly seen and, as expected, both their recalls and the way that the questions were answered, as well as the reports about how they set about learning, showed that they reacted to the questioning through adopting a surface approach. However, in the other group, the reaction did not simply involve moving towards a deep approach. Some students did, others did not. A fundamental reason underlying this was differing *interpretations of what was demanded of them*. Only about half the group interpreted the demands in the way intended. The other students handled the task in very much the same way as was found in the study by Marton described above. By focusing their attention on the most conspicuous tasks, they were able to foresee what they would have to face after reading (recalling the text and summarising it in a few sentences). These participants then *technified* their learning, again concentrating solely on perceived requirements. They could summarise, but not demonstrate understanding. This concept of technification requires some additional comments, since it reflects a rather fundamental observation that has been made in the studies where attempts have been made to influence the approach people use.

A common idea in these studies has been to observe and describe, in as great a detail as possible, what characterises a deep and a surface approach respectively in terms of the kind of learning that people engage in. On the basis of this knowledge, it ought to be possible to influence people who do not spontaneously adopt a deep approach to behave in a way similar to those who do this in a given situation. For example, since it could be observed that it was characteristic for students using a deep approach to clarify for themselves in an explicit way the main points and lines of reasoning in the text that they were reading, it is very common to assume that if one makes other students perform the same kinds of activities, this would mean that they too would be using a deep approach. However, it is obvious from the two studies reported here, and from other similar investigations (see, for instance, Dahlgren, 1975), that this kind of logical reasoning does not always lead to the expected results when applied to human behaviour. It is important to realise that the indicators of a deep approach, isolated in the research, are symptoms of a rather fundamental attitude towards what it takes to learn from texts. Thus, one cannot treat these observations on what characterises a deep approach as pointing to casual factors that can be isolated and manipulated through rather simple means to achieve the desired end. Instead, if we take the study by Säljö as an example, what happened was that some students *made it an end in itself* to be able to give a summary of the text after each chapter. In this way, their learning was geared towards the objective of fulfilling this particular demand, and again the task can be solved through *mentioning* the various parts of the text at a very superficial level. This is thus an example of the process of *technification* of learning resulting in poor performance. The functional mechanism underlying this process is that the perceived demands become so predictable that students believe they can handle them through a very shallow interaction with the text. They simply use their knowledge about what is going to happen later to economise on their efforts. This, as was pointed out earlier, is a very common human reaction, and we should not be surprised to find students behaving in such a way.

Taken together, these studies illustrate that although in one sense it is fairly easy to influence the approach people adopt when learning, in another sense it appears very difficult. It is obviously quite easy to induce a surface approach and enhance the tendency to take a reproductive attitude when learning from texts. However, when attempting to induce a deep approach the difficulties seem quite profound. How are we to understand this?

If we return for a moment to the nature of this distinction as it emerged in our studies, the fundamental difference between approaches has been described as one of whether students interpreted the text itself as what was to be learned, or conceived the text as the *means* through which they sought to grasp the meaning underlying the words and so to change their conceptions about historical developments, economic processes, or whatever. The fact that even when students have been encouraged through various means to adopt a deep approach redefine the situation in a way which will make it expedient to use a surface approach, should tell us something about the strong mechanisms operating within educational contexts in support of this reproductive mode of learning.

Learning and Motivation

One of the factors contributing to the partial failure of these attempts to induce a deep approach by manipulating the "demand structure" of the learning situation is the relation between the learners' motives and the ways they go about learning. Learning or reading out of interest, a wish to find something out (i.e. due to intrinsic motivation), can reasonably be expected to be linked with a deep approach. On the other hand comments from students who had adopted a surface approach showed that they had tried to memorise the text because they felt that this was required of them. Surface approach and the motive of fulfilling the demands raised by others (i.e. extrinsic motivation) seem to go together. This relation between approach to learning and motivation to learn was the topic of Fransson's (1977) study.

His premise was that intrinsic motivation is not so much something one creates but rather something one finds. If we want to utilise people's intrinsic motivation, we must focus on what they are interested in and link the study material to it. Once again, the material used was in the form of a text, but the text was chosen in such a way that it could be considered to be of immediate interest to one of the groups that participated in the experiment, but not the other. The text was about the examination system in the Education Department. The group which was assumed to be interested in the text was made up of first-year students in the department. The other group consisted of sociology students who were not taking Education. In addition, each group was randomly divided into two subgroups. One of these subgroups was subjected to treatment that was assumed would create extrinsic motivation while the other subgroup was left alone. This subgroup were told that after they had read the text they would be asked to give an oral report and that their report would be video-recorded (the equipment was prominently displayed). The source of the extrinsic motivation was thus the utilisation of people's fear of "making a fool of themselves". When the text had been read, each group was, in fact, treated in the same way; they were all asked to write down what they remembered of the text.

After the sessions the students were asked to fill in questionnaires indicating how interested they were in the text, and how anxious they felt while reading it. Of course, not all the students from the Department of Education were interested in the text, nor were all the sociology students uninterested in it. Not all the subjects found the idea of being video-taped particularly threatening, but on the other hand some of those who were simply told they would have to write down what they could remember after having read the text, became very nervous. Some of the subjects who did not usually become nervous in other situations of a similar nature, did not become nervous this time either while others did. All this came to light during the interviews that were held after the experiment. The analysis showed that the main effect on approach to learning came not from the experimental situation *per se*, but from the reported experiences of the students — whether they *felt* interested, threatened, or anxious. Then the results produced a clear picture. Intrinsic motivation, absence of threat (extrinsic motivation) and absence of anxiety, both independently and together, were associated with a deep approach. Threat (extrinsic motivation), anxiety and absence of intrinsic motivation similarly correlate with a surface approach. In fact *all* students in the 'relaxed' condition who were interested and non-anxious used a deep approach, while *all* those who felt themselves threatened, anxious, and uninterested adopted a surface approach when they read. The conclusion that can be drawn from this experiment is that if we want to promote a deep approach, we should above all keep in mind the students' own interests at the same time as we should try to eliminate the factors that lead to a surface approach (irrelevance, threat and anxiety).

Approaches to Learning and Conceptions of Learning

There is, however, a paradoxical circular relation between approach to learning and motivation to learn. As the results quoted in the previous section suggest, intrinsic motivation (interest) seems to lead to a deep approach and extrinsic motivation (concern with demands) to a surface approach. On the other hand, adopting a surface approach means that the learner focuses on the "text" or tasks in themselves and not on what they are about. But it is hardly possible to be interested in a "text" unless one is paying attention to what it is about. Not being motivated by an interest in the "text" tends thus to lead to the adoption of a surface approach, and the adoption of a surface approach tends to block any interest in the "text". In order to unravel this circularity we may need to move to a superordinate level of description.

Säljö's (1975) above-mentioned study showed that the two groups participating in the experiment on the whole behaved differently because of the difference in the kind of questions they expected to follow their reading. On the other hand, there was a great variation both in the process and outcome of learning within the group which was given questions intended to induce a deep approach. In our view, this was due to the participants' different perceptions of what was required of them. The differences between contrasting experimental groups reflect the effect of context on learning. The differences within the same treatment, however, logically must originate from a variation in something which the participants "brought with them" to the experiments. Their perceptions of the task reflect their past experiences of similar situations, and so mirror differences in their preconceived ideas of what it takes to learn.

Säljö (1979) carried out an interview study in which he asked a group of adults what learning meant to them. Analyses of the transcripts produced five qualitatively different conceptions, to which a sixth has subsequently been added (Marton *et al.*, 1993). Learning was seen as:

1. A quantitative increase in knowledge.
2. Memorising.
3. The acquisition, for subsequent utilisation, of facts, methods, etc.
4. The abstraction of meaning.
5. An interpretative process aimed at understanding reality.
6. Developing as a person (added subsequently).

According to the previous line of reasoning, in a learning situation, which is the "same" from an external point of view and to which the participants adopt different approaches, we would expect the observed variation in approaches to be closely linked with a variation in conceptions of learning held by the participants on a more general level.

This was indeed one of the questions which van Rossum and Schenk (1984) set out to illuminate. They used an open-ended questionnaire to identify the conceptions of learning held by the students. The answers showed a clear correspondence to Säljö's categories. The students also had to read a piece of argumentative prose, give an account of its content, and report about their experience of learning. The design of this part of their study was very similar to that of the Gothenburg experiment already extensively discussed in this chapter. And van Rossum and Schenk also found that students' experiential accounts of how the learning task was carried out could be classified in terms of deep and surface approaches respectively. Furthermore a close correlation between conceptions of learning and approaches to learning was found (see Table 3.3).

TABLE 3.3

Relation between conceptions of learning and approaches
(from van Rossum and Schenk, 1984)

| Conceptions | Approach to learning | | |
	Surface	Deep	Sub-totals
1. Increase in knowledge	6	0	6
2. Memorisation	19	4	23
3. Fact acquisition for utilisation	8	7	15
4. Abstraction of meaning	1	11	12
5. Understanding reality	1	12	13
Sub-totals	35	34	69

In addition to matching the expectation of a relationship between conceptions and approaches, Table 3.3 seems to support Säljö's (1979) remark that the main dividing line goes between the third and fourth conception. Or modifying Säljö's earlier view somewhat, we can say that the first and second conception on the one hand, and the fourth and fifth, on the other, seem to have similar relations to approaches to learning. The third conception appears to be intermediate between the others. Though the conceptions refer to what learning is seen as, on the next subordinate level within the two pairs, there are "what-how" relations between the conceptions. The quantitative increase in knowledge (the first conception of learning) is achieved reasonably by memorisation (second conception). On the other hand, we improve our understanding of reality (fifth conception) by abstracting meaning from what we read, see, hear (fourth conception). The second and the fourth conceptions thus represent the "how" aspect of the two different answers to the "what" questions reflected by the first and fifth conceptions respectively. The first one of these two pairs of conceptions is closely linked to the surface approach, not only empirically, but conceptually as well. Indeed, it appears as a generalised version of the special experience of learning, which has been termed "surface approach" (orientation towards memorisation, seeing learning as a more or less passive transmission of what is on the paper into the head of the learner).

A similar relationship seems to hold between the second pair of conceptions (the fourth and fifth) and the deep approach. Especially in the context of normal studies, the distinction between conception (aiming at a better understanding of reality by abstracting meaning from what is presented) and approach (focusing attention on what the presentation refers to) seems to become blurred. As we pointed out earlier, a deep approach, in the context of everyday studying, primarily refers to the realisation of the fact that the studies one is engaged in deal with some aspect of the "real world" and thus by studying, one is trying to improve one's understanding of it. This is a view more or less identical with the one expressed in the fourth and fifth conceptions of learning; its investigation became the focus for much of the subsequent work in phenomenography (Marton, 1994).

The most recent work on conceptions of learning has been examining possible cultural differences in the conceptions themselves and in the relationships between them. For example, there has been considerable interest in what has been called the 'Chinese paradox' — that Chinese students seem to put much effort into memorising the material they are asked to learn, and yet they also seem to acquire a good understanding of it. Interviews with students in Hong Kong (Marton et al., 1995) have indicated that high school students there seem first to seek understanding, and then try to commit that understanding to memory — a phenomenon which is not dissimilar to the ways British students carried out their revision for Finals (Chapter 9 and Entwistle, in press).

In this latest work, Marton has explored not only the previous depth dimension in the hierarchy of conceptions, but also a temporal dimension which separates *acquiring* from the subsequent *knowing* and *using*. The depth dimension was also elaborated to distinguish between committing *words to memory*, committing *meaning to memory*, understanding *meaning (text based)*, and understanding the *phenomenon (reality based)*.

> Committing meaning to memory is more complex than committing words to memory, because meaning implies a distinction between words and meaning. Understanding (meaning) is more complex than remembering (meaning) because both imply permanence, but the former implies an act of constituting (or finding) meaning as well. (Marton *et al.*, 1995, pp.28–29)

In the responses of students, there also seemed to be a shift away from surface approaches and towards deep approaches, as pupils met increasing volumes of material in the later years of secondary education.

Conclusion

In Chapter 2 it was argued that the outcome of this kind of learning should be described in terms of the conceptions of the phenomena learned about which have been reached through learning. As one of the most immediate implications for teaching, on the other hand, attention is drawn in Chapter 15 to the importance of knowing what conceptions students already hold about the phenomena to be introduced to them. And it is exactly in transitions between preconceived ideas of the phenomena and an improved understanding of those phenomena, where the most important form of learning in higher education is to be found. Chapters 1 and 2 both showed, however, that this conceptualisation of learning differs radically from the one underlying the way in which learning has been dealt with in psychological research.

The research described in this book is an attempt to draw attention to outcomes of learning which seem to coincide with the aims of university lecturers (as seen in Chapter 1), and yet are currently under-emphasised in the teaching methods most commonly adopted, and not reached by the many students who still conceptualise learning in terms of reproductive requirements. To the extent to which students and teachers share an understanding of what it means to learn, we should expect improvements in the quality of learning in higher education — and indeed in education in general. The third part of this book explores the implications of this research in more detail, after looking at the experiences of teaching and assessment which students report.

Acknowledgements

The research reported here was financially supported by two separate grants from the Swedish Council for Research in the Humanities and Social Sciences, one to each of the authors.

CHAPTER FOUR

Skill in Learning and Organising Knowledge

LENNART SVENSSON

Introduction

In the preceding chapter, the distinction between deep and surface approach was presented. This distinction is used throughout the book as a general framework for describing differences in learning. Within this general framework, differences between people in their ways of organising learning materials are distinguished. It is the aim of the present chapter to pursue further the question of organisation in learning and to specify in greater detail the nature of the relation between the activity of the learner and the outcome of learning. This will be done by use of the concept of skill in learning and by further describing the meaning of approaches to learning. In the present chapter the term skill will be used to refer to the nature or quality of an interaction. The term skill is used in a way similar to that of Bartlett (1951, 1958) and Singleton (1978). Bartlett gives the term skill a very broad meaning and makes the concept a fundamental one in describing all human activity. Singleton summarises the meaning skill has to Bartlett and his colleagues in the following way.

> Sir Frederick Bartlett and his colleagues in the Psychology Department were talking and writing about the concept of skill as the fundamental unit of behaviour. This made entire sense to me but not apparently to very many other people because the movement dwindled rapidly with the retirement of Sir Frederick in 1952. It got lost within performance studies which were essentially behaviouristic and stimulus-response in origin, a quite different style of thinking from the gestalt approach of skill psychology. (Singleton, 1978, p. xi)

Instances of reading, listening, writing and problem-solving, which are the kind of interactions dealt with in other chapters of the present book, can be considered to represent skills. Such skills are conditions for and parts of learning, and the quality of learning is dependent upon the quality of the skills deployed. The purpose of this chapter is to discuss the most important general characteristics of skill in learning. An important change which takes place when one moves through the successive levels of the educational system from primary school to higher education concerns the learning tasks dealt with. The knowledge and the phenomena which students are required to deal with increase in scope and complexity. Thus there is an increasing requirement to deal with complexity and to some extent a corresponding development of knowledge and skills. Differences in complexity have important implications for the meaning of skill in learning, and organisation, as we shall see, is the most important element in dealing with complexity.

Organisation is also the aspect of the treatment of the learning material most closely linking the qualities of knowledge and outcome of learning described

59

in Chapter 2 and the approaches to learning described in Chapter 3. The main differences in knowledge described in Chapter 2 are of an organisational or structural character and they are related to corresponding differences in the approach to the content of the task Here we shall discuss skill in learning by further exploring the concept of organisation. The centrality of organisation to skill in learning will be examined through a consideration of the learning of different and successively more complex kinds of subject-matter, learning facts, and learning organised wholes.

The main concern in this chapter is with the nature of learning for understanding. Learning for understanding does involve learning facts. However, the learning of facts may involve only very limited understanding. This is why it is so important to consider the learning of larger wholes and the role of organisation in learning for understanding. The concept of deep approach emphasises the thinking about the world of which facts form a part, in contrast to memorising facts as isolated units of information. The concept of holistic approach, which we introduce here, suggests that, in learning for understanding within a deep approach the student forms wholes corresponding to complex phenomena of the world, including facts and their interrelations. It is the skill of forming integrated wholes that constitutes the most central aspect of skill in learning through understanding.

In this skill dealing with facts as parts of larger wholes is crucial. The nature of learning facts within the development of understanding, thus becomes the starting point of this chapter. In dealing with the question of learning in the two subsequent sections, we shall first describe and discuss the skill of understanding and then comment on what learning from understanding might involve.

Learning Facts

Facts refer to parts of the surrounding world. Unlike, for example, nonsense syllables, facts have an inherent meaning; indeed, referential meaning is a basic characteristic of a stated fact. As we shall see, organisation is fundamental in the learning of facts as it is bound up with referential meaning.

Understanding facts

The importance of organisation and of referential meaning to remembering and learning facts will be illustrated by discussing an experiment carried out with adults by Katona (1940) in the USA. In his discussion of two main processes of learning, learning by memorising and learning by organising, Katona used a series of numbers, 581215192226. He instructed a group of adults to group the figures in threes and reproduce them. After a short period most of them could reproduce the series. This illustrates the marked effect brought about by the simple grouping of the numbers compared to memorising the figures as a series of isolated items. When asked one week later if they still remembered the figures, the adults considered the question unfair, as they had not been told that they would be asked to recall the numbers later on.

Another group of subjects in Katona's experiment were merely instructed to learn the series. Some of them then discovered a regularity in the series. They found that the series could be structured in a series of numbers from lower to higher with alternating differences of 3 and 4 between numbers, as follows:

$$5 \quad 8 \quad 12 \quad 15 \quad 19 \quad 22 \quad 26$$
$$\quad 3 \quad 4 \quad 3 \quad 4 \quad 3 \quad 4$$

Those who discovered this principle of organisation returned the material to the experimenter. They did not need to repeat the series and they were able to reproduce it without any faults. One week later they could still reproduce the series and after four weeks had elapsed three out of five still remembered the principle although only one of them could remember that the first figure was 5. (Indeed, this principle can easily be explained to a subject and will be readily remembered, even though the subject has not discovered the principle for himself.)

In Katona's experiment, another group of experimental subjects was given the same figures in the same order, but presented in the form of a factual statement: "The Federal expenditures in the last year amounted to $5812151922.26". The subjects in this group made rather more errors in recalling the exact figures compared with the earlier groups we described. However, several of them remembered the approximate sum of money a week later (about $5,810 millions, or 5.8 billions). Where, as here, the series of figures is treated as a part of a fact, skill takes on a different meaning. The series of figures is attended to as a whole, as a sum of money, and moreover as a specific sum related to a part of reality. And in contrast to the case of remembering the figures as such, they are not given equal importance, for although they are still in the same order, there is a gradual decrease in the importance of the exact figures as we move from the beginning to the end of the series. This decrease in importance is determined, of course, by the meaning which the figures now have. Thus we see how organisation and referential meaning together constitute the fact. The organising principle is therefore not, as in the previous case, simply a mnemonic device dependent on grouping the signs or on discovering the alternating differences of 3 and 4. In the learning of facts, we have to consider organisation together with referential meaning.

It is through their combination with words that the figures in the above example are given their referential meaning However, words may be treated as isolated units, as in research on "free recall", where the subjects have had to learn lists of words or names. In this research, the phenomenon of grouping has been very clearly demonstrated, for although the words in the lists are presented in a random order it is found that the subjects arrange them into groups when learning the lists. The grouping is made on the basis of the meaning of the words. This kind of subjective organisation has been well demonstrated by, for instance, Tulving (1962, 1968) and Marton (1970).

Here, we are mainly concerned with series of related words expressing a fact, as in our example of Federal expenditure above. The example concerned a rather isolated fact. We now turn to another example where the fact is presented together with other facts in a reading text. In other words, the facts are located within a text, and have been organised in a way which reflects the subject-matter of that text. The text is an article by Dahllöf (1968) entitled "New facts about the open faculties". This article was used in an investigation by Svensson (1976), and parts of the data from the same investigation were analysed by Marton (1975b) and have already been referred to in Chapters 2 and 3. The content of the article has already been summarised in Chapter 2.

In the article, Dahllöf presented statistical tables showing that pass rates differed between different groups of students (e.g. male/female, younger/older students, arts/science students) and that they differed between the traditional and newer universities. He then presented cross-tabulations showing that the more significant differences in pass rates were found amongst particular groups of students and between different kinds of universities — for example, the pass rate was high amongst younger men studying liberal arts at the traditional universities of Uppsala and Lund, but it was low amongst younger male arts students at the newer universities.

If we now compare the problems posed by dealing with the facts about pass rates presented in this article with that given in the Federal expenditure example, we can see that there are very considerable differences. One important difference concerns the degree of specificity with which the facts are remembered. In the Federal expenditure example, the only fact to be remembered is the sum involved, and there may be some differences in the specificity with which this is recalled (e.g. as 5.8 billion or as 5.812 billion dollars). In the case of the article, however, there is at one level the exact pass rates and at another, the fact that there are differences in pass rates in a particular direction. Indeed, the direction of the difference is easier to remember than the precise pass rates or the exact difference. The reason for this stems from the relation between this fact of the direction of difference, on the one hand, and on the other, the rest of the message of the text and the previous knowledge of the learner. It is difficult to find other facts that support the remembering of an exact pass rate. It is much easier to find support in other facts for the direction of the difference.

The supporting facts presented in the text concern a general reference to differences between the universities in terms of the environment in which students study. Two specific differences are mentioned: that there are more job opportunities in the big cities and that group solidarity might be more highly developed at the older universities. A weaker sense of solidarity would mean that students in the large cities do not study quite as hard, while the wealth of job opportunities in the cities might divert them from studying. These supporting facts therefore make it understandable that the pass rate is lower in the big cities. They mirror the direction of differences in the pass rate, and they suggest that perhaps these differences can be seen in terms of a cause-effect relationship. In this case, then, organisation and reference aid the remembering of the direction of difference.

What may also help in remembering the difference is its relation to the overall organisation of the content of the text. The overall organisation is that of 'facts-conclusion' and the differences in pass rates have a direct relation to the conclusion, which is that if any measures are to be taken, they should be selective ones. The basis for this conclusion is the differences between groups of students, some of whom had a satisfying pass rate while others perhaps did not. Here, again, we can note that it is not necessary to remember any specific differences at all (nor even the correct direction of the difference) when recalling the point being made. The organising principle here — the structure of the text in the form 'facts-conclusion' — is the chief organising principle of the text. If understood, it very strongly supports the recognition that there are differences between groups of students. There was a clear difference in the use of this organising principle between students, and this difference also represented the main variation in understanding the text as a whole: we shall therefore turn to this in the section about learning organised wholes.

Learning from understanding facts

Whether a performance is to be considered skilled or unskilled varies in accordance with the criteria specified. This can be illustrated in relation to the example of Federal expenditure. Let us assume that students are asked a question about the size of the Federal expenditure, and one gives the answer "5.8 billions" while another answers "approximately 6 billions". If the criterion of performance is precise recall of the text, then "5.8 billions" represents a better performance. If, however, the criterion of performance is one in which the fact about Federal expenditure is to be understood as having meaning in the surrounding world, then the definition of skilled performance changes. Here, let us assume that the student answering "5.8 billions" has simply committed the fact to memory without grasping its meaning; and that the student answering "approximately 6 billions" has recognised its referential meaning. With the grasp of the referential meaning as criterion, the more precise answer represents unskilled performance, and the less precise one skilled performance. What has actually been learned through reading the text cannot easily be determined. The referential meaning that facts have is not necessarily fully acknowledged by students in their learning of these facts. The facts may be treated merely as units of information in a learning task. This, of course, means that there is a crucial difference in what might be learned: it might be something about the surrounding world or something about the text.

The description of learning also has to be based on some knowledge about what the students' conception of Federal expenditure was prior to reading the text. Turning to the second example we gave, on differences in the pass rates at Swedish universities, we can examine the role of previous knowledge as a basis for understanding and learning facts. In this example, it is reasonable to assume that the students already know what percentages and differences in percentage are, and that they know the meaning of the groupings of the students. Lack of knowledge in any one respect may cause problems in understanding the fact of the difference. Another problem may be that some students have not previously encountered cross-tabulations, and so fail to grasp their meaning. Although a student might not understand the meaning of the cross tabulations because of a lack of prior experience of them, the student could have overcome this deficiency with the aid of the discussion which accompanied the tabulations. In other words, by grasping the organising principle and the referential meaning according to which the fact of the difference was to be understood, the student would be able to make up for a lack of knowledge of cross-tabulations. Indeed, the most interesting aspect of skill in learning is that students are able to overcome deficiencies in previous knowledge. To learn to use previous knowledge, to organise and to extend meaning are important aspects of skill in understanding and learning. To develop these qualities is to learn how to learn.

Learning for Understanding

In the preceding section of the discussion, our concern was with the understanding of a fact or facts. In the last example we gave, the differences in pass rates (which constituted the facts we focused upon) appeared within the framework of a more complex unit of meaning — i.e. an article which was structured according to the principle 'arguments conclusion'. Indeed, we saw that the learning, remembering and understanding of this fact was related to the organisational and referential setting in which the fact was embedded.

In more complex learning, however, the aim underlying a learning task involving material such as an academic text is not the learning of facts, but rather the learning of an organised whole in which certain facts are embedded. This represents a very significant shift. The aim has become the learning of the organised whole, through a grasp of the interrelation between the parts which make up that whole. Within this organisational and referential framework, a specific fact is often of no consequence. It often does not matter whether the fact itself has been remembered or not, and it may not even matter if the fact has not been understood. In this section, we shall be concerned with the learning of organised wholes, defined as units of distinctive parts which are interrelated.

Understanding organised wholes

We shall continue with the earlier example of a text about university pass rates to give a description of qualitative differences in the understanding of the text as a whole. As we saw in Chapter 2, the different understandings which students had of the overall meaning of this text could be seen in terms of four qualitatively different categories of outcome. The four categories were the following:

A. *Selective measures.* If one wants to increase the pass rate, one should take selective measures, i.e. measures for some groups of students and not for others.

B *Differential measures.* If one wants to increase the pass rate, one should take different measures for different groups.

C. *Measures.* One should take measures.

D. *Differences.* There are differences in examination pass rates between groups of students.

The four categories represent different treatments of the message of the article. In category D, "Differences", the students have focused on some of the facts but have merely grouped them together without organising them into a whole. This is also true of the students holding outcome C, "Measures". They consider a concern for measures as just another unit of meaning. It does not have the character of a conclusion related to certain arguments and, in fact, it is in contradiction to what was argued in the text, since the author's concern was to question whether any measures were needed at all.

Categories 'A' and 'B' represent organised wholes with a facts conclusion structure. The specific structure, however, is not the same in each case. Outcome 'B' has the quite common structure that there are differences between groups of students and that the groups therefore have to be treated differently. Outcome 'A' has a more complex structure and is equivalent to the author's message. The differences between groups of students mean that in some groups the pass rate is in line with expectations, while for others it is not. Therefore, if any measures are needed, these measures should be directed only towards those groups where pass rates are below expectations. In other words, it is stressed that nothing need be done about certain groups of students, so the measures to be taken should be selective.

The four categories of outcome are thus based on four qualitatively different ways of organising the content of the text when reading and remembering it, i.e. they represent four different skills which each lead to different understandings. At the same time there is a more fundamental difference between the skills embodied in categories A and B and those embodied in C and D. It is the difference between organising the content into an organised whole or merely ordering and grouping parts. In one of the original Gothenburg investigations (Svensson 1976 and 1977), the first way of interacting with the text and organising the content was called a *holistic* approach to and understanding of the text and the second way was called an *atomistic* approach and understanding.

Within that investigation, the difference between a holistic and an atomistic approach was found to be the most crucial difference between interactions with complex learning materials. The difference is one between merely delimiting and ordering parts of the material interacted with, compared to integrating parts by the use of some organising principle. As our earlier discussion implies, there are usually important differences too within these main categories of approach and organisation. Within the atomistic approach, the parts may be differently delimited, internally integrated and ordered. Such differences will also exist within the holistic approach, but here the main difference will concern the principles adopted in organising the parts into a whole.

Several general principles of organisation such as narratives, argument-conclusion, principle-example and cause-effect are often commonly recognised as essential to a given material. It is, in most cases, not common for a learner to use a different principle of organisation from that suggested by the material; for instance, the form argument-conclusion instead of principle-example or narrative instead of cause-effect. The level of agreement amongst individuals about the organising principle of course also reflects the experienced clearness or ambiguity of the material. The relatively high degree of agreement which usually exists creates a situation where the main difference becomes one between those recognising and using the principle of organisation and those not doing so, i.e. between a holistic and an atomistic approach.

Although the fundamental difference between holistic and atomistic understanding in many cases is the main difference among a group of persons, this may not always be the case. Different learning materials lend themselves more or less readily to the identification and use of a main principle of organisation. In some cases, everyone in a given group may very well use an atomistic approach while in other cases all will use a holistic approach. This does not exclude the fact that individuals display some degree of consistency in their approach to similar kinds of material; a degree of consistency, however, that varies between individuals.

Another kind of difference to that between a holistic and atomistic approach can be seen in the following example, which does not focus on interaction with a text or message, but on relating to and thinking about a physical phenomenon. The example is taken from an investigation of university engineering students' understanding of physical phenomena (Johansson, 1981; Svensson, 1989). The students were asked to describe and explain a number of different physical events. The present example, which has also been discussed in Chapter 2, concerned what happens when a car is driven in a straight line on a motorway at a high constant speed. The first question put was "What forces act on the car?", and there were further questions concerning the different forces, their interrelation and effects. The most general and fundamental principle used to organise the whole phenomenon was that of cause and effect. An atomistic approach, then, would have meant not using this principle, but giving the "causes" and "effects" as unrelated parts. However, the relevance of a cause-effect relation as the superordinate one is apparent to all of the students in this instance. The difference that does emerge concerns how cause and effect are delimited and related, i.e. it is a difference within the category of holistic approach. It broadly corresponds to the difference between the two holistic categories of "Selective measures" and "Differential measures" in our earlier example. Those two categories represented two different ways of relating arguments and conclusions about university pass rates. As far as the organisation of the present example is concerned, the force or causal aspect is related either to velocity in the sense of motion or to change in velocity, i.e. to acceleration. This difference in the delimitation of the effect (and in the relation between cause and effect) is the most fundamental difference which can be observed in the students' organisation of the phenomenon.

The first mode of organisation, based on motion as effect, represents an Aristotelian conception and the second, based on acceleration as effect, represents a Newtonian conception of motion. The difference is one of the most important ones in the history of the science of physics. The Newtonian conception, although it is more complex, is not more holistic. The complexity involves greater and better distinctions within the description of the whole. Thus, the Newtonian conception not only involves more complexity in terms of differentiation of more aspects or parts (like constant velocity in addition to acceleration as a special case of motion) but also better fidelity to the material organised. (A similar observation can be made concerning the difference between the two corresponding categories in our earlier example about university pass rates.) This combined difference in complexity and fidelity we might call *completeness*. Thus we have emphasised two main differences in the skill of understanding; the difference between a holistic and an atomistic approach and distinct differences in completeness within a holistic approach. While this in no way exhausts the variation in important qualitative differences, these two differences can be considered to be the most important ones.

The quality of the interaction, the skill, is dependent both on the person acting and the material being acted upon; it is a *relational* phenomenon. Moreover, holistic and atomistic approaches are not seen as characteristics of individuals, but as individuals' way of relating to specific materials. It was for this reason that the concept of approach was introduced by Svensson (1976). The concept emphasises the possibilities of openness to and dependence on a given learning material as well as on the past experience of the individual. It was used in preference to the concept of process which emphasises certain given forms or mechanisms by means of which material is processed. It was also used in contrast to the concept of strategy which sometimes seems to emphasise the dependence of interactions on predefined plans — something which is not prejudged but left open when using the concept of approach. This accords with a more general emphasis on the fundamentally creative nature of human activity.

Learning through understanding

The atomistic approach represents a type of skill which is restricted in terms of the learning which it makes possible. This skill means, at best, learning of parts if these are new to the learner. This is a severe restriction since the understanding of the main point or the significant meaning of a message or the fundamental nature of a phenomenon is dependent on holistic organisation. A shift from an atomistic to a holistic approach thus constitutes the most significant of any improvements in understanding and learning. To learn to organise the content into a whole is the main problem of learning to learn. However, we must also consider the fact that there is a great variation within both the atomistic and the holistic approaches.

Within the atomistic approach to complex material, there is a variation in how atomistic the approach is. This variation corresponds to the degree of organisation of parts. The most atomistic approach means a memorisation of very specific details. A less atomistic approach means the integration of details into bigger parts and into main parts. There is also a variation in completeness, i.e. in the complexity and fidelity of the treatment of parts, which has its counterpart, as we have already seen, in the holistic approach. Such variations, of course, make a considerable difference to the understanding of the message or the phenomenon and to what might be learned by means of this understanding.

Such variations within the atomistic approach also mean, in effect, that some learners are holistic in relation to parts of the material while others are atomistic in relation to these same parts. This is important not only to the understanding of these parts but also to learning to learn. The less atomistic the approach is (the more holistic in relation to parts it is), the easier is the shift to a thoroughgoing holistic approach. An important aspect of learning to learn takes place within the atomistic approach when there is understanding and learning of progressively larger parts and an increasing completeness in the understanding of parts. But the biggest stumbling-block occurs when the progression halts and learning becomes fixated to memorising parts of a certain complexity. Learning to learn then becomes equivalent to learning to memorise as opposed to learning to organise.

Within the holistic approach, there are also variations in understanding and learning. We have already discussed differences in completeness. As far as learning to learn is concerned, an improvement in completeness means improved analytical and interpretative skills, which are skills in learning. This is a part of learning to learn within the atomistic approach too, but only in relation to parts of the material. And since learning materials vary in complexity, to be atomistic in relation to a very complex material may involve more organisation, analysis and interpretation, than to be holistic in relation to a rather simple material. This is because the precise meanings of a holistic and an atomistic approach are not fixed but are instead a function of the learning material concerned. The distinction between the two approaches centres upon the main difference in approach to a given learning material. And just as the nature of the learning material may vary, so the meaning of the main difference in approach may vary too.

There is the further problem of the difference between understanding or performance and learning. Learning is equivalent to what is new to understanding. What has been learned may be many very different things, ranging from previously unknown specific facts to an entirely fresh conception of a very complex subject matter or phenomenon. What is new in the latter case cannot be ascertained solely on the basis of what has been understood in a particular instance, but is dependent on the previous understanding of the subject matter or the phenomenon, i.e. to describe learning fully we have to describe qualitative changes within a developmental perspective.

What may also have been learned, in addition to a new understanding, is the skill of learning, i.e. of how to deal with learning materials. Skill in learning is dependent upon sensitivity to the material and the exploration both of the content of the material and of the relevance of organisational principles to the content. In any particular learning situation, there may be a complex interplay between two groups of elements. On the one hand there is the content of the task and its organisation. On the other hand, there is the student's previous knowledge and his or her approach to the task, where the approach encompasses a particular intention, a way of thinking about the treatment of the task, and an attempt to organise the material.

To be skilled in learning, then, means to be deep, holistic and complete in approach and understanding. As we have already suggested, the most important aspect of this is the open exploration and use of the possibilities inherent in the material, allied to a consideration of relevant previous knowledge. It is this kind of exploration of relevant knowledge and of relevant principles of organisation that represents skill in learning in the deepest sense, and it also represents learning to learn in its deepest sense.

Skill in Studying

In this closing section of the chapter, we shall be concerned with the relationship between skill in learning and skill in studying. This relationship is an important one which is often overlooked. The term "study skills" is a common expression which has generally been used to refer to techniques of studying such as notetaking, underlining, summarising and so on.

Interesting though these techniques are, they represent relatively superficial and peripheral aspects of the activity of studying. To see these techniques as skills in themselves is misleading, for this has the effect of isolating them from the student's thinking about the content of the study task of which they form a part. Thus, for example, underlining should be seen as a part of reading a text and notetaking as a part of listening to and making use of a lecture presentation.

On similar grounds, even the skills of reading, listening, writing and problem-solving do not in themselves constitute skill in studying, for they cannot be considered in isolation from the main units of the activity of studying as it takes place in educational settings. In an educational setting, such skills are practised within the framework of a course structure which is also linked to an examination system. And it is these assessed courses which comprise the main units of study activity (Svensson, 1976, 1977, 1981). In its widest sense, then, skill in studying describes the quality of students' performance on a study task which is embedded within a course. Consequently, our focus continues to be that of skill in performing a task, but we are now considering a more extensive task which encompasses, in varying combinations, the kinds of tasks we examined earlier.

What the task and the skill mean depends on the amount of material assigned and read, the time allocated for its study, and the form, conditions and result of the examination. Skill in studying involves the display of understanding of a given material through special skills of performance in examinations. However, examinations are normally very restricted in their form, content and duration. This means that very little of what has been understood by the student can be demonstrated in the examination, and selection is therefore necessary. This creates several problems, especially in higher education where the volume of material which students are expected to study is substantial. Since study success rather than understanding is what matters, and since this is defined as success in examinations, it seems unnecessary to understand more than what is demanded in the examinations. It is thus in the interests of students to be selective and to focus their studying in accordance with the examination. In practice, examination performance may very much depend on students' memory of the material, even in cases where tutors are aware of the shortcomings of examinations and would like performance to be dependent on a broader and deeper understanding.

In being selective, students can, broadly speaking, opt for one of two possibilities. One is to tackle the problem by selecting specific parts of the course material which they consider important and which, by themselves, are not dauntingly large. The students, therefore, see the examination as requiring them to remember and understand accurately and in detail these "correct" parts of the material. The other possibility is not to select *from* the material, but to select *within* it. The students place much more emphasis on overall structures and meanings than on specific details. They see the examination as requiring them to remember and understand details only insofar as these details exemplify or corroborate broader structures and meanings. The first of these possibilities constitutes a surface or atomistic approach and the second a deep or holistic approach.

The problem for the students is that the adoption of a deep or holistic approach is not explicitly required of them. What approach the students adopt is therefore likely to depend upon their previous knowledge and experience. If they are accustomed to taking a deep or holistic approach, they are likely to be able to cope with much larger units of course material. If they are not used to treating course material in this way, their experience of larger units of course material may become steadily less rewarding to them personally and less rewarding in terms of their examination performance.

The reason for this may have less to do with the content of the examinations as such than with the demands of large units of course material. As we noted earlier, it is easier to remember something that is part of a larger organised whole. It is also more efficient and more pleasurable to aim at and achieve deep and holistic understanding. The cumulative nature and increased complexity of course content presents considerable problems, however, if the approach adopted is a surface or atomistic one. Instead of the pleasure of understanding, there is the hard work of memorising increasingly more complex and steadily larger units of material. If students adopting such an approach are fortunate as well as industrious, they will manage to pass their examinations by dint of extensive memorisation while also gradually modifying their approach and learning what is required for understanding. But what often happens is that the students cope initially, when the amount of material to be digested is relatively small, but find that as the volume of material increases, studying becomes increasingly more arduous, tedious and likely to result in failure (Svensson, 1976, 1977). Academic success may be most easily achieved by students whose previous knowledge and experience has already equipped them to cope with the learning of complex organised wholes. These students will select within the material as described above. However, to those students who select from the material there is very little feedback telling them that this approach will be detrimental in the long run. The understanding displayed and accepted in examination performance to a considerable extent represents short-term memorisation. Relatively soon after the examinations are over, most of it will have been forgotten. In the long-term, the retention of understanding will depend upon the integration between what has been learned and previous knowledge and experience — that is, on the degree to which the students' conceptions of the world around them have been transformed by what they have understood. However, integration is not an inevitable part of skill in studying, rather it represents a problem.

The student has to balance two competing requirements: the need to deal with a large body of material in a short time, and what is required in the painstaking construction of integrated wholes. Achieving the latter demands insight, confidence and even independence and stubbornness on the part of the student. This is extremely unlikely to be found among students relying on an atomistic approach and already pressed by the increasing risk of failure. On the other hand, its achievement may in some extreme cases lead to failure if, in allocating study time, the student places integrated understanding above the requirements to learn a specified range of materials, as demanded by the examination system. Here, the paradox is that although in most cases academic failure results from problems with understanding, in some cases it may result from a devotion to thorough understanding.

To reiterate our main concluding point, skill in studying is not equivalent to skill in learning. Moreover, the benefits of skilled learning go beyond a better knowledge of a specific body of subject-matter and its long-term retention and application to new material. Ultimately, improvements in skill in learning which stem from any particular course unit are not specific to the content of that unit. They are improvements in the skill of understanding and of learning to learn. The student becomes more skilled at extending his or her understanding through an exploration of new and more complex material. Defined in this way, learning requires a relative absence of stress and a confidence in one's own thinking that are not always fostered in educational systems.

CHAPTER FIVE

Learning Orientations and Study Contracts

LIZ BEATY, GRAHAM GIBBS AND ALISTAIR MORGAN

Introduction

Students join higher education with different aims. For some there is a wish to continue their study of a particular subject, while for others their main concern is to progress towards a chosen career. For many students, however, their own reasons for joining the university are affected by outside pressures from, for example, family, school or employment. Then, students must discover what it is possible to gain from the experience of higher education and how to study in order to achieve their own, individual goals.

This chapter describes the differences in students' *orientations to learning* which affect their study patterns and strongly influence their experience of learning. The interviews on which this research is based, carried out with Open University students and in Surrey University, showed that students develop more or less explicit strategies to work in particular ways in order to gain maximum value from the experience. This does not mean that they work equally hard however, and the focus of their effort will be on different aspects of the experience. It is also clear from studies described in earlier chapters that students differ in their sophistication as learners. For some, therefore, greater effort does not yield a better outcome of learning. In understanding student learning, we need to look at the interaction between orientation, approach, and conceptions. We also need to consider how far students develop and change during their period in higher education.

To highlight students' overall experience of learning or their perceptions of gains from study, consider the following replies to the question—"What have you learnt from the course?". The quotations from six students, who had just completed a foundation course in Social Science at the Open University, show that it is possible to gain very many different kinds of things from the same course (Taylor *et al.*, 1982).

> I've learnt about the different disciplines and about the way the society's changed over the centuries since the industrial revolution and how this has changed everything.

> ... well basically an insight into methods of looking at different things. I mean, it was so broad, it has set things in perspective and so it's a good introduction to different facets of the subject. The way different disciplines will look at something, different attitudes of the sociologist and the more specific examination of an individual that a psychologist would make.

> I've learnt, I think, this business of being sceptical is quite a big thing. Questioning things a lot more. I think probably to live in the future, if I don't carry on with Social Sciences that's probably the most valuable thing that I

72

feel that I personally got from the course. When I read a newspaper or watch television or something I find that I am a lot more questioning than I used to be.

I think the biggest thing is the confidence—that perhaps I am not as stupid as I thought I was.

I suppose I'd have missed a lot of what I've learnt in relation to my work about the psychology of work and that kind of thing and perhaps thinking about things a bit deeper. Whereas I was inclined to take decisions fairly quickly on certain things, now I do have certain experience having studied a bit of psychology and sociology in places and I do try and perhaps see how things are going to interrelate and affect people—spend a bit more time on it and be a bit more thoughtful than I was before.

I think it's given me different ideas as to how I'll approach my course next year. I will take notes which I didn't do this year — I didn't know really what to do and what not to do this year. So I'll do quite a lot of things differently. I think I'll just approach the whole learning bit, if you like, differently next time. And what else have I learnt? — I suppose on a personal level I've learnt to use my time effectively.

Besides gaining an understanding of the course content, which may be the teacher's main aim, students mention the personal and affective aspects of study; gaining in confidence, changing in attitudes, and increasing critical awareness and scepticism. As teachers and researchers, we may be too ready to accept students' assessment grades and their understanding of the course content as the sole measure of success. It is clear from these quotations, however, that from the students' point of view other aspects can be equally important.

In higher education in recent years there has been a focus on transferable skills for future employment. The kind of higher education most useful to future employers has become an area of intense debate and courses have increasingly included more emphasis on transferable skills. In Britain, the Enterprise in Higher Education programme has been successful in supporting this movement (Elton, 1994). In describing the learner's orientation to education, we must take account of both institutional and personal contexts for study. What are the formal demands of the assessment system? What sort of understandings are valued and rewarded by the formal curriculum? What are students' aims and purposes in engaging in a course of study?

The Social Context of Learning

The institutional context

In previous chapters the outcome of learning has been described as a change in conception of some concept, issue, or aspect of the world. The quotations above show the diversity of these changes, while subsequent chapters will indicate the ways in which the institutional context and the learning environment influence the outcomes of learning.

A similar interpretation of the effects of assessment was provided by Becker, Geer and Hughes (1968). In *Making the Grade*, they show how the "grade-point average perspective" pervaded the entire course experience for students and provided the background for their study. The grade-point average perspective involved a "definition of the situation" by students who identified grades as the most important force leading their actions. Students felt that getting good grades defined success and that gaining these grades was of primary importance for their college career.

> There's an awful lot of work being done up here for the wrong reason. I don't exactly know how to put it, but people are going through here and not learning anything at all... There's a terrific pressure on everybody here to get good grades... There are a lot of courses where you can learn what's necessary to get the grade and when you come out of the class you don't know anything at all. You haven't learned a damn thing, really. In fact, if you try to really learn something, it would handicap you as far as getting a grade goes.

The conflict between "getting the grade" and "really learning something" can be seen as an unintended side-effect of the assessment system. The pervasive influence of assessment defined the institutional context for studying—the grade-point average became the "Camp currency".

At a more general level, the interaction of the education institution and the students can lead to particular sub-cultures. Clark and Trow (1966) described this interaction as follows:

> Two broad sets of factors shape the nature of the orientations and relationships of students in college. The first set flows from the character of the larger society. Students come to college with certain resources — material, moral, intellectual, emotional and cultural. These resources are largely determined by the life experiences the students have had, and these in turn are shaped by the status they and their parents have held in the larger society. The prior social locations and experiences also shape aspiration: the kinds of lives the students envisage for themselves in a rapidly changing society. The second set of determinants derives from the nature of the colleges themselves; their historical development, their value climates, their structural features, and the shaping environment thus provided for student life. A college is not simply an aggregation of students, it also has qualities and characteristics which are to some extent independent of the people who fill its halls and offices at any given moment.

In our terms, Clark and Trow were showing how distinctive sub-cultures emerged from the differing experiences of institutional and personal contexts of learning with four main analytical categories used to describe these sub-cultures. They are not describing types of student, as a student may well participate in several sub-cultures, and the actual sub-cultures that exist may well combine aspects of more than one type. Rather the typology can be seen as "a heuristic device for getting at the processes by which social structures shape student styles of life in different kinds of colleges". The four main sub-cultures were labelled collegiate, vocational, academic and non-conformist wthin the framework shown in Table 5.1.

The collegiate culture is the stereotype of college life, a world of sport and campus fun — some gesture is made to studying, but only in terms of the minimum requirements to gain a degree. The vocational culture is focused on getting a qualification and gaining employment; here the engagement in ideas and scholarship may be seen as a distraction, equivalent to sport and social activities. The academic culture, present on every campus, is the sub-culture of serious intellectual effort applied to the world of knowledge and ideas. Students pursue knowledge and understanding. Their symbols of the institution are the library, the seminar group and teaching staff with the same inclinations. The non-conformist culture differs from other cultures in its detachment from the college. Students are involved with ideas and learning but their points of reference are off-campus groups. There exists in this distinctive student style a somewhat aggressive non-conformist and critical detachment from the college. Clark and Trow summarised this typology of sub-cultures in terms of two main dimensions — the degree to which students are involved with ideas and the extent to which students identify with the college or institution.

TABLE 5.1

Types of Orientations of the Four Most Distinguishable Student Subcultures.

(from Clark and Trow, 1966)

		Involvement with Ideas	
		much	little
	much	ACADEMIC	COLLEGIATE
Identification			
with College	little	NON-CONFORMIST	VOCATIONAL

Clark and Trow use the term 'orientations' to mean the "defining elements of student sub-cultures in which they appear as shared notions constitutes right attitude and action towards the range of issues and experiences confronted in college". This general use of orientation is rather different from what has been defined in this chapter as a student's *learning orientation;* the aims, values and purposes for study — the personal context of study.

The personal context

How do students come to be taking a particular course? What are the aims and purposes in undertaking a course of study? With adult students these questions are particularly important because of the voluntary nature of the education they are engaged in.

The concept of motivation has been used to explain variations in students' capabilities for studying. However, there are problems with the use of this concept. Firstly, it has been used in so many different ways, there is a lack of precise definition with regard to its meaning (Peters, 1958; Parlett, 1980). Secondly, it has been used as an explanation of behaviour, which may not take enough account of the conscious control learners have over how and what they study. Motivation is seen as a drive, students are viewed as being driven by factors out of their control. Similarly, some goal direction theories tend to view students as responding to stimuli, rather than actively constructing their own behaviour patterns. The foci of traditional studies are the motivational factors which push and pull students towards particular goals, for example, to pass an examination.

Such ideas about motivation are based on theories derived from other contexts which have been imposed on student learning without sufficient consideration of their ecological validity. Subsequent work on motivation, in relation to study processes (e.g. Biggs, 1978), has, however, developed constructs more closely associated with the study situation and students' intentions. The description of personal context for study or learning orientation develops this work further, to provide a more holistic description of students' motives and purposes.

Learning orientation is defined by "all those attitudes and aims which express the student's individual relationship with a course of study and the university", (Taylor *et al.*, 1981). It is the collection of purposes which form the personal context for the individual student's learning. The idea of an orientation assumes that students have an active relationship with their studying. From the point of view of learning orientation, success and failure is judged in terms of the extent to which students fulfil their own aims. Orientation does not assume any state or trait belonging to the student; it is a quality of the relationship between the student and the course rather than a quality inherent in the student, and so may change over time. The analysis of learning orientation, therefore, does not set out to type students, rather it sets out to identify and describe types of orientation and to show the implications of different types of orientation for the approach a student takes to learning.

Orientations to Learning

An interview study of students' orientations to learning at Surrey University (Taylor, 1983) identified four distinct types of orientation. These were *academic orientation,* where the student's goals involved the academic side of university life; *vocational orientation,* where the student's goal was to get a job after university; *personal orientation* where the student's goals were concerned with their personal development; and *social orientation* where the student's goals focused on the social side of the university life. The first three of these orientations could be divided into two sub- types according to whether the student was directly interested in the content of the course or whether they were studying the course more as a means to an end. These sub-types distinguished in each case between intrinsic and extrinsic interest in the course. Taylor found that the concerns that students had while studying at university were intimately connected to the type of orientation they had, and that these orientations and their concerns helped to make sense of the amount of effort the student put into different aspects of the course and university life (see Table 5.2).

A further study at the Open University (Taylor *et al.*, 1981) found all these categories, with the exception of the social orientation, among students taking the Social Science Foundation Course, *Making Sense of Society.*

TABLE 5.2

Student's learning orientations

Orientation	Interest	Aim	Concerns
Vocational	Intrinsic	Training	Relevance of course to future career
	Extrinsic	Qualification	Recognition of qualification's worth
Academic	Intrinsic	Intellectual interest	Choosing stimulating lectures
	Extrinsic	Educational progression	Grades and academic progress
Personal	Intrinsic	Broadening or self-improvement	Challenging, interesting material
	Extrinsic	Compensation or proof of capability	Feedback and passing the course
Social	Extrinsic	Having a good time	Facilities for sport and social activities

The Complexity of the Learner's Orientation

It is important to recognise that the categories and sub-categories used to describe orientations are simply an analytic framework and not descriptions of the types of student found in the sample. In fact, any particular student's orientation will usually be a complex mix of two or more of these orientational types. For example, many of the Open University students could clearly be seen to have mainly a personal orientation to learning, but many of them also showed evidence of vocational or academic orientations. To illustrate these joint orientations, and the complexity of individual students' orientations, here is an example of a student who, while primarily personally oriented, shows aspects of a vocational orientation.

> Well I hope to stop myself from turning into a complete cabbage—and to widen my views on life and the problems —eventually I hope to get a degree and possibly that will help me to get a job one day which I would like to do. But I think that is very much a secondary consideration.

This quote shows clearly the primary personal aims, and the secondary vocational aims, of this student. We can expect that both these aims will affect the student's approach to the course and a detailed description of the orientation, including the relative strength of these aims, should help us to understand the particular student's approaches to studying.

Similarly, where a student shows signs of having both personal and academic orientations, both aspects will affect the student's relationship with the course. A student who is personally oriented, but also academically oriented, might be interested in personal development, but more in terms of the ideas to be explored in the subject than in becoming more capable in a general way.

> I am interested in man, in society and I realise how narrow a view I have about the way society works, about what other people feel and do and why they do these things. I got a bit from doing the A-level last year and I hope that I get an awful lot more from doing the Social Science Foundation Course this year.

In this quote one cannot distinguish clearly between the two orientations— they seem to mingle together as one orientation in terms of the student's own experience. However, the separation produced by the use of these <u>analytic</u> categories of orientation helps to unravel a student's particular orientation and to see the implications for approaches to studying. Further examples from the interview transcripts help to elaborate these categories of educational orientation.

Academic orientation — intrinsic   *Intellectual interest in the discipline*

This category of orientation is characterised by students who are primarily interested in studying a particular subject 'for its own sake'. They are intellectually interested in the subject and are interested in studying at a higher level. Most students with this orientation already had some experience of the subject before coming to university and so tended to be 'syllabus free'. They want to follow up aspects of the subject beyond the defined syllabus. One student at Surrey University had taken this to an extreme.

> I wanted to do sociology … the interesting thing about sociology is that a part of it is called the sociology of education and in studying education I had become more aware of it in a more objective way. You start to see the place it has in society. You see sociology isn't a nine to five study, it's a continual thing in your social life — you are being a sociologist … You are assessed so you've got to do a certain amount of course work… I copy as many essays as I can and do that minimum amount of work in psychology and philosophy. In sociology I just try and do as much reading as I can and then when I write essays I always bring in much more. But I hardly ever answer the question; I am always much too concerned with other things of interest to me.

So, the main concern of these students with a dominant intellectual interest in the subject is to be allowed to follow their own intellectual interests. In the interview, these students often mentioned particular lectures which had fired their enthusiasm for parts of the course and they particularly appreciated parts of the course which allowed them freedom to choose their own topic, for example, project work in the third year. They tended to criticise parts of the course where this sort of choice was restricted.

Academic Orientation — extrinsic   *Educational progression*

In this category students are primarily interested in *progression* through the educational system. They tend to have chosen the course because they had been successful in the subject at school, rather than study from an intellectual interest in the subject; that was thought of as 'the next step'.

> I wanted to do something and I've done evening classes, but it wasn't really enough. I don't know, I've got through that sort of stage.

> Well basically I am studying it because I did three 'A' levels and one of them was sociology. English doesn't seem too good really unless you want to teach and economics — well I find the maths difficult... I suppose most of my work is for assessment. I do tend to try to work—to do my best as I can in essays because they're assessed. If you try to work hard you'll get a good mark then you haven't got much pressure when it comes to the exams.

Within this category, students are interested primarily in passing the courses and getting the degree. They tend to be competitive and to lay great stress on getting good grades. In contrast to the intrinsically interested academic students, they tend to be 'syllabus bound' and in some ways may be described as 'model' students, in that their essays were always in on time, and they work evenly over all the subjects in the syllabus. The students with this orientation prefer to have clear guidelines as to what is required for assessments and to criticise parts of the course where there is little guidance.

Vocational orientation — intrinsic   *Good training*

One of the courses studied at Surrey University was a degree in Hotel and Catering Administration and, as one might expect, many of the students who were studying the course were vocationally oriented. There was, however, a profound difference in concerns of students according to whether their aim was to get a *qualification* in order to get a job in the industry or whether their aim was to be *trained* as hotel managers. The latter were intrinsically interested in the course and were critical of any parts of it that they thought were irrelevant to their future careers. They tended to place emphasis on the practical side of the course and to like the industrial year best of all. Since their interest was in becoming trained, students with this orientation tended to work hard on the course while they could see its relevance to their chosen career.

At the Open University students are sometimes thinking not of a future career but of a current one.

> It appealed to me because the reaction of people is terribly important and it is not just seeing the reaction — I want to know the reason people react under various kinds of circumstances. So far, all I have is observations you know; experiences. It's important because I hope it will help me to

understand people more. But I am not going to use the qualification at the end of the day so that side of it is not important to me.

As we see here, this category is characterised by vocational concerns and an intrinsic interest in the course.

Vocational orientation — extrinsic   *Qualification*

I'm in for a third (class degree) at the moment. I think I'm better than a third but I'm not that bothered — I don't think our degree is recognised that much by industry. So you could say that it is not that important. As long as I'm getting a pass mark or reasonably above, then good — I'm not going to go all out to do the best I can. I go out to get a reasonable mark.

The orientation a student has helps to explain the differential effort put into studying by different students. The above student, for example, did little beyond the minimum requirements of the assessment system. The amount of effort he was willing to make is understandable, given his aim of getting a degree in order to get a particular kind of job, and his belief that the grade of degree would not matter.

For the Open University students with this orientation there was sometimes the fear that an employer would not recognise the worth of their degree and this caused some anxiety. However, the expectation of many of them was that the degree would help them in promotion.

To get into this apex (top of the hierarchy) is going to be quite hard ... okay I've got two sets of professional qualifications but need this one to go with it. Because in a lot of people's eyes, particularly management trainers and development people, a degree is everything — it proves you've done something — you've trained yourself to think and express yourself clearly.

For this student, the choice of degree subjects was only important because the employer had to be able to see the relevance of these courses to the job. However, for those students who were hoping that the degree would qualify them to start a new career, the choice of course was less important and often a hit or miss affair. This was in contrast to those who were intrinsically interested in the training aspect of taking a course; then its relevance became crucially important to them personally.

For some of the Open University students, the degree course was seen as a way of ensuring that they could get a job sometime in the future. This was particularly so for women with young children.

I've got nothing behind me absolutely nothing. No qualifications — I've only had odd jobs before. As soon as the child is old enough, I'll have to get a job. Somebody said, "the O.U... that's your best bet". It's an education basis; something behind me. You know, if I go for a job now I haven't got a chance, no way. And I know nothing except factory work and that's not what I want. I'm not all that bright but I'm not thick either. So I want something so I can go and get a decent job.

Personal orientation — intrinsic   *Broadening*

This category is characterised by students who are personally oriented and interested in being tested or improving themselves as individuals. The intrinsically interested student is concerned more with the *broadening* effect of education and is using university study as a means of changing. In some ways, the university is seen as a sort of finishing school, a place where new ideas and challenges can be used for self-improvement and to improve the ability to cope with life.

> Its a broad course, and I think it is an excellent course for someone like me who wants enrichment of life having missed the opportunity earlier in life.

In the course, and in all the other aspects of university life, these students look for stimulation and challenge. They are concerned with the content of the course, only insofar as they can see its usefulness as a vehicle for change and personal development.

> The topics I like I will and sit and read for ever — if I think it will be useful to me then I'll do more but some things aren't that useful.

This personal orientation is very common among Open University students and among mature students at Surrey University. For these students the incentive to join the university often comes from a feeling of frustration with their life.

> I hadn't thought about that at all but I felt that I had to do something. I thought I was going to go round the bend being at home and I wasn't raring to go to get a job. I like looking after the house and the baby and that sort of thing, but somehow I wanted to do something else.

> I suppose it was waking up one morning and finding I'm 35, sort of male menopause. I can't sit around here watching T.V. for the rest of my life — let's do something.

The importance of this course to these students concerned how it might change them as people, making them more able to cope with life and making them more interesting people. They saw their study as purely of personal significance.

> It is important to me because it is the only thing that is me, and that only I am doing. It doesn't matter to anyone else results wise, how you get on, and I think it is purely you doing it and you getting something out of it for yourself.

Again, the choice of course was almost irrelevant and was likely to be chosen by means of elimination of the alternatives, rather than by positive choice. These students hoped that the social science course would help their understanding of everyday life. The broadening aim was summed up in their response to the question about their expectations of the course and what they wanted to gain from it.

> Well I expect a better insight into the way other people (are). I think one tends to be very biased; you live your life and that is the way it is. I'm hoping that I'll be able to see things from different points of view and not to

be too single minded about things. I hope at the end I'll be able to converse with people more easily without getting nervous.

Being at home it is easy just to go to coffee mornings and just to watch play school which are all right in themselves but it is not the end. I would hate to think of myself doing that this year, next year and the next year afterwards. And also I would like to think that it might make me more interesting really — I want to feel that I've had an exciting day and I've learnt something today or read something today and so hopefully enrich me as a person.

Personal orientation — extrinsic   *Compensation*

Extrinsic personal orientation is seen most clearly where students are doing the course to test their own capability. They want to find out if they are capable of a degree and if so, to what level. These students are more concerned with grades and feedback than with the content of the course. This orientation again is prevalent among Open University students. It can be seen as a sort of *compensation* for the lack of further education in the past. Students' reasons for joining the university for this orientation are to do with a feeling that they have been deprived of opportunities in the past or incorrectly judged by the education system. Through Open University study they hope to prove to themselves and to other people that they are capable of higher education.

It's something I've always wanted to do. For personal reasons between me and my parents I didn't go to university when I should have done. I've had a hankering ever since to discover whether or not I could have done it.

I suppose I want to prove something to myself. The one piece I have read said it was the most difficult way anybody had yet devised to get a degree and I thought — well, if I can do it at least it will prove something to me if to nobody else, and I'd like to.

Almost as soon as they start the course it becomes important to these students to succeed in passing the course, or at least in studying the course.

It is important, yes, now I've started it is going to be quite important. I feel that I don't suppose I had a challenge ,not ever probably, not for me to have to do it myself, so it is important. I have to prove, perhaps to myself that I can stick to it and do it. It is important, but just to me.

I'd say fairly important. I feel it's going to be the only chance I've got to do this and if I drop out of it I won't get another chance, not in the foreseeable future and by then it will be too late.

Personal satisfaction, …. It won't help me with my job, I don't intend to go marching off in six or seven years time clutching my B.A. and demanding a super job somewhere. I just want to do it to see what happens.

Social orientation   *Having a good time*

This category is characterised by students who appear to have social aims which influence the way they go about working:

> Put it this way, I would have gone to university anyway — it was irrelevant which course.

> The outside activities that I do — (radio, film unit, and sport) are very important. There is a lot to do outside and in some respects I tend to put off work because of them. If there's something to be done, I'd rather do that than something else. Then I try to keep it balanced — from the point of view of university education. This side of it is just as important as the academic side, if not more important, I suppose because you can always study in a correspondence course or something like that, but you can't get this kind of social thing and development anywhere else.

Social orientation appears to be extrinsic almost by definition; as it cannot be related to the course itself. But students often have aspects of vocational or academic orientations as well. Social orientation seems to affect the decisions students make about how to spend their time and may mean that the course is allocated a certain percentage of the available time and social activities the remainder.

Very few Open University students show this type of orientation, almost certainly due to the nature of the teaching, which is mainly by course materials sent through the post . However, some students place a high priority on tutorials because these provide an opportunity to meet people. The university life at a conventional university does, in contrast to this, provide numerous social activities, and at Surrey some students appeared to have these things in mind when they decided to apply to university.

Study Contracts

If we look at what students say that they gain from university study, we can see a mirror image of orientation type. The quotations below, for example, show an extrinsic personal orientation at the beginning of the year and a perception of gain at the end of the year which is a direct match.

At the beginning of the year, one student said:

> I didn't do much at school — I got to my mid twenties and I started to think — perhaps you're not as stupid as you thought. I have to prove to myself that I can stick to it and do it.

At the end of the first year of study, a comment was:

> I think the biggest thing is the confidence and perhaps I'm not as stupid as I thought I was, well perhaps I didn't think I was stupid anyway. But I can do a foundation course so we'll see what happens from there.

The following example shows a match between an intrinsic vocational orientation and the perception of gain at the end of the year. Again comparing first and final years, we find comments like:

I think I chose the social science course possibly because the sociology is more related to day-to-day environment — things that I do. I cover Personnel at work so it seemed to be a useful vehicle. I wanted a broader knowledge of the basic things I'm doing on a daily basis.

If I hadn't done the course I would have probably missed a lot of what I have learnt in relation to my job in dealing with people — the psychology of work and that kind of thing. I was inclined to take decisions quickly and now I do have certain experience in psychology and sociology, in certain cases I do try and perhaps work out how things are going to interrelate to people — perhaps more thoughtful than I was before.

In the study of orientations (Taylor, 1983), the longitudinal data also showed that there was a logical consistency between students' orientations and their reported study patterns over time, including the efforts they expended on different aspects of the course. For example, one of the students with an academic, intrinsic orientation already mentioned, said:

My attitude is both instrumental and interest, really, because you are assessed and so you've got to do a certain amount of course work and, eh, I copy as many essays as I can and do the minimum amount of work in Philosophy and Psychology. And in Sociology, I just try to do as much reading as I can, and then when I do write essays I always bring in much more, but I hardly ever answer the question. I'm always much more concerned with the things that are of interest to me.

Although this student, not surprisingly, did not get good marks, he nevertheless could describe a coherent rationale for his study behaviour. This shows a remarkable contrast in strategy with the following quotation from a student who has an academic extrinsic orientation.

All the work I do is geared for the assessment. It seems to me you could do a lot of background reading but I don't think it's really necessary. I mean, if I was particularly interested in something I would, but I'm not the sort of person who reads round a lot. You don't have to do an awful lot of reading to do quite well. I do what is necessary for the assignments and that's all the work I do really.

The use of the term *study contract* describes this relationship between the students' orientations and the way that they go about working and studying on the course. One student says to herself, "If I want to get a 2i and get onto that professional qualification course, I am going to have to put a lot of effort into the course particularly on assessments". While another student says to himself, "Well, getting the degree guarantees me a suitable job, so I will concentrate my efforts on those parts of the course which will provide me with the best training programme".

By study contract we do not mean the type of learning contract which some courses use to negotiate the specific learning objectives students will pursue within a course. Rather this contract is internally negotiated by the students with themselves. It becomes visible in an interview through descriptions of concerns and study patterns. Students vary in their awareness of the strategy they are using. While some students have a way of describing their approach in strategic terms others describe what they are doing without, themselves, making conscious links between their aims and their studying. The links nevertheless are implied by the relationship which is visible in the longitudinal data and which shows the consistency of their concerns over time.

The situational context of a student's aspirations and the opportunities offered by the course are part of the calculation students make about how to expend their efforts. Of course, students do not always live up to their own good intentions and they are not always so logical in their choices. There are, however, clear indications of long term planning and internal negotiation. It is the students' own ambitions and interests, and their knowledge of themselves, which show us that this internal contract is being made. The effectiveness of this contract depends on good information. The students can only work on the basis of that knowledge.

> I'm aiming for an upper second because if I want to go on to a postgraduate course I will need an upper second for either Vocational Guidance or Educational Psychology. And really, the higher (class) you get for the job the better, really being realistic. If there's a shortage of jobs they are going to take the one with the highest degree.   *(Vocational extrinsic)*

Whether or not this analysis is correct, the student's beliefs and orientation help to form a study contract which involves working consistently hard with a strong assessment focus. For such students, changes in the assessment system crucially affect their study contract and they may need to change their study patterns to take this into account — they may need to work more or less hard. The above student with this orientation in a highly competitive job market had to work much harder than the student quoted below who, although he shared the same extrinsic vocational orientation, had calculated that he needed only to coast along to his degree.

> Most of my work is to get marks. It shouldn't be that way, but it is. I do some background reading, but it is still for assessment. I'm in for a third at the moment. I think I'm better than a third, but I'm not all that bothered, because I don't think our degree is recognised much by industry anyway, and so you could say that it is not that important. As long as I'm getting a pass mark, or reasonably above, that's good. I'm not the sort of person to go all out to do the best that I can. I go out to get a reasonable mark.

This analysis re-emphasises the strategic approach many students take and shows why some students need to take this approach while others do not. The study contract is affected most by changed circumstances which cannot be anticipated by the student. Particular points of re-negotiation occur at times such as after a sandwich placement or after examination results. It would be foolish, perhaps, for students to continue working for really good class of degree when their continuous assessment results mean that it is out of their reach. The longitudinal research shows students making calculations and formulating strategies which are much more subtle than simply working hard or less hard. The effort and what it is expended on depends on what particular blend of outcome the student wants — i.e. on their orientation alongside their knowledge of how easy or difficult it will be for them to get what they want.

The concept of study contract does, however, capture the differing and changing attitudes which students show in the interviews towards the outcomes of their university studies. It shows that for any outcome there is a payment in terms of effort, and that some students may not have to 'pay' as much as others. It also shows that an understanding of differing approaches to learning depends on seeing not only their individual learning orientation, but also their perspective and knowledge about the external context of the course. This concept demonstrates the need to value individual students in a more holistic way and to provide students with accurate information about all aspects of a course. It also points to the importance of the students' awareness of the impact of their decisions on their future. Otherwise, many students will make their study contract on the basis of poor information both about the course and about the consequences of their choices.

Conclusion

We have established that a *learning orientation* provides a useful construct for understanding a student's personal context for study. It encapsulates the complex nature of a student's aims, attitudes, purposes for studying. Moreover, learning orientation is not an invariable property ascribed to a student. It describes the relationship between the individual and both the course of study, the institution and indeed the world beyond the university. It can also change and develop over time. Learning orientation is an important construct as it contributes to our understanding of what students learn. Besides the qualitative differences in learning outcomes described by Dahlgren (Chapter 2), which focus on the variations in how students understand specific concepts, students' overall perceptions of gains from studying can be understood in relation to orientation. Students' perceptions of gains from study, illustrated in the opening quotations to this chapter, can be related, logically and empirically, to their learning orientations. The powerful influences of the student's idiosyncratic purposes in studying, and of the student's perceptions of the learning context within the institution, are already clear.

Many lecturers seem unaware of the very different orientations held by their students, and as we saw in Chapter 1, tend to blame students for laziness (or lack of motivation). They thus assume that there is a single reason for being at university or college—to obtain the highest level of qualification. No doubt that was the lecturers' orientation: they almost inevitably had, or developed, a strong academic orientation.

The research described in this chapter serves as a strong reminder that most students have a complex mixture of reasons for continuing their education, and few of them aspire to the pinnacle of academic achievement towards which lecturers seem to believe they should be striving. Students study in a strategic way to maximise their achievement but within their own definition of what achievement means.

Part II

Experiences and Conceptions of Studying

CHAPTER SIX

Reading and Everyday Conceptions of Knowledge

ROGER SÄLJÖ

Introduction

The written word is a powerful strategy for communicating. As Olson (1977) has observed, the introduction of writing systems has had important consequences historically, both for cultural practices in Western society and for the cognitive processes of individuals. In its capacity to store segments of the collective experiences of a people or a culture, the written word puts a premium on a different set of cognitive activities than does the spoken word. "The documented statement", Havelock has argued, "persisting through time unchanged, [releases] the human brain from certain formidable burdens of memorisation while releasing the energies available for conceptual thought" (Havelock, 1963, p. 60). Thus as a cultural and technological device the written word has had significant consequences for the development of scientific, abstract thinking, for the mode in which the knowledge which has been accumulated is passed on from one generation to another, and, consequently, for the development of society at large.

A basic notion underlying the research reported in this book is that our capacity to understand and master learning phenomena is intimately linked to our ability to talk about this only vaguely defined concept in a precise way. A vital ingredient in our research activities has been to consider "the actor's definition of the situation" (Dale, 1973, p. 179) as worthy of scientific inquiry and to recognise that human action does not take place in a social vacuum, nor is there one universally best or most basic way of construing reality — of "world-making", as Goodman (1978) puts it. This excursion into the fascinating topic of how people make sense of what they read is therefore to be conceived not merely as an inquiry into human capacity for learning in a narrow sense, but also into fundamental processes of knowledge-generation and mediation in a complex and dynamic cultural and scientific milieu where a multitude of — sometimes competing — conceptions of reality (Marton, 1981) can be found.

Reading and Learning

The vital role played by the written word in our society is a strong reminder of the fact that the ability to read cannot be adequately considered as a mere technical skill denoting the ability to decipher strings of letters on a page (see Edfeldt, 1981 and Gibson and Levin, 1975 for an analysis of the nature of the reading process). A core feature of much of the reading that is carried out in academic contexts is that individuals are required to see something in the outside world — be it the structure of physical objects, an historical development resulting in major social changes, or evolution — in a perspective which is not a familiar part of everyday thinking. Consequently in the kind of reading that we do as students in order to learn, our present understanding of the world around us is often challenged, and this, we suggest, causes problems that have considerable pedagogical significance.

From the technical point of view, the Gutenbergian invention of book printing was a rather limited step; from the cultural and social point of view it must be understood as representing an immense leap forward, making it possible for a writer or scientist to share ideas and findings with a large number of anonymous communication partners with whom he or she had never had — nor perhaps ever would have — any personal contact. Viewed in this perspective the written document, so much a part of university and college life today, is really a quite specific form of communication placing a particular set of demands on the reader in terms of the attitudes and intentions with which it is approached.

As a preliminary to studying the phenomenon of learning through reading, it is necessary to recognise that the kind of reading undertaken in universities and many other educational contexts is in certain important respects different from the kind of reading (of a novel, for example, or a daily newspaper) which typifies other contexts. A very obvious difference is that in the latter case we select what and when to read, while in the educational context freedom of choice is constrained. Students normally have to read the literature specified in course requirements, and they generally do so at a time and in an order specified in the curriculum. This means that while reading in the everyday context of the novel or newspaper reflects a choice to engage in that particular kind of activity at that particular point in time, the reading that we do to fulfil the demands of the educational system is often carried out with a different set of initial commitments on the part of the reader.

Expressed differently, what varies between contexts in which reading is done are the *premisses for communication* (Rommetveit, 1974) that guide our way of making sense of what we read. When trying to understand how students approach the task of learning through reading, it must not be assumed that reading done in different contexts constitutes one and the same cognitive activity; that it can be reduced to a single, basic model of information processing characteristics of individuals irrespective of their intentions and the situations which they encounter. At the very least great caution must be exercised in making this an initial assumption if the concern of the research lies in revealing what the act of learning through reading is like to the individual reader. Indeed, as will be shown in this and subsequent chapters, there are good grounds for striving towards "thick descriptions" (Geertz, 1973) of learning, i.e. descriptions which reveal the meaning of human thinking and acting "when these are no longer defined in isolation, but rather... infused with the demands and traditions of the socially and culturally defined networks in which they exist" (Säljö, 1982, p. 47).

In one sense it might appear unnecessarily thorough to delve into problems of reading in a book which has the explicit aim of dealing with teaching and learning at university. Surely we can assume that students at this advanced level of the educational system can read in a sufficiently skilled way as to be able to cope with their textbooks? However, we do not merely expect students to read, we also expect them to gain something from their reading, i.e. we expect them to increase their knowledge of the world and their competence in understanding and handling various aspects of reality. This demand for learning through reading can be seen as adding yet another layer of difficulty to the process of reading, and it imposes criteria and restrictions which are different from those that apply to other kinds of reading that we do. The pedagogical context often — although by no means always — contains rather severe restrictions on the kind of interpretation of a particular piece of writing that is relevant or 'correct' *in that particular situation of teaching and learning.* In 'private' reading the demands for a 'common' interpretation of a text may be less meaningful, although it is quite easy to find instances where only one interpretation might be relevant, e.g. in the case of a brochure containing directions for mending or assembling an object.

In summary, then, when reading to learn students are expected to develop cognitive activities which enable them to accomplish something more complex than is generally assumed. Reading, as considered here, is a strategy for taking part in ways of conceptualising the world that are frequently abstract and unrelated to everyday experiences in any obvious way. This poses a central problem for contemporary education. Many of the insights and statements encountered in text-books, even those encapsulated in a brief passage or two, may be the product of centuries of discussion and reflection. This should alert us to the enormous intellectual investment which underpins our present conceptualisations of the world. In investigating how students learn from reading, we are thus not merely studying the mastery of a particular technique of communication. Our inquiries concern how insights and alternative 'versions of the world' are reproduced and mediated to large groups of students under the particular premisses for communication characteristic of educational institutions.

Outline of the Empirical Study

The empirical study from which the findings to be reported here derive (see Säljö, 1982), was designed to continue the inquiries into the processes and outcomes of learning described in Chapters 2 and 3. Again the work can be characterised as taking place in what Reichenbach (1938) refers to as a 'context of discovery', the object of inquiry being a more detailed understanding of how students make sense of what they read.

The study comprised five main parts:

(i)   An initial interview concerning the participants' usual methods and habits of study, their conceptions of phenomena such as learning, knowledge, etc.

(ii) The reading of a text which served as learning material.

(iii) An interview session during which the participants were asked to:
   (a) summarise the main point of the text;
   (b) give a free recall of the text;
   (c) answer questions on how they set about reading and learning in this particular situation;
   (d) answer a set of questions on the content of the text.

(iv) A discussion of the experience of learning in this controlled situation as compared to real life.

(v) Finally, the participants took two standardised tests, a vocabulary test and Raven's Progressive Matrices.

Each session was run individually with each participant. All communication during phases (i), (iii) and (iv) was tape-recorded. The tapes were later transcribed and the transcripts then served as the data-base for the analysis. No time-limits were imposed during any of the various phases, with the exception of the vocabulary test.

In total 90 participants took part in the study. They were recruited by telephone, and the names of prospective candidates were taken at random from the registers of various educational institutions. The 90 participants represented a much wider variation in terms of age and level of formal education than in earlier Gothenburg studies. Their level of formal education fell into one of three broad groups: short (6 – 9 years), intermediate (12 years), and high (at least 14 years of education, i.e. this group had at least two years of successful studies at the university behind them). The youngest participant was 15 and the oldest 73 years of age.

Broadly speaking, the rationale underlying the selection of participants was to match 'conventional' students at the three levels of formal education to adult students with comparable educational experiences. Thus, the three groups of adult students were not only older than their 'conventional' counterparts but had also had extensive experience of work outside school. Common to all participants was that, at the time when the study was carried out, they were taking part in some kind of education or were just about to start doing so.

In view of the complexity of the empirical material and of our specific concern with understanding how people make sense of what they read, the present discussion will make use of six participants as *exemplars*, demonstrating the major patterns which emerged from the analysis. The function of the exemplars is thus to provide concrete illustrations of ways of 'reading' the text which were characteristic of the entire group of participants, and which can be seen as indicative of significant differences in approach and outcome. The criteria which are valid in judging the merits of this task of discovery differ from those that apply to the (equally important) task of verifying the existence of the patterns and relationships described (cf. Glaser and Strauss, 1967).

The six exemplars were also chosen so as to represent the variation in age and level of formal education characteristic of the entire group of participants, as indicated in the following summary:

- Suzy was 43 years old and just about to start her studies at a college of adult education after having been a housewife for the past 12 years. The subjects she had chosen were Swedish, English, History and Civics. Her previous educational experience consisted of 8 years of first-level education, which she had finished at the age of 15, and occasional evening courses run by a voluntary educational association.
- Sean, aged 16, had just finished basic comprehensive school and had begun his studies at upper-secondary school.
- Stan, 47 and a primary school teacher, was a university student at the

time of the study. He had almost completed his degree in Swedish Literature and English, and he held a diploma of the Institute of Printing.

- Dick, 16 years of age, had recently finished basic comprehensive school and had started his studies at upper-secondary school.
- Dora was just about to commence her first term at university at the age of 38. She had trained initially as a laboratory assistant, but for more than 10 years she had been a housewife.
- Dave, a university student, aged 23, was just about to qualify for the award of his first degree. His studies included Russian, Economics and Political Science. Since the age of seven, Dave had spent only one year outside the educational system, working in a bank.

The text which the participants were asked to read is 3,750 words in length, and is divided into three sections, without sub-headings. The first section (850 words) deals with the phenomenon of classical conditioning and starts with an example of how, as a result of being tortured, a prisoner has been conditioned to respond with convulsions at the mere sight of the pair of electrodes which have been used to torture him. Following this, the basic principles and terminology of classical conditioning, which the example illustrates, are described. The second part of the text (550 words) contains a corresponding presentation of instrumental conditioning. Besides briefly introducing the basic principles (the idea of reinforcement as a means of controlling behaviour, punishment, shaping) the name of Skinner is mentioned and his Skinner-box is explained.

The rest of the text deals with learning through language and mainly contains a presentation of some findings from our own previous research. First an attempt is made to introduce the idea of qualitative differences in approach to learning in terms of the distinction between a deep and a surface approach. This is followed by a presentation of qualitative differences in the outcome of learning which are related to these differences in approach. This is done by means of an example illustrating how different people recalled a passage in a text, some focusing on conclusions while others focused on reproducing the text as such or on the superficial mention of various parts of it (as has been described in Chapters 2 and 3). The text thus had a clear pedagogical intention and the general mode of presenting results and knowledge from scientific studies corresponds to what can be found in many other texts having similar aims (the text is a chapter from a book of readings in psychology used at upper-secondary school). Several examples are used to illustrate and back up the general statements made and principles presented.

Findings

As a preliminary to discussing the kind of text which has been used here as an object of learning, it is essential to make a distinction between the <u>information</u> it contains and the <u>messages</u> it is intended to convey. Thus, in addition to presenting information such as names, technical terms, descriptions of famous experiments, etc., the text is obviously written, to use Rommetveit's (1974) phrase, "to make something known" about learning. What it intends to make known about learning can be described at different levels of generality. For instance, at the most general level the text has been written so as to provide some kind of map in terms of which learning processes and events can be understood. However, within the text there are also many statements which have an obvious message character, i.e. they make something known about learning without necessarily providing any new information of a more specific kind. The fundamental nature of this distinction between messages and information when considering this text as a means of communication will become evident below.

Since the text introduces the field of learning as an area of scientific inquiry, it also aims to introduce basic technical terms such as conditioning and stimulus, and to show the reader how different everyday behaviours and processes can be interpreted. As an aid to understanding, the author employs various techniques such as simplification and analogy to adapt the content as well as the linguistic form to the assumed interests and preconceived notions of his readers. The text opens with a rather dramatic scene from a Greek prison where a man is being tortured with electrodes. After having been exposed to this torture for some time, the prisoner has only to see the electrodes and he responds with convulsions. Following this example, it is pointed out that what the prisoner has been going through can be described as an instance of learning, and an explanation is then given of how the illustration can be explained within the framework of learning. The following excerpt is the very beginning of the text:

> On the same day they applied the electrodes in a new way. Instead of placing them in the usual way, behind my ears, they rubbed them over my whole body—my arms, legs, everywhere. It felt like having a drill-bit in me, drilling in until you feel like you're going to fall apart. It was like being in the middle of a whirlwind, you feel like a piece of straw in a threshing machine. One of the leather straps broke and so they quit. I was very afraid. One of them listened to my heart. He said something to me, but I couldn't understand. Then they put me on a stretcher. I couldn't collect myself. I couldn't think about anything. Lethargy.

> I don't remember if it was Karagounakis who came in afterwards, I only remember the stretcher and the leather bench, of course. New preparations. This time I had the feeling that everything was electrified. I got a shock as soon as I saw the electrodes, even before they had touched me with them. The man who held me was surprised. He only moved it in front of my eyes and I felt the current the whole time. He moved the electrode behind my head, where I couldn't see it; then I felt no electric current. Then he touched the back of my head slightly with the electrode and I jerked. The others came nearer to watch. They tried with the electrode from different angles. It made no difference where they put it, as soon as it came into my field of vision I felt the current. That day they didn't ask any more questions. They laid me on the stretcher and took me back to my room …

> This example from a very unsettling event in one of the Greek military

junta's torture chambers at the close of the 60's describes one form of learning in a dramatic way. Normally we don't feel shocks just from seeing electrodes or electric plugs of various kinds. However, the tortured prisoner in the example above had been exposed to experiences which caused him to react in a way quite unlike what he would have done had he never been tortured with electric current. We can say that this new reaction was learned.

   This form of learning is called CLASSICAL CONDITIONING. Contact with the charged electrode (is the unconditioned stimulus).

In looking at how the participants dealt with this particular passage, several interesting, and unexpected, observations can be made. Starting with excerpts from the recalls, we can see how Dick, Dora and Dave retold this passage.

Dick: Yes, it starts with a story about conditioning, classical conditioning. They had taken an example there about a man who was being tortured with electrodes and things in a Greek torture-chamber. On several occasions he had been given electric shocks and sort of become afraid of them. After that it was enough for him to see them to feel the electricity pass through his body. He didn't have to get any electricity, it was enough just to see them. But if they took them away so that he didn't see them then he didn't feel any electricity. That was classical conditioning.

Dora: First he described what's called classical conditioning. There was a man who had been tortured with electrical … equipment, and it got the effect that he just had to see these electrodes and then he'd feel the pain … And this was what they called classical conditioning.

Dave: A Greek was being tortured by the Greek junta and this was used as an example of classical conditioning, that is of conditioned responses. The person who was being tortured also got to see the electrodes, which gave the electrical shocks and gradually he sort of felt the electricity in his body just by seeing the electrodes. This I suppose is an example of classical conditioning which was investigated and discovered by Pavlov…

The point here is that it is evident that in these recalls this passage is reconstructed in very much the same way as it was used by the author, i.e. what is brought into focus by the writer through the torture scene is jointly attended to by the reader. Consider now other ways of reconstructing this passage. The following recall of the text is given by Suzy:

Suzy: There was a lot said about Skinner and, for instance, Ivan Pavlov and the psychologist Ebbinghaus and research results. That's always fun to read about. And then all this, there were some statistics about Chile, for instance, and that's interesting and I've always been interested in South America … and Spain too. And then there was something about the torture methods of the Greek junta and you sort of got bad feelings when you read about that kind of thing, even if it's interesting.

Here the torture passage is mentioned as if it were in itself part of the main theme of the text. There is no indication that Suzy reconstructs the passage as subordinated to the theme of learning (or classical conditioning), which is the "talked-about state of affairs" (Rommetveit, 1983, p. 16) with which the passage is used by the author. This tendency of not maintaining the 'vertical' relationship in the text typifies the accounts of a substantial proportion of the participants in the study. To borrow an expression from *Gestalt* psychology, what appears problematic is to discern the 'figure-ground relationships' that are used in the text, i.e. the relationships between what is in the forefront of the discussion and that which forms its background.

Another example of how this passage was perceived yields signs of similar problems:

Interviewer: Do you remember the very first example in the text, I mean the example that the whole text started with?

Sean: Yes, it was about torture, a man was being tortured ... under the Greek junta.

Interviewer: Could you tell me a bit about it?

Sean: Well, first ... he was lying on some stretcher, this man. And, how there were people around him exposing him to different kinds of experiments. They had electrodes and touched his body and ... before they had started torturing his body he'd scream. And then they took the electricity and all that behind his head so that he couldn't see when they approached his body... And then they attached them to his skull and ... then they examined his heart and,... yes, well I don't remember anything else. I do remember though that it all ended with their leaving him on his own...

Interviewer: Why was it placed here, this example, do you think?

Sean: Yes, it was to show through violence one can get people to learn other things than what they have learnt before...

Interviewer: What was this an example of, this.

Sean: It was an example of ... how the junta tried to ... Well, it was probably some opponent of the Greek junta and they tried to get him to get rid of ... to forget everything that he had learnt earlier on ... they tried to indoctrinate him ...

Here we can note two features that are interesting from the point of view of knowledge mediation through reading. First, although Sean recounts the torture scene at considerable length and quite accurately, he does not say anything about the process of conditioning which was obviously the reason why the passage had been selected as an appropriate part of the present text. Again from a communication perspective this can be considered as a distortion in the figure-ground relationships of the text. The phenomenon which the author attempts to 'make known' is conditioning (as a variant of learning), and it is this which is the 'figure' and the torture scene from Greece—in spite of its prominence in the text—which is the 'ground'. Sean in his recall, or decoding, reverts this figure-ground pattern, and focuses on the torture scene as if it were itself 'the talked-about state of affairs'.

Second, when Sean, having been prompted by the interviewer, does subordinate this passage to the general theme of learning, he states that it is intended to illustrate how violence can be used to 'teach' someone something against his own will, and that this is a specific form of learning. Now when the excerpt about the prisoner is considered in isolation and not as a part of this particular text, this appears to be a perfectly appropriate mode of recalling it. It can be considered, and used, as a story illustrating how torture is used for political purposes, to brainwash dissidents. In that sense this recall is a reasonable and perfectly coherent mode of retelling this section, but — and this is our point — not *of reconstructing its message within the overall framework of the text.* If the communication situation were to be construed as allowing the reader a free choice in determining what to attend to, and in whatever way was felt to be appropriate, any further discussion on criteria of 'correctness' of interpretations would be futile. However, if we assume that in this particular pedagogical context the power of decision over what is being talked about is asymmetrically distributed (in the sense that the (possible) expansion of the reader's conception of reality relies on his or her temporary subordination to the line of reasoning suggested by the author), then the apparent failure to 'agree on' what is being talked about can be understood as a problematic element in the process of mediating knowledge.

To give another illustration of the problems of establishing intersubjectivity between text and reader, we can take a passage which was an example to illustrate something general. The passage dealt with the difference between a deep and a surface approach to learning, which has been examined in previous chapters of the present book. The example used was about the training of graduate professionals and of sub-professionals in developing countries as compared to industrialised ones. It was pointed out that in developing countries, this proportion is often very unfavourable, while in the industrialised countries it is much better (meaning a higher proportion of sub-professionals to professionals). The countries used as illustrations were, on the one hand, Chile, and on the other the USA and Sweden, and the occupational groups used as concrete examples for the comparisons were doctors and nurses.

Neither Suzy nor Stan relates this passage to the topic of learning. What is said about Chile is treated as if it formed a part of the main theme of the text itself, and not as if it were a means to concretise differences in the outcome of learning.

Suzy: And then all this, there were some statistics about Chile, for instance, and that's interesting and I've always been interested in South America... and Spain too..

Stan: There were examples from the situation in Chile, where there were three doctors to one nurse or something like that, from a Swedish point of view a very bad proportion and even more so compared to America where there were seven nurses for every doctor, I think. That's the kind of picture that I very vaguely have. I mean, its the same impression that you get from reading the newspapers, for instance, about how things are in the underdeveloped countries.

By contrast, Dora and Dave clearly perceive that the information about the education of doctors and nurses in different countries has the status of an example.

> *Dora*: Then there was a discussion about the value of different kinds of learning and well, there were other students who had to read another text and they also had to relate this text. It was a text which examined the working relationship between professionals and sub-professionals.

> *Dave*: Here they account for yet another example of experiments on how a text was read. They had read about this relationship, that qualified professionals need a large number of special assistants to be able to function properly and there was an example of doctors versus nurses. Thus, a doctor should ideally have a greater number of nurses than the other way around. And then they had seen what these persons got out of this text and...

This contrast between the two groups of exemplars was again apparent at a later stage in the interviews, when participants were specifically asked why this particular example had been introduced. The responses given by Dick, Dora and Dave provide further confirmation that they have grasped the illustrative function of the example. Suzy, however, states that she does not know why this example was placed in the text, while Sean again assumes that the information given was an integrated part of the text's main theme. He appears to have interpreted the text as dealing with classical conditioning, instrumental conditioning, learning through language and the education of professionals and sub-professionals in various countries.

> *Sean*: It depends on when it's written... If it's written before '73 or ... before the fall of Allende in Chile or ...

> *Interviewer*: Oh, well, it's older than that ...

> *Sean*: It's older ... well, then I think they want to show ... how well Chile has been developing and how the development has been in comparison to these other countries.

Stan, on the other hand, perceives that this passage has the role of an example, but he is completely mistaken about what it exemplifies.

> *Stan*: Yes, in that context it should probably have some ... be associated with some kind of behaviour, ... type of behaviour. The behaviour of different countries or ...

To sum up at this point, what has been seen can be described as different ways of making sense of two segments of this particular text. Yet the difference between the two groups of exemplars is less a question of what is understood and remembered than of the extent to which what the author attempts to make known is reconstructed. Suzy, Sean and Stan do not seem to have any difficulties in understanding the two passages *per se*. Rather what appears problematic, it seems, is to discern and to attend to the particular aspects of these illustrations that are relevant to the line of reasoning adopted by the author.

Suzy, Sean and Stan seem to have adopted what Svensson (see Chapter 4) calls an *atomistic* approach. In consequence, in terms of the figure-ground analogy they seem to construe figures that are only partially related to the ones suggested by the author. However, and this seems important, their ways of making sense of these paragraphs are not wrong in any absolute sense and do not violate basic rules of language use. Nor is it reasonable to assume that general intellectual deficits would make it impossible for Suzy, Sean and Stan to reconstruct the messages as intended. (Indeed it should be noted that the performances of Suzy and Stan on the Vocabulary Test were far superior to that of Dick.) Our search for an adequate interpretative framework must instead focus on the assumptions held by these readers/learners about the nature and purposes of this task and the criteria of understanding relevant to this particular situation. Before attempting this, however, let us comment on some other findings indicating differences in how the exemplars made sense of what they had been reading.

In continuing our search for the nature of the inter-subjectivity established between the reader and the text, we shall add some observations from two other sources that reveal interesting differences. The first source was a very open and non-directive question asking participants to give their general reaction to the text. It was phrased as "Well, what did you think of this text?". A striking difference is once again apparent. Consider first the accounts given by Suzy, Sean and Stan.

Suzy: Well, I really think one should have had more time on it. 'Cos after all one gets a bit distracted and I find it difficult to concentrate on reading.

Sean: I think that ... what was said at the beginning about different methods of learning was rather interesting. To see how ... that there are very different ... many different methods for learning things.

Stan: Well, I found it very interesting.

Interviewer: In what way?

Stan: Because I'm rather keen on that sort of thing and the arguments presented. Maybe it's an illusion, but I think you learn something from such things... You sort of learn. At the end there were also such nice comments about deep structure and surface structure. Such things fascinate me very much.

These excerpts contain general reactions to the test as a learning task and some comments about how interesting it was found to be. Dick, Dora and Dave also comment on their interest in the text, but add a very specific remark.

Dick: Well it tied in with the questions we discussed earlier, sort of. Why some people find it easier to learn and remember, and how you remember things and so on.

Dora: Well, it is about the very same thing that we're doing right now... That's what's so funny about it, I think.

Interviewer: Yes... How do you mean ... ?

Dora: Well, I mean what we talked about earlier, it relates very closely to what I was saying ... It all comes back here in this.

Dave: It was interesting. We had just been sitting here talking about learning and of course I thought about that. What was said corresponded to a certain degree with the ideas I had and it was interesting to get it confirmed all this about the activity and so on and thinking independently. That's what I also said is the most important thing about learning, that you should be able to apply it in a wider context and not just churn it out by heart.

What is added in these comments is an explicit recognition that the text deals with the very same situation as was discussed in the initial interview. These participants, in contrast to their counterparts above, thus spontaneously react by pointing to the thematic continuity between two different instances of communication, the interview and the text. Furthermore, throughout the continued questioning they compare what they themselves had said about learning with what was said in the text. A striking difference between the two groups of participants thus concerns to what extent the content of the text has been explicitly seen *as offering the possibility of changing (or confirming) the conception of learning that the individual brought to the situation in relation to the conception presented in the text.* According to the view of human learning introduced earlier in this volume and described as characterised by changes in conceptions of reality, it is, we would hold, *precisely in such encounters between different conceptions of the same phenomenon, or between different 'versions of the world', that new insights may result, i.e. that learning can occur.*

The second source of data to be commented upon here derives from the concluding interview, where the participants were encouraged to report on the associations they had been making while reading and to explain to what extent and in what way the text had reminded them of things they had experienced or read about. Here too clear differences between the two groups can be discerned. Dick, Dora and Dave constantly talk in terms of the overarching theme of learning and the various scientific investigations and experiments they refer to are always explicitly accounted for as illustrations of learning. They also explicitly and spontaneously make comments which indicate an active attempt to identify the 'talked about state of affairs', as is illustrated by Dave:

Interviewer: Can you describe how you went about reading the article?

Dave: I didn't look the article over first, instead I started reading it straightaway, something that I don't usually do, usually I'll skim through them rather quickly sort of to see what it's all about... But here I just read the introduction and then I understood what its slant would be... I understood that it would be going to deal with different forms of learning...

Suzy, Sean and Stan, on the other hand, do not seem to be directed towards identifying what the author attempts to make known in the same active way. They have difficulties in identifying and expressing what theme the author addresses, as is exemplified by the following quotation from Suzy.

Interviewer: What did you see as of most importance in the text? What did the person who wrote it want to get across? Could you say that in just a few sentences...

Suzy: Wanted to say? Hm, it's difficult to say really.

Interviewer: Hm, what title do you think you would want to give to this text?

Suzy: What title to give it,... well,... in the introduction there it referred back to the Greek junta. Then there was a lot of research stuff and then there... Well, there were sort of a lot of different things which come in there all the time like ... No, I need to have more time to sort of get ...

The questioning also yields signs of differences in how the two groups of participants inject meaning into what they read and what kind of associations the text evokes. The statements given by Suzy, Sean and Stan imply that they had been reacting to the text, and to the various parts of it, in a way that was not related to the messages the author intended to convey. They atomise the text and they use the parts which they themselves have singled out as a basis for injecting meaning and for associating. In so doing they miss the intended relationship between parts and 'wholes', and the possibilities of profiting from the insights offered by the author are, we would assume, impaired.

Reading with the Intention of Learning

In accordance with the logic of research adopted in this volume, our search for an interpretative framework encompassing differences in how the participants made sense of this particular text should focus on possible *internal relationships* between approach and outcome (cf. Marton and Svensson, 1979). In other words, in <u>functional</u> terms, it should focus on what the participants were doing in this particular communication situation, and the assumptions they held about it.

As will have been evident to the reader, the two groups of participants focused on here were selected since their approach to learning could be identified as instances of a deep (Dick, Dora and Dave) or a surface (Suzy, Sean and Stan) approach. The latter display indications of what has been described in Chapter 3 as a surface approach (an orientation towards memorising, focusing on the text *per se* rather than what the text is about, etc.). But a further salient difference was found to reside in their *conceptions of knowledge and learning*. These differences in conception, as we saw in Chapter 3, are linked to differences in approach. Thus Dave Dick and Dora see knowledge as offering an improved understanding of reality through the abstraction of meaning, while for Sean, Stan and Suzy on the other hand, knowledge is equated with 'information' or 'facts' which are learned through memorisation (Säljö, 1982, pp. 76 – 91). How then can the relationship between approach and conception help us to understand how the text is apprehended by Sean, Stan and Suzy?

The point we wish to make is that this subjectively coherent picture of what knowledge is and <u>how</u> one learns *serves as a premiss for, and a limitation upon, the sense-making activities assumed to be appropriate when approaching a discourse with the intention of learning.* If this conclusion is valid, the major learning problem in this instance is that a surface approach seems to imply that the text is not decoded on the premises on which it was written, and the reader, in his or her role <u>as learner</u>, does not seem to be directed towards reconstructing its messages. In this sense, a surface approach implies a violation of the fundamental rule of role-taking summarised by Rommetveit (1983) when analysing dyadic interaction in terms of the "constellation of the speaker's privilege and the listener's commitment" (p. 16). In the present case the privilege of deciding what is brought into focus in the dialogue between text and reader lies with the text (and its author) and the commitment or responsibility to determine what is being meant lies with the reader.

In comparison to oral communication the written discourse thus implies a different distribution of responsibility for controlling the progress of the 'dialogue'. Once writers have encoded their message, it leaves their charge: reconstructing what is made known is at the discretion of their readers. This means that even in cases where messages are interpreted as running counter to what the readers themselves happen to know or assume, the reader must—in one way or another—provisionally accept the line of reasoning followed by the author while they are reading. Thus, the reader/learner must grant to the writer the active role in directing the dialogue, provisionally accept the premises the writer has introduced, and search for the messages or 'wholes' pointed to by this anonymous communication partner.

At a general level, this seems to be a significant part of the problem which Suzy, Sean and Stan have in reading this kind of text. Since their implicit assumptions of learning and knowledge lead them to focus on 'information' they can see no obvious way of dealing with much of what is said in the text nor with the general line of reasoning developed. In fact, *they act as if they lack what we might call a cognitive category corresponding to a conception of a phenomenon.* This of course does not mean that they did not have any preconceived ideas about the phenomenon of learning prior to the reading of this particular text. What it does mean is that they do not see it as the purpose of the general situation they are in to confront their preconceived assumptions with the ideas presented by the author. For them, changing one's conceptions of reality is not what has come to be associated with the specific task of learning in this kind of context.

Concluding Comments

To recapitulate, it follows from what has been said that the distinction between a deep and surface approach is not meaningful in all contexts. If the distinction is to be useful in analysing how people learn, the learning material should have the same general character as that used in the studies presented in this and in previous chapters, i.e. a text which presents arguments, scientific principles and constructs, and/or is intended to provide a coherent way of explaining or analysing a phenomenon. Should the learning material be of a different kind, (listing, for example, German prepositions which take the accusative case), this distinction might not be at all applicable or enlightening. Learning of this latter kind has very much the character of acquisition of information, and mastery of the task is probably to a large extent a function of the time and energy one devotes to memorising. The pedagogical problems in such situations are obviously different from those dealt with here.

Instead, the question of what approach a person uses when learning through reading becomes critical when we deal with texts which have a message character. In such instances our research indicates that a surface approach is associated with decisive difficulties in understanding. Furthermore, the conception of the *what* and *how* of learning which underlies this approach makes it rather difficult to deal with the more provisional and conditional types of reasoning which are quite often found in this kind of text ('assuming that A and B are related, we find that the process C can be explained in the following way...'). To a large extent it seems as if the premises underlying this kind of reasoning and the qualifications imposed are disregarded by the students in the learning process, and what are left as appropriate 'targets for learning' are more definite statements shorn of such qualifications and with a more factual appearance (see Säljö, 1982, for a fuller discussion).

A discourse of the kind used in the present study is thus not a list of unambiguous and fixed statements about the world. Instead it can be conceived as a conscious attempt to reorganise current 'versions of the world' and to provide conceptual tools and contexts for understanding that have emerged from scientific experimentation and theorising. From a communication perspective, the text is an <u>invitation</u> to attend to some more or less familiar aspects of reality within a framework that may not be part of our everyday thinking with respect to this class of phenomena. The reader is offered the possibility of expanding his or her current repertoire of 'world-versions' and of adding alternative ones which might never present themselves as a result of day-to-day experiences. However, this is only a <u>potential</u> which is dependent for its realisation on the approach the reader/learner uses.

A conclusion of our examination of learning approaches would thus be the somewhat paradoxical statement that to quite a large extent it is *the intention to learn from the text which leads people to misunderstand it*. When a text is defined as an object of learning this seems to affect how it is made sense of, and prominence is given to *criteria of relevance* which are not those adhered to in other reading situations. The distortions of the 'figure-ground' relationships in the text, the problems encountered in discerning the 'vertical' dimension of the text (the horizontalisation phenomenon), and the more general difficulties in grasping the contextually relevant meanings, are not, we can safely assume, characteristic of how Suzy, Sean and Stan relate to written texts in other contexts. Were this to be a problem characteristic of their reading in general, it could be interpreted as a severe dysfunction. It is our assumption, however, that the crucial process of decoding a text on the premises on which it was written, is the natural mode of acting in everyday reading situations. In such situations, reading is characterised by a *voluntary and self-induced decision to attend to a written discourse in which there is a genuine and momentary desire to find out what is 'made known'*. A basic feature of a deep approach therefore seems to be that this attitude is <u>also</u> maintained in a situation where there may not be such an initial commitment on the part of the reader, but where the reading is undertaken in response to a request or requirement.

It also follows that we can view students' approaches to learning from texts, and their conceptions of knowledge and learning, as social phenomena that evolve as a response to long exposure to educational situations. There are many factors which might be seen as reinforcing this way of learning: overloaded curricula, forms of assessment requiring the more or less verbatim recall of facts and even the design of text books, which can present knowledge in such a neatly parcelled way that there is scope for little beyond mere memorising. Nevertheless, to suggest that schools may encourage a surface approach is not to level an accusation, for the conception of learning endorsed in schools is modelled on what this concept is commonly assumed to refer to in society at large. A static and factual conception of knowledge is not an invention of schools, as many critics seem to assume; it is a part of common-sense thinking. Without going too deeply into this fascinating topic, the dominance of a factual view of knowledge among teachers and learners can be seen as a consequence of its domination of the larger cultural context of Western everyday thinking, where there is a strong tradition of construing knowledge in absolutistic terms. As Douglas (1971) observes, "Absolutist (non-situational and non-contextual) thought is not the product of some mad scientist. Absolutist thought is a fundamental part of Western thought" (p. 39). What we have referred to as a 'fact' stands as a symbol, unreflective and taken-for-granted, of what knowledge should look like, and it is thus not particularly surprising that educational activities often start from this platform. Nor should we be surprised that students have difficulties when this definition of knowledge is challenged (see Perry, 1970).

But can the conclusion be drawn that a deep approach is more efficient than a surface one? We hope the reader has been able to conclude that this is not necessarily the case given a long tradition in education of what characterises pedagogic situations. A surface approach is obviously a rational approach to the way in which schools "do business" (Becker, Geer and Hughes, 1968). In higher education, however, the demands of learning are in many cases of a different kind, since students have to work much more independently and have to deal with a substantially larger volume of written material. In that setting, a surface approach can be detrimental.

The problems students encounter in reading are thus not merely — as is commonly assumed — efficiency problems, a question of speeding up teaching and learning in a one-dimensional process of fact-gathering. Our literate culture has made possible a conceptual development in which a multitude of 'world-versions' appear and are continually modified. A dynamic conception of knowledge, a commitment to seeing reality from new and previously unfamiliar perspectives, is thus built into the scientific enterprise itself. Though this is self-evident to the trained academic, it may appear as strange and unfamiliar to the student. Coming to terms with it causes pedagogical problems which are bound up with changes in conceptions of reality and the expansion of intellectual repertoires.

Scientific texts offer new 'versions of the world', or fragments of these, and the act of learning through reading may thus be seen as entailing an implicit commitment to transcend assumptions about reality which are firmly grounded in our everyday experiences. In our culture, knowledge deriving from personal experience and therefore 'true' in the everyday realm may have to yield to an alternative mode of conceptualisation which stems from a scientific 'version of the world'. A distinctive feature of collective and individual learning in our scientific mode of thinking is thus an "increasing capacity for emancipation from immediate 'bodily engagement' in ... objects and events" (Rommetveit, 1974, p. 43). This is the process of abstraction and detachment from the world close at hand which writing *per se* has made possible, and which confronts us today with pedagogical problems in our attempts to convey its insights to coming generations.

Acknowledgements

The research reported here has been financed by the Swedish Council for Research in the Humanities and Social Sciences.

CHAPTER SEVEN

Contrasting Conceptions of Essay-writing

DAI HOUNSELL

In every work regard the writer's end
Since none can compass more than they intend

Alexander Pope, *Essay on Criticism*

Introduction

In the arts and social sciences, essay-writing is the undergraduate's Amazon. Throughout a degree course, the processes of studying often proceed along a river of coursework essays — the equivalent of one essay every ten days in some universities (Nimmo, 1977). Essay-writing occupies this central place within higher education because it serves two fundamental purposes: it is both a tool of assessment and an avenue to learning.

The coursework essay has not always had a part to play in assessment. Until the 1960's, the only essays which directly determined degree results were generally those written in final examinations where students wrote from memory under severe time constraints. Over the last two decades, however, formal recognition has increasingly been given to the 'coursework' essays which students write as part of their everyday studying. Compared to the exam answer, coursework essays give students an opportunity to draw upon a wide range of sources and allow time for sustained reflection. Collectively, therefore, they can play a key part in assessment by providing a reliable record of the student's achievements over a substantial span of time. The adoption of coursework assessment has also been seen as a counter to the debilitating anxiety of 'sudden-death' examinations, although the consequences may be to redistribute stress throughout a course rather than to remove it altogether (see for example Heywood, 1969; Baumgart and Johnstone, 1974).

As a learning activity, essay-writing makes particularly exacting demands of the student. The student must not only apprehend and make sense of a topic, but go further and communicate what he or she knows within the framework of a formal, ordered statement. Essay-writing thus involves putting learning on display. But the task of constructing meaning is made doubly difficult because the student usually has to venture beyond the comparative security of lecture and seminar notes. Other sources have to be tracked down, digested, their relevance to the topic weighed in relation to all of the material at the student's disposal. Finally, what the student chooses to make use of has to be marshalled and deployed within a discussion of the topic. As a learning activity therefore, the process of essay-writing is inherently more complex than reading and listening, and its product may reflect even more strongly the personal sense which the student has made of what he or she has learnt.

These two purposes of learning and assessment co-exist uneasily. The potential for conflict was first shown in the classic American study *Making the Grade* (Becker *et al.*, 1968) which has already been referred to in Chapter 1. As one of the students interviewed observed:

> There's an awful lot of work being done up here for the wrong reason.... There are a lot of courses where you can learn what's necessary to get the grade and when you come out of the class you don't know anything at all. You haven't learned a damn thing really. In fact, if you try to really learn something, it would handicap you as far as getting a grade goes ....
> (Becker et al., 1968, p. 59).

This comment illustrates one of the main findings of Becker and his colleagues. The ways in which students went about learning were influenced by their pursuit of grades, and this could lead to a conflict between the requirements of grade-getting and students' desires to learn in a personally satisfying way. As Chapter 13, "The Context of Learning", will show, these tensions between learning and assessment seem to be a persistent phenomenon which has been found in many other studies.

A further source of tension has been less widely recognised. In discussing essay-writing, it is tempting to make inferences from other domains of written expression, but the parallels are sometimes too easily taken for granted. There is a gulf between, say, the specialist author and the undergraduate essay-writer which extends far beyond differences in knowledge or experience. The nub of the problem is the idiosyncrasy of essay-writing, which arises from the setting in which the activity takes place. Firstly, the knowledge of students is generally, though not invariably, inferior to that of their tutors. They may be hard pressed to communicate anything which the tutor does not already know. While the success of the specialist author comes from prompting readers to see some aspect of the world in a fresh way, the success of students may lie in the degree to which they can articulate and validate views of the world which are already familiar to the tutor. Secondly, specialist authors generally choose their own theme and write because they have something they want to communicate. For students, however, the initial stimulus comes from outside, not within. They are required to say something on a given theme whether or not they feel drawn to the topic and whether or not they feel they have something to say. Indeed, essay assignments are what Shaughnessy (1977) calls *stipulative*: not only topic but mode of expression, depth of treatment, sources, length and preparation time may all be specified in advance. These contextual features determine the conditions of studying in a formal educational setting, but they do not necessarily create an ideal medium in which learning can flourish. The student's concern to make sense of a problem may come into conflict with the obligations of the task as assigned. Britton and his colleagues have sketched out the consequences of conflict:

> The strategies a writer uses must be the outcome of a series of interlocking choices that arise from the context within which he writes and the resources of experience, linguistic and non-linguistic, that he brings to the occasion. He is an individual with both unique and socially determined

experience, attitudes and expectations; he may be writing voluntarily or, as is almost universally the case in the school situation, he may be writing within the constraints of a prescribed task. This he either accepts and *makes his own* in the process of writing, or he perfunctorily *fulfils his notion of what is demanded;* and his choices are likely to vary from occasion to occasion and from task to task. (Britton et al., 1975, p.9, my italics.)

So far we have looked at the incidence and purposes of essay-writing and the potential for conflict within it between learning and assessment and learning and studying. Viewed in any of these ways, essay-writing would seem to be a crucial area for discussion and investigation, yet what we find instead is a puzzling neglect. In some books on undergraduate teaching, essay-writing is hardly mentioned at all, while in others it has been consigned to the corner cupboards of "private study" or "marking problems". Even in study skills manuals, where essays are normally a prime concern, there is a preoccupation with form rather than substance. Accomplishment in essay-writing is often seen in terms of style or bibliographic finesse or as a matter of systematic planning and organisation. Amidst the flurry of technical tips, it is hard to get a sense of the student as a "maker of meaning" (Perry, 1977) or of writing as "a struggle to give meaning to experience" (Berger, 1979).

Previous Research

The neglect extends also to research (Hartley, 1980, p. 64). Most studies of undergraduate essay-writing derive from an interest in the reliability of essay-grading rather than in student learning (see Rowntree, 1977, pp. 188 ff.; and more recently Byrne, 1980). There are two notable exceptions. The first is a study by Hughes-Jones (1980) of students' perceptions of the reasons for success and failure in exams and essay work. Interest was a prominent factor in accounting for both successful and unsuccessful essays — a finding which echoes an earlier distinction between "involved" and "perfunctory" approaches to written work by secondary school pupils (Britton *et al.,* 1975). The second is a questionnaire study of the essay-writing procedures of 80 Psychology students (Branthwaite *et al.,* 1980). The main findings of the study focus upon dimensions associated with academic success in general: one dimension involved "confidence, self-assertiveness and being in control, as opposed to being pessimistic, unenterprising and being externally constrained", while the other was typified by "the presence (or absence) of concentrated, individual hard work" (Branthwaite *et al.,* 1980, pp. 103–4). Other findings, however, are more specific to essay-writing. One of these concerns a difference between first- and second-year students: the second-years appeared to be "more product-orientated and more aware of the variety of ways in which one could go about essay-writing" (p. 104), and they were more likely to go beyond the recommended texts and to share their ideas with others. A marked mismatch was also found between what students felt tutors were looking for in essays and tutors' own criteria. While originality and understanding were high amongst the criteria advanced by students, none of the seven tutors who also took part in the study mentioned originality and only one mentioned understanding.

This lean harvest of findings reinforces rather than removes the impression of neglect. How students experience essay-writing, what the demands posed by essay-writing tasks might be, and what significant variations might exist between one discipline and another — all these are unexamined questions. As a learning activity, essay-writing remains virtually uncharted territory.

Background to the Study

In the remainder of this chapter, we begin to explore this territory, drawing upon the findings of a study of 17 second-year History undergraduates and 16 second-year Psychology undergraduates (Hounsell, 1984b). The students took part in two sets of semi-structured interviews, each focusing upon a recent essay prepared for a specific course module. The students were invited to describe both the content of the essay and how they went about preparing it, to draw comparisons and contrasts with other essays written for the course unit concerned, and to discuss various aspects of the activity of essay-writing and the course setting within which it took place. The students were invited to bring to the interviews copies of their essays and other associated notes and materials. In analysing the interview transcripts, the aim was to examine the students' experience of essay-writing as a learning activity against the backcloth of the two course settings. For reasons of space, the discussion which follows deals in the main with the findings for the History students. It outlines essay-practice within the course module concerned and the students' perceptions of the context in which they prepare their essays, as a preliminary to exploring the main findings of the study, which concern differences in the students' conceptions of what an essay is and what essay-writing involves.

Essay-Writing in a History Course

The History students are prolific essay-writers, spending on average almost two-thirds of their working time writing essays. Overall essay workloads vary as a function of different combinations of the five course modules taken by second year students, but some of the students say that they have to write a total of between 18 and 20 essays over the year as a whole. Within the particular course module investigated, students submit three essays of 2,000–2,500 words in the first two terms and an extended essay of 3,000–3,500 words in the final term. The average time spent on a History essay is 13–15 hours, but individual estimates range from eight hours in the case of one student to nearly 30 hours for another. Students normally have four weeks in which to prepare the essay, and the tutor for the course module usually recommends books to be consulted. Then, as one student says, "You go away and get on with it". The first three essays are linked to fortnightly seminars, where students submitting an essay summarise its contents and respond to questions. The fourth, 'extended' essay is prepared during the final term and draws on primary sources — for example, edited collections of documents such as correspondence and Acts of Parliament. Teaching during the term consists of four lectures, each of which introduces and comments upon one of the four topics assigned and relevant source documents.

The context in which essay-writing takes place is outwardly exceptionally well-organized. Essays are woven into the structure of the course module, titles are announced well in advance and allow some measure of choice, sources of reading are well-signposted and the tutor's written comments on essays are acknowledged as consistently thorough. In the students' perception, however, this is a less than ideal context for essay-writing. Most of the students not only comment on what they see as a heavy essay workload but feel this has unfortunate consequences for how their time is allocated. For example, (using fictitious names, here and elsewhere):

Tom: I mean, basically I'm a full-time essay-writer.

Edward: [The School of History emphasises] that you shouldn't concentrate on essays, because they're very narrowly focused, and you don't do yourself any good by concentrating on them. But everyone finds that, I mean, you've just got to do your essays. And they're the ones that get marked.... And that certainly doesn't give you enough time for general reading.

Moreover, there is a widespread feeling that the essay workload leaves little time to dwell on any one essay or to spend much time subsequently reflecting on the tutor's written comments. As Chris puts it:

I've got so many other things to do, (laughs), essays to do, I just sort of churn them out.... You know, think of something else, get on to something else.

In addition to this source of tension between learning and the requirements of studying and assessment, there is a further contextual feature which is striking. Although students may discuss an essay with the tutor individually if they wish, this is an opportunity which is only very seldom taken up. Equally, the students say either that they do not discuss their essays with one another or that if they do so, discussion is never about content or how one might approach a particular essay:

Martin: It's all centred around marks, really.

Graham: They talk to each other about how they haven't finished it on time, and, oh, 'I have to get an extension', and this kind of thing. But they don't actually discuss essays.

Essay-writing seems therefore an essentially private activity. There is evidently little or no discussion of the problems or processes it entails.

Conceptions of Essay-Writing

In analysing the interviews, the unit of analysis initially adopted was that of the individual essay task. The aim was to look for evidence of differences in how students went about essays which might parallel the well-established distinction between deep and surface approaches to academic reading (see Chapter 3). As the analysis proceeded, however, it became apparent that essay-writing, as an activity, had distinctive meanings for the students which extended beyond the particularities of any one essay assignment and which lent a broadly consistent character to their essay-writing. In other words, the most fundamental difference to emerge from the interview analysis lay in the students' *conceptions* of what an essay was and what essay-writing involved in the discipline concerned. In the case of the History students, three qualitatively distinct conceptions were identified, and these can be summed up as *argument*, *viewpoint* and *arrangement*. At the core of each conception is a global or overall definition of an essay, and it is this definition which gives the conception its distinctive character.

The essay as argument

This, the most sophisticated of the three conceptions, is represented in the following examples:

Chris: Being able to construct an argument, that's where for me, this plan sheet here is, like, the key to that because, I get everything in a logical order where everything's building up, you know, and point 1, boom, boom, boom, boom, like that. And so I try to aim that, come the end of the essay, that no matter what they thought before that, the logic of the argument and the evidence produced is such that, even if they don't agree with my interpretation, they've got to say it's reasonable, reasonably argued. And I think that's one of the things I'm good at, is argument, and constructing an argument.... Tutors aren't looking for sort of, eloquence of style and so on, it's more the argument you present providing it's fairly clear.

Tom: [The tutor] will be looking for a very well-structured essay, very well-balanced. [The tutor] likes you to, you know, weigh the evidence up and come to some sort of conclusion.

Will: ... whereas in an essay you really have to think about something, and then... well, just keep thinking about it as regards to all the reading and the evidence you're going to use.

Interviewer: So it stimulates you to think in a way you don't get from other things?

Will: Well, you have to follow a coherent argument, basically. And that's the only time you have to — like in a lecture you don't and in a seminar you just usually state your point of view on a certain point. You don't form an actual, coherent argument, along a broad theme, really.

Each of these students seems to share a common definition of an essay, seen as *an ordered presentation of an argument well-supported by evidence*. And if we penetrate beyond this global characterisation, three sub-components of the definition can be disentangled. The most important of these is an interpretive sub-component:

Graham: [Essays] crystallise your ideas on a topic. You learn to put forward a logical argument.

Edward: You've got to look for arguments, and prove yourself. I wrote an essay last term in English, and I didn't even use a textbook for it, I just used a text. And I got as good a mark for that, or as good comments, as I would for any History essay. And yet for me it was just reading a text and putting my own opinion forward. Whereas in History I mean you've got to take other people's ideas, and mould them into your own argument.

Essays are thus seen as concerned with the presentation of an argument in which ideas have been "moulded" or "crystallised", as these students put it, into a single entity. An argument therefore pivots upon a distinctive position or point of view on a problem or issue. Within this global definition, the interpretive sub-component is superordinate, subsuming the other two sub-components. The first of these is an organisational one. A distinctive point of view is not merely advanced but presented in a way which is "coherent" or "logical":

Edward: Conclusions are just, you've really got to just tie everything together then, you've got all your strands of argument. But then conclusions, since I've come to University they've become less important, I think, 'cos your argument should be developing all the way through the essay anyway.

This sub-component therefore reflects a concern with an essay as an integrated whole, in which the point of view to be presented underpins and informs the structural conventions of introduction, main text and conclusion.

The second of the two subordinate sub-components of the definition is concerned with data in the form of evidence substantiating or refuting a particular position or point of view. For an argument to be authentic, it must be demonstrated and buttressed by supporting evidence:

Kate: ... I think I've got a balanced argument, a convincing argument, putting in enough facts, and reference points, to back up what you're saying... I suppose I could've written the essay saying that the 'court' and 'country' divisions were very pronounced by this time, and if I'd been able to back it well enough, then logically I should get the same mark, but I don't really think that that view is convincing enough to be able ... to present it.

This global definition, therefore, can be seen as comprising three sub-components, representing specific stances towards three elements of essay-writing:

Data   The subject-matter which provides the raw material or bedrock of essays.

Organisation   The structuring of essay material into a discussion of the topic which follows a particular sequence or order.

Interpretation The meaning or meanings given to essay material by the student.

These three elements, which emerged from intensive analysis of the interview transcripts of both the History and the Psychology students, may be considered as *core elements* of essay-writing. They are crucial to an understanding of any given global definition of an essay in two ways. Firstly, the particular stance adopted towards each core element forms a sub-component of the global definition. And secondly, the character of the definition is also determined by the interrelationship of these sub-components. In the global definition we have just examined, organisation and data are hierarchically related to interpretation, since decisions on how the essay is to be organized and what evidence is to be marshalled are dependent on the distinctive point of view to be adopted; but this is not always the case, as we shall see.

The essay as viewpoint

At first glance the conceptions of *argument* and *viewpoint* might seem to entail the same definition of an essay:

> *Alan:* There must be a technique to writing the perfect essay. Um, I suppose you've got to have a clearly defined argument and a plan of what you're going to do, already written down, so you can always refer back to it, and then start from there.

> *Rick:* It's a discipline to getting it, to getting your argument down on paper in a constructive and in a literate sort of fashion … If you didn't do an essay at all and just had tutorials, instead of essays, you'd then learn more but you wouldn't be able to express it so well.

Indeed, both definitions share a concern to present a distinctive point of view and a concern with essays as integral wholes. What sets them apart, however, is the sub-component of data. In the case of two of the five students associated with this conception, the role of data in essays is not explicitly considered. References to data are very sparse and take the most indirect of forms. For the remaining three students, there are some indications that the function of data as evidence has been acknowledged, but the general impression is one of a lack of concern with this sub-component. In this conception, therefore, the global definition reflects only the alliance of interpretation to organisation: an essay is seen as *the ordered presentation of a distinctive viewpoint on a problem or issue.*

The essay as arrangement

Within the conception *arrangement*, an essay is defined as *an ordered presentation embracing facts and ideas.* This definition is largely tacit rather than made explicit by the students concerned. It is strongly implied in the students' accounts of their essay-writing procedures (analysed below), and it can be gleaned too from an examination of its sub-components. In the stance taken towards interpretation, ideas are viewed disjunctively, as collections of essentially discrete thoughts. It is considered useful or important in an essay to express whatever ideas or opinions one might have, but there is no concomitant concern to marry related ideas to form a unified position or point of view:

> *Donna:* I think [tutors] are asking us to look at secondary sources and just see what we think about them. But — they do want our own ideas, but I think it's limited when you've only got secondary sources.

Sue: What's distinctive is that I'm here expressing myself, and what I thought, and what my ideas are, in certain subjects, on paper. It's very important to know, it's a gauge how well the course is going. Obviously if you're not coming up with the right ideas, or certain ideas, and aren't able to express yourself, then I think that obviously you've got problems.

The references to organisation are characteristically flat, expressing a commitment to essay structure which is apparently devoid of any consideration of what organising principles might be appropriate:

Pattie: I usually start off with a quote, and then finish with a quote. I find that's the easiest way to start it. But I think the worst thing is starting an essay. Once you get halfway through you're alright. The first few pages ...

And where there is a concern with data, the standpoint is at base a quantitative one, displaying a conscientious coverage of sources rather than a regard for evidence supporting a point of view:

Interviewer: What do you see as your strengths as an essay-writer?

Pattie: ... I think, the um, the presentation: I tend to put quite a few quotes in, and put them down as references.

Interviewer: What's studying History at University about?

Donna: I'm not quite sure what it is. I don't know. I don't think we get a lot of our own ideas into it. I know we're supposed to but we seem to be reading books, and criticising what people think, more than actually — it's sometimes annoying when you're doing an essay, and you don't really know enough facts, but what you're doing is sorting out other people's interpretations, and you feel that you can't really criticise them yourself because you don't know the source material. And so, um ... I don't know. It just seems to me as though you're reading about a period, and trying to fit your reading into an essay. It just seems like a lot of facts more than anything else.

Finally, what also typifies this global definition is the lack of integration between the three sub-components. In the first two contrasting conceptions, it is the articulation of a distinctive point of view or position which gives an essay its fundamental meaning: the sub-components of organisation (in the *viewpoint* conception) or of organisation and data (in the *argument* conception) are the vehicles upon which this interpretive stance is conveyed. A decisive characteristic of essay-writing as *arrangement*, however, is that the three sub-components are not hierarchically related. Indeed, interpretation, in the form of whatever ideas and thoughts one has, assumes an almost incidental status relative to the other two sub-components of organisation and data.

Essay-Writing Procedures

Thus far we have looked at differences in conception in relation to how History essays are defined by the students. But we can also find evidence of such differences in the students' essay-writing procedures. We look firstly at essay preparation — the initial stages of reading, taking notes, and clarifying what will be said in the essay.

When a student conceives of essays as arguments, as in the following example, the elements of interpretation ("his argument", "you make a case") and data ("you've got to back it up with actual facts") are seen in interrelation:

> *Interviewer:* What are you looking out for in individual chapters? What will you be getting from them?
>
> *Chris:* Well, really things that are relevant to the question in hand. I try to find the author's own particular view, his argument, and also really just to really plunder it for facts. Whether the facts that he gives, you know, whether I agree with his argument or not, I think that the main thing in an historical essay anyway is that you make a case and back it up with actual facts of what happened, and evidence. Sometimes I just go through a book very quickly and just jot down fact after fact after fact, and, you know, events, what people said, or sometimes I write out quotes, from the time. What people actually did and said. And then I have a good body of things that actually happened that I can then ... use to support what I want to say. So in a book I'm looking for A, his argument, and then B, facts and evidence.

Preparing an essay therefore entails being attentive both to arguments and to evidence, and the essay emerges out of the interplay between these.

In a conception of essays as viewpoints, however, the element of data is much less in focus, and there may be indications that reading is directed by a preconceived view of the line the essay will take:

> *Martin:* Well, I must admit, I had a set idea on the question. And so I went in with that attitude, I got the books, um, again, the same process of going through them, doing the reading, taking notes, analysing, condensing the notes down and then writing the essay out. I mean, it's much the same process, and I knew that it was what [the tutor] had thought as well... It was exactly what [the tutor] thought, but I believed in it myself as well.

or even that the interplay of interpretive stance and supporting data is deliberately overridden:

> *Rick:* Usually, on the whole, I try and make the facts fit my argument anyway, sort of, or I try and start with the argument in my head anyway. I'll change it, you know, the facts they say...

Where essays are seen as arrangements on the other hand, the procedures described seem uninformed by an interpretive focus. Material is assembled in relation to the topic assigned rather than a point of view to be advanced, as in the following account of an essay entitled 'How greatly did English government and administration differ at the end of Henry VIII's reign from the beginning?':

> *Frank:* [I chose this question because] it was one that I could deal with systematically, in a way. I could deal with you know, Privy Council, financial

administration, Parliament, all these things in turn. It's reasonably easy for research, that sort of thing.... I already knew a bit about the subject from lectures, so I had a good idea of what I was going to do in the first place. So basically I was collecting the different things I was going to deal with; just put them down on a piece of paper, used the indexes of books, looked it up, and then I dealt with each in turn, collecting material from the different books. I did that ... in rough, and then, when I copied it up, like this, you know, ironed it out a bit, and reorganised it, and put it how I wanted it.

The absence of an explicit interpretive focus is similarly evident in the construction of essay answers, where the students' accounts appear flat and mechanical. There is no apparent criterion underpinning the arrangement of the material:

Pattie: You don't put any waffle in, you don't put anything in that's not necessary, not needed, 'cos you just ... you just try and let it flow.

Donna: I read through my notes and try to split it up into sections, so that I can get an essay plan. And then I number the sections. It'll just be usually 1, 2, 3, 4, and sort of, how I argue the name to the group, whatever it is, say, religious conflict, and go down like that. It might not necessarily be in the right order, but then I'll mark it through, and then I'll decide what order it's in. I usually get — probably not in the right order, but it's hard sometimes because various topics merge into each other and you never know how to separate it. Sometimes there's no distinct line, and you get, put bits in the wrong bits, and things like that.

Alternatively, the problem of organisation is side-stepped, either by resorting to a chronological sequence or, as in the example below, through reliance on an external source:

Sue: If I haven't formulated a very definite plan, and if I'm not quite sure how my essay's going to go, then I'll probably take a main theme in a book and work through that way. I mean in History you might have a problem about whether to deal with ideas, sort of, a chronology, which approach to use.... And if I have got a problem like that, then I'll use the authority, you know, the book, and work through their way.

Where by contrast the conception is of essays as arguments or viewpoints, questions of organisation and interpretation are seen as interrelated. The structure of the essay is determined by and subservient to the distinctive position or point of view advanced, as in an account of an essay entitled 'Was Tudor Government at any time a despotism?':

Alan: Well first of all I did an introduction, 'What is a despotism?' And then sort of blasted down a few characteristics, then I discussed these ..., like, that uh, that Tudor Government wasn't based upon Divine Right, it was based upon the law. Then I went on to discuss the argument for Tudor despotism, and then try and take, uh, the elements of those who argued for, and argued against them. I tried to keep to the argument, keep the argument very trimmed and streamlined.... My conclusion was, the Tudor Government wasn't a despotism because these particular characteristics of despotism weren't fulfilled.

Striving for a unity of essay structure and interpretive stance also entails attention to the parts which make up the whole:

> *Kate:* Every paragraph, I sort of make sure I'm making a relevant point. Is it clear what point I'm making or am I just waffling?

There is an obvious parallel here with what Laurillard (1978) and Ramsden (1981) in their descriptions of a deep approach have called, respectively, "keeping the end-point in mind throughout the solution process" and "integrating the parts into a whole".

Essay Content

If the differences identified in the students' conceptions of essay-writing are valid, then we should also expect indications of these differences in their accounts of essay content. These accounts could not be analysed in their entirety because of the large number of essay topics tackled and the almost limitless range of library sources upon which the students could draw, but it was feasible to adopt the stratagem of focusing upon essay conclusions as the key criterion. This analysis showed that, generally speaking, when asked about their conclusions, in the *argument* conception the students stated what their conclusion to an essay was, while in the *viewpoint* conception the conclusion was stated or students said they had arrived at a conclusion but did not specify what this was. Where the students held the *arrangement* conception, on the other hand, they either did not refer to any conclusion, said the essay was not concluded, or outlined a conclusion which merely reiterated the substance of the essay title.

The analysis of essay content was also taken a stage further, however, by scrutinising the students' 'extended' essays, which were confined to four topics. The overriding aim was to look at the extent to which the essays mirrored conceptions, regardless — it should be stressed — of the historical plausibility of the content or its accuracy. Here only two examples are discussed, both of which are essays on the topic 'What were the main sources of friction between Charles II and the Cavalier Parliament, and how far were they inherent in the Restoration Settlement?'. The essays are respectively by Chris and Frank. As a result of the analysis of the interview data, Chris was ascribed to the *argument* and Frank to the *arrangement* conception.

Chris's essay

Chris's essay comprises 17 paragraphs totalling 4,200 words. It begins with what he subsequently describes as a "brief overview of the constitutional arrangements of the Restoration Settlement".

PANEL 7.1 *Chris's essay, 5th paragraph*

This brief overview of the constitutional arrangements of the Restoration Settlement gives the impression that the future should be promising enough, but by the middle of the decade the honeymoon euphoria had evaporated and sharp conflicts between crown and parliament had emerged, despite the amelioration and promise of the Restoration. Nevertheless, it is misleading to think of the relations between Charles and the Cavalier Parliament as one of constant friction, because there were many issues that caused no friction and long periods of give and take and relaxed relations in which the process of government functioned quite well. But for the purposes of this discussion I shall concentrate on areas of conflict, even though this may give a distorted impression of relations between King and Parliament. As we shall see, all but one of the sources of these conflict areas were inherent in the Restoration Settlement. There were areas of ambiguity in the Settlement which led to friction over finance, the use of suspending and dispensing power, and the armed forces. Then there were two main areas of out-and-out conflict; the religious controversy and foreign policy. I shall deal with each issue in turn by considering its relation to the Restoration Settlement and by tracing its development during the life-time of the Cavalier Parliament, although it will quickly be seen that all these issues overlapped and affected one another.

The opening paragraph outlines events from Charles' arrival in Dover in May 1660 to the election of the Cavalier Parliament twelve months later. Paragraph 2 suggests that the "underlying premiss" of the Restoration Settlement was "the belief that historical events were cyclical" and a widespread belief that the country had returned to its situation prior to the 1641–2 crisis. The legislation of the intervening years had thus been nullified or its status clarified "in an attempt to construct a lasting settlement". Paragraphs 3 and 4 go on to outline the principal legislative measures of the Restoration Settlement enacted by the Cavalier Parliament.

Paragraph 5 (see Panel 7.1) sets the previous discussion in context and indicates the course which the remainder of the essay will follow. While "this brief overview", Chris says, might give the impression of a "promising enough" future, sharp conflicts had emerged by the middle of the decade. Chris goes on to sketch out his view of the essay question, identifying five sources of friction categorised in two groupings. This framework explicitly maps out the sequence adhered to in the remainder of the essay. First, Chris discusses areas of conflict which arose from ambiguities in the Settlement: finance (paras. 6, 7 and 8), the armed forces (paras. 9, 10 and 11) and suspending and dispensing powers (para. 12). Second, he deals with areas of out-and-out conflict: the religious controversy (paras. 13–15), and foreign policy (para. 16).

PANEL 7.2 *Chris's essay, concluding paragraph*

We have identified five principal sources of friction between Charles and the Cavalier Parliament that we have also seen were to some extent inherent in the Restoration Settlement. The areas of ambiguity in the settlement, that is: finance, the armed forces and the prerogative rights of suspending and dispensing power and of determining foreign policy were areas that left room for a considerable development of royal power. However, when the Crown attempted to enhance its power by exploiting these ambiguities and by exercising its prerogative rights, which though not formally confirmed by the Restoration were assumed to have been maintained, Parliament rose to the challenge, attacked and usually prevailed. Religion was the one area w[h]ere specific Restoration legislation directly led to conflict since the overwhelming Anglican resurgence represented by the Act of Uniformity and the Clarendon Code was committed to fighting any Pro-Catholic and Pro-French policies of the King even though it involved an unprecedented invasion of the royal prerogative. This reveals the shallowness of the Restoration's upholding of royal supremacy in the constitution. Nevertheless, the conflicts of the 1660s and 1670s did not spark off another civil war since they were all kept at the political level and the Restoration Settlement held together despite two changes of dynasty in 1689 and in 1714 because Parliament had become the lynch-pin of government.

The concluding paragraph of Chris's essay is shown in Panel 7.2, and recapitulates the five principal sources of friction discussed. Furthermore, returning to a distinction he had made in paragraph 5, Chris states that religion was the only one of the five areas where specific Restoration legislation directly led to conflict. Chris ends with some general observations about the constitutional maintenance of the royal supremacy and the containment of the conflicts of the period.

Having summarised this essay, we can analyse it by trying to assess how far it reflects a conception of essays as argument in relation to the three sub-components of the global definition.

Interpretation. Chris clearly takes up a distinctive position or point of view on the essay question. He responds to the first part of the question by identifying five main sources of friction which he categorises in two groups, and he responds to the second part of the essay question by seeing all five areas as to some extent inherent in the Restoration Settlement, but with the area of religion seen as a special case.

Organisation. The essay is underpinned by an explicit interpretive framework, announced in advance as a preliminary to a more detailed examination, and reiterated in the essay's concluding paragraph. The essay thus mirrors a concern with essays as integral wholes. Introduction, main text and conclusion share the same organising principle, which is founded upon the interpretive position which Chris advances.

Data. Similarly the bulk of the factual references which appear in the essay are aligned to Chris's interpretive framework. References to relevant data are subsumed within each point raised, and thus become the evidence which substantiates each of these points. The opening four paragraphs are the single exception, but since they are described as providing the background to the constitutional arrangements of the Restoration Settlement, their evidential status and their relation to the main concerns of the essay are clearly specified.

Frank's essay

Frank's essay comprises 33 paragraphs totalling 3,700 words. The opening paragraph, shown in Panel 7.3, can be seen as the introduction to the essay

PANEL 7.3 *Frank's essay, opening paragraph*

The years of the Cavalier Parliament, which opened in 1661 and was not dissolved until 1679, were marked by increasing points of friction between King Charles ll and Parliament on such crucial matters as the political and religious settlements, foreign policy and the royal finances, many of which were related to the question of the balance of power between King and Parliament.

Frank notes the growing friction between sovereign and Parliament on "such crucial matters as the political and religious settlements, foreign policy and the royal finances", and comments that many of these were linked "to the question of the balance of power between King and Parliament". The paragraphs which succeed it represent an implicit structure which is adhered to throughout the essay. Paragraphs 2–32 follow a clear chronological order beginning with the Convention Parliament in 1660 and ending with the dissolution of the Cavalier Parliament in 1679. The majority of these paragraphs start from or are focused upon one or more Acts of Parliament, Parliamentary measures, Treaties, or Declarations by the Crown, (17 paragraphs in total); or they deal with a series of events such as those surrounding the impeachments of Charles' First Minister, Clarendon, in 1667 (4 paragraphs) and of Danby in 1678–79 (2 paragraphs). At intervals throughout the essay, a small number of paragraphs (paras. 3, 18, 27) set earlier or later paragraphs within a broader context. Paragraph 18, for example, foreshadows the topics of foreign policy, religion and money which are prominent in succeeding paragraphs.

Panel 7.4 shows the final paragraph. Frank concludes that the period saw "much friction [between King and Parliament] in such fundamental and interrelated issues as religion, the political settlement, finance and foreign policy".

PANEL 7.4 *Frank's essay, concluding paragraph*

The years of the Cavalier Parliament saw much friction between Parliament and the King's government in such fundamental and inter-related issues as religion, the political settlement, finance and foreign policy. The result, by 1678, was a strongly Anglican, anti-Catholic religious settlement with a uniform Anglican Church based on the Book of Common Prayer, and the end of religious toleration. A strongly royalist political settlement was initially introduced although this was partly eroded by Parliament's increased use of their power of the purse to control the government's policies, particularly in the raising of armies and hence in war and peace, and their use of statute to scotch the King's tolerant and pro-Catholic policies. The outcome of the Restoration Settlement, therefore, reflects the friction between King and Parliament in these years, particularly over religious toleration and the closely connected Catholic problem.

He suggests that this resulted in "a strongly Anglican, anti-Catholic religious settlement" and that the initially strongly royalist political settlement became eroded by increasing intervention by Parliament. The outcome of the Restoration Settlement therefore "reflects the friction between King and Parliament in these years", particularly on questions of religion.

Interpretation. There is little to indicate that Frank has taken up the distinctive position or point of view characteristic of a conception of essays as argument. Four areas of friction are suggested in both the introductory and concluding paragraphs of the essay, but these are tagged on each occasion with the phrase "such as" rather than explicitly identified as the main sources of friction. Similarly, the second part of the essay question is only touched upon in the final sentence of the essay, where a connection is posited between one area of friction and the Settlement, but no assessment is made of how far the former was inherent in the latter. In sum, then, the interpretative component seems closest to the incidental thoughts and ideas characteristic of a conception of essay-writing as arrangement.

Organisation. There are intermittent references throughout the essay to areas of friction (religious toleration, for example, and foreign policy) but these do not provide a framework underpinning the essay. The structure followed is a chronological one in which specific parliamentary measures or sets of events mark out the route the discussion follows. In sharp contrast to Chris's essay, therefore, the organising principle adopted is not determined by the essay's interpretative stance. A concern with essays as integrated wholes would not, of course, be invalidated by a chronological sequence if there were also an attempt to relate the chronological account to the focal issue of the main sources of friction and their degree of inherence in the Restoration Settlement. However, Frank's stance towards the focal issue is unclear and the links between introduction, main text and conclusion are not clarified.

Data. For similar reasons, the use of data seems informed by quantitative considerations rather than selected as evidence confirming or refuting an identifiable position or point of view.

Conceptions and Approaches

Amongst this group of seventeen History students, three distinct conceptions of essay-writing were identified. These differences in conception were apparent in how an essay was defined, in the students' essay-writing procedures, and in the content of their essays. The criteria adopted in the interview analysis have also been validated by two independent judges [1] . Similar differences in conception have been found amongst the group of Psychology students who took part in the larger investigation, and both sets of findings are discussed elsewhere – in relation to essay planning (Hounsell, 1984a), the quality of feedback (Hounsell, 1987), and the notion of academic discourse (Hounsell, 1988).

The differences in the History students' conceptions are reflected in their combined coursework essay mark for the History course module concerned. Taking only the fourteen students who can be ascribed without qualification to one of the three conceptions, four of the five students with an arrangement conception have marks below 60 per cent, while all four students ascribed to the viewpoint conception have marks in the range 60–64 per cent. Only two students have marks of 65 per cent or more, and both are students assigned to the argument conception. There is no striking relationship with final degree results, but any such link would inevitably be tenuous, since the course module investigated forms only a part of each student's scheme of studies and assessment is strongly weighted towards examination performance. What, then, of the relationships between these and other findings on student learning?

The conceptions which have been identified are of essay-writing as an activity embracing more than a single essay task. As descriptions of students' experience, therefore, they occupy conceptual ground between, on the one hand, the generic conceptions of learning described by Säljö (see Chapters 3 and 6), and on the other, the contrasting conceptions of a specific learning task represented in a deep and surface approach. And as we might in consequence expect, there are conceptual links which span this spectrum of constructs.

Firstly, the most sophisticated conceptions of learning and of essay-writing entail definitions which are made explicit. The students can readily articulate and discuss the activity as they conceive of it. The activity has therefore become an "object of reflection" (Säljö, 1982) which can be appraised and tackled purposively. Secondly, to conceive of essays as arguments is to see oneself as a "maker of meaning". An essay offers a way of understanding or making sense of a problem or issue which is interpretively distinct, logically coherent, and firmly rooted in the available evidence. In this ar*gument* conception, then, as in both a deep approach and a thematic conception of learning, there is a concern to abstract and construct meaning through an active engagement with the subject-matter.

The quest for meaning is also characteristic of a conception of essays as *viewpoints*, but the holistic focus of a deep approach is here only partly manifested. Ideas are interrelated and integrated but interconnections between interpretation and data tend to be unplumbed or overridden. The completed essay may constitute an ordered argument underpinned by evidence, but has not grown out of a consideration of the range of interpretive options open. This conception also shares the defining features of the multistructural level in the SOLO taxonomy referred to in Chapter 2. At this level, as applied to examples of learning tasks in History, inconsistencies or conflicts encountered in data are ignored or discounted so that a firm conclusion can be reached (Biggs and Collis, 1982, pp. 36 ff.).

Contrasting observations can be made concerning the *arrangement* conception where the definition of an essay tends to be tacit and implied, and where essay-writing seems to involve passively restating and regurgitating what has been gleaned from source materials rather than attempting to make coherent sense of them. This closely parallels Säljö's first and second conceptions in which learning has an essentially factual and reproductive character and is, as Säljö has noted elsewhere, largely "taken-for-granted" (Säljö, 1982, pp. 76–82). Furthermore, in both the arrangement conception and a surface approach, the activity is seen unreflectively and mechanically. Material is collected, ideas are advanced, and the discussion is given a structure; but these subsist as a collection of discrete procedures which lack a unifying purpose. The meaning of an essay lies less in what it says than in what the completed essay represents: outward stipulations met, a course requirement fulfilled. This constitutes learning-as-studying but not learning-as-understanding.

Conceptions and the Study of History

Of the three conceptions identified, it is the conception of essay-writing as argument which is espoused by the School of History. First-year students are advised that "Writing an essay is an exercise in handling historical evidence and building it into a convincing argument", and in our own investigation this same concern was expressed in comments by the tutor on individual essays. How is it, then, that two other conceptions apparently persist, especially when the students are such prolific essay-writers?

In the case of the students who see essay-writing as *arrangement*, the very frequency with which essays are prepared may help to account for the persistence of the conception. As the earlier discussion of context showed, the History students' opportunities for reflection seem limited: essay-writing is an essentially private activity and the need to "churn the essays out", as one student puts it, leaves little room to dwell on the merits or demerits of any one assignment. The consequences may be especially acute as far as this particular sub-group is concerned, for what also distinguishes these students is a perceived gap between their aspirations and what they achieve in their essays, combined with uncertainty about what essay-writing entails. And since the School and the tutor explicitly indicate what is required in a History essay, the uncertainty these students feel cannot evidently be resolved by information-giving, but represents a more fundamental problem. Indeed, there is an echo here of Säljö's analysis in Chapter 6. The students do not share the premises of their teachers, and so fail to grasp the messages the teachers convey about the nature of essay-writing (Hounsell, 1987), as the following comment seems to illustrate:

Interviewer: What do you think the tutor was looking for in this essay?

Sue: He's obviously looking for a much more sort of, detailed approach, I would say. Although on my last essay he did say that I spent too much time explaining things, and I ought to be arguing and interpreting more, and so I was trying to argue and interpret all the way through this, as well as obviously having to bring in details. And I just wondered if by doing that I haven't tended to generalise a bit. Because when I start to argue and interpret I generalise a little bit…. I think he's looking for argument and interpretation, I just think he's expecting a lot of, uh, more detail perhaps as well.

In the case of the students who see essays as *viewpoints*, however, the persistence of the conception may be indicative of a more general orientation to academic studies of the kind discussed in Chapter 5. These students tend to place a premium on originality and to see essay-writing as a medium for self-expression. To Alan, for example, writing an essay can be fulfilling because "It's a work of art. [*Ironically*]. Your latest album's coming out next week". For these students, interpretation is closely bound up with their own ideas, thoughts and feelings.

Interpretation is also given pride of place by the students who conceive of essay-writing as *argument*, but the latter talk not simply of "what I argued" or "my argument" but of "the argument" and of "having an argument". It is as if their interpretive stance has taken on an objective existence: it is no longer "my argument" but something which might be argued by any individual on the basis of the evidence presented. Equally strikingly, this seems linked to a further characteristic of these students, summed up in Graham's comment that learning to put forward a logical argument in an essay is very important because "it's what History's all about". These students seem to share the view of Bennett (1974) that:

The difference between the scholar's book and the candidate's answer is, in History at any rate, almost entirely one of degree and hardly at all one of kind, for both are products of the same type of thought and both are judged in the same way. (Bennett, 1974, p. 1)

This perspective upon essay-writing can be seen as a way of coming to terms with the tensions between learning and studying and learning and assessment outlined at the beginning of this chapter. Whatever reservations these particular students may have about their essay workload and its consequences, they see themselves as practitioners, in their essay-writing, of the discipline of History. And perhaps too, in mastering the fundamentals of argument, the students have transcended the discipline; for argument is a universal of academic discourse and the currency of reasoned debate in society at large.

Note

1. In deciding the appropriate category to assign an essay, each judge was given a set of coding instructions and a sample of uncoded interview extracts. The level of agreement reached, without consultation, was 84 per cent in both cases.

CHAPTER EIGHT

Styles and Approaches in Problem-solving

DIANA LAURILLARD

Introduction

Problem-solving tasks are set as a regular part of the course work on most courses in science, mathematics and technology, and in some social science courses as well. They are seen as an important part of the students' work because they require the application of knowledge and principles to new situations, thus testing and reinforcing the students' real understanding of what they have learned. Knowledge without the ability to apply it is rightly seen as a very poor commodity, and teachers therefore regard problem-solving exercises as an important part of learning.

We can assume, for the purpose of this chapter, that the problems being set for students have a purely educational value; that it is not so much the solution that is of interest, as the process of reaching that solution. We can thus define a problem-solving task as one which 'engages the students in thinking about the subject matter in ways designed to improve their understanding of it'. Problems may sometimes be set to give students practice in some procedure, such as solving quadratic equations, but students learn little from this, other than a facility with the procedure itself. Such problems do not fit into our definition. We are concerned only with problems intended to develop in the students at least a greater familiarity with their subject, and perhaps a better understanding as well.

The teacher faces a difficult challenge in designing problem-solving tasks that fully serve this educational function. Such tasks should help the students to weave the factual knowledge they have into their own conceptual organisation, by enabling them to elaborate the relationships between concepts and to impose structure on the information they have. If they do less, then the exercise can easily become a meaningless mechanical manipulation, and loses its real educational potential. Naturally, for many teachers the choice of problem-solving tasks is circumscribed by the traditions of their subject, and there is relatively little creative effort involved in designing such tasks. Even when there is, it is more likely to be for the sake of the elegance of the problem, rather than for its educational value. But the design of problems is important because the cognitive activity inherent in a particular problem-solving task determines the way the student will think about the subject matter. 'Bookwork' problems will encourage bookwork solutions, requiring very little cognitive effort on the part of the student. A more imaginative problem that challenges the student and invites him to construct new ways of combining information will promote a better understanding. The point is illustrated neatly by Dahlgren's question to economics students about the cost of a bun (Chapter 2). They were practised at defining the laws of supply and demand, but their lack of basic understanding was revealed by their inability to break out of familiar patterns of thinking to answer a very basic but unusual question.

If we can establish the characteristics of a good problem-solving task we must then ask how successful it is in practice. This brings us back to the main theme of this book. Here we ask "what are students' experiences of learning from problem-solving?"

In this chapter, we begin by considering how problem-solving has been studied in the past, and how this relates to recent studies of the students' experience of problem-solving. We shall find that students' approaches to problem-solving can be described in terms of the deep and surface approach already introduced in Chapter 3. This categorisation is developed further to include a theoretical analysis of the internal relations between the students' learning processes and the nature of the subject matter content. The aim overall is to clarify the nature of learning from problem-solving which may then enable us to use it more efficiently as a teaching method.

Ways of Approaching an Understanding of Problem-Solving

Human problem-solving has been a continuing concern of psychologists, and they have developed different ways of investigating it. In this section, two well-established approaches are introduced, namely *Gestalt* psychology and Human Information Processing, while the next section develops a critique of them based on empirical studies using qualitative methods.

There are important differences between these two theoretical analyses of problem-solving. Gestalt psychology describes human cognition in terms of the quality of our perception and thinking, while information processing theory categorises the *mechanism* of our perception and thinking. Not surprisingly, therefore, the two types of theory produce very different descriptions of problem-solving.

Gestalt Theory and Problem-Solving

The essence of Gestalt psychology is to emphasise the structural quality of the way in which we perceive, think about, and feel, the world around us. This structural quality is wholeness ('Gestalt' means 'whole'). In order to see something, we focus on some part of it — like a word on a page. We select a part from a whole. In focusing on the foreground or 'figure' we thereby create a background or 'ground'. The essence of our perception is that each part exists by virtue of its relation to a whole, and can itself be seen as a whole. By emphasising this structural quality of human cognition, the Gestalt psychologists make the assumption that there is always some underlying structure within our perception of a situation, or experience, or task. They also regard relationships between parts and wholes within that structure as constituting the forces that drive our productive thinking.

Wertheimer (1959) applied these ideas to exercises in elementary geometry to show how Gestalt theory can be useful in understanding problem solving. The theory suggests, for example, that the best way of discovering how to find the area of a parallelogram is not by being taught a rule or algorithm, but by finding the underlying structure of the problem, and thereby solving the problem in a meaningful way. The reasoning process might run as follows: the parallelogram is essentially a rectangle in the middle, plus two extra triangles:

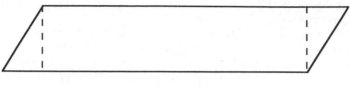

FIGURE 8.1(a)

We know how to find the area of a rectangle, so the area of the middle part is known. We are left with the two triangular parts. They are not rectangles, but by rearranging the diagram they do fit together:

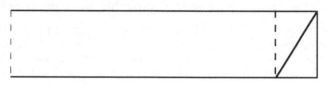

FIGURE 8.1(b)

and that makes one large rectangle with the same area as the parallelogram. Hence the problem is solved as 'area = length x height', where the reason for this is now apparent: the solution is generated from the visual restructuring of the problem statement. Wertheimer (1959, p. 239) describes this kind of process as follows (my parentheses):

> When one grasps a problem situation, its structural features and the requirements set up certain strains, stresses, tensions in the thinker. What happens in real thinking is that these strains and stresses (e.g. what to do about the triangular parts) are followed, yield vectors in the direction of improvement of the situation (i.e. they fit together to make a rectangle which it is easy to find the area of), and change it accordingly (i.e. draw the reconstruction). (The solution) is a state of affairs that is held together by inner forces as a good structure in which there is harmony in the mutual requirements (i.e. the reconstruction is equivalent in area to the original, but also allows us to calculate the area) and in which the parts are determined by the structure of the whole, as the whole is by the parts.

What Wertheimer has done here is to explain the process by which we can solve a problem, not in terms of a procedure, or a series of steps, or even a strategy, but in terms of the way in which we perceive the whole problem situation. The forces that drive our thinking along the steps to the solution are created by our perception of the structured requirements, in other words what the 'givens' of the problem need to become the solution. Such an account of problem-solving emphasises the importance of the <u>meaning</u> of the problem for the student. When we draw on Gestalt theory to think about problem-solving, it is inconceivable to think of teaching children to solve problems by some rote method.

There are two main difficulties in applying Gestalt theory to the kinds of learning and problem-solving that occurs in the classroom. One is that the problems researched are of a particular character—geometric, algebraic, mathematical. It is not clear how far the theory can help us with different kinds of problems, (e.g. experimental situations or engineering problems) which have very different structural characteristics from those often discussed in the literature. The second problem is that the focus is always on the <u>problem</u> and the student's perception of it. But from the student's point of view, the problem situation is not just the content of the problem as given but includes also the <u>context</u> in which it is given. Wertheimer himself makes the same point in his introduction to *Productive Thinking*, p. 12.

> The nature of the topics discussed permits us to deal with thought in terms of "relatively closed systems", as though thinking about a problem were a process that occurred independently of larger issues. Only occasionally shall we refer to the place, role and function of such a process within the personality structure of the subject and within the structure of his social field.

Again, in the conclusion, he describes the problem-solving process as:

> ... a partial field within the general process of knowledge and insight, within the context of a broad historical development, within the social situation, and also within the subject's personal life. (p. 240).

We can imagine this broader context by considering the problem from the student's viewpoint. Does he just have to find the area of the parallelogram, or does he also have to do it in the way the teacher wants? If so, he may wonder whether or not he could get away with doing it his own way, or even consider the consequences of not doing it at all. It is a far more complex 'problem' than we might at first suppose, and all these issues have some kind of bearing on what precisely the student does with the content of the given problem, as we shall see later in the chapter.

Information Processing and Problem-Solving

The Gestalt account of problem-solving tells us that the structural quality of our perception assists the solution process, and when we fail to solve problems, this amounts to a failure to perceive the structure of the problem situation. By contrast, information processing theory focuses on the <u>mechanism</u> of the problem-solving process. Both theories begin by looking at the ways in which people go through a problem-solving process, but they do it in different theoretical contexts, and so focus on different aspects of the situation. Information processing looks at the procedures that people adopt, and integrates these into a more deterministic account of how humans solve problems. It is characteristic of this type of account that it should be capable of supporting a computational model, which "aims at the representation of a psychological theory of problem-solving". (Boden, 1978, p. 143). This approach to theory within cognitive psychology led to the development of a new field within instructional design, which experimented with the computational modelling of students' problem-solving processes, especially for the construction of intelligent tutoring systems. The origins of this approach can be traced to the work of Newell and Simon, who developed a program called 'General Problem-Solver' (Newell and Simon, 1972). They derived a psychological theory of human problem-solving from an analysis of people attempting to solve 'brain teaser' problems. The theory was based on the idea that human cognition is dominated by heuristic processes. Their analysis of protocols revealed these heuristics, which could then be represented in a computer program capable of solving the same problem in a similar way. Failures to solve problems could then be seen as failures either to apply the correct heuristic, or to use one at all.

The general heuristic procedures, such as means-end analysis, creating sub-goals, or working forwards and backwards can be applied to any problem. The General Problem-Solver used these heuristics, together with an appropriate representation of the problem, to generate the specific heuristics for that problem. This, the theory states, is what a human will do when confronted with a new problem, i.e. use general heuristic procedures, together with an appropriate representation of the problem, to generate a specific solution. The value of the theory lay in its description of the heuristics of human problem-solving in a form capable of computational modelling. This opened up the possibility that, if computers could model ideal human problem-solving, then they could also be expected to model flawed problem-solving procedures, by perturbing that ideal in specific ways. This would be valuable in an instructional context if, by modelling a flawed problem-solving strategy, the program could generate the same incorrect result as a student. Since the program would then have a representation of the flawed strategy (e.g. as deleting one step in the correct procedure), it would be able to advise the student on how to correct the flaw (e.g. "Have you forgotten the following step?"), and thereby provide individually adaptive tuition. This intriguing idea led to a number of computer-based experiments with attempts to model students' problem-solving behaviour, mainly in mathematical subjects (see Wenger, 1987, Chapters 9 – 12 for a survey of these experiments).

One of the greatest theoretical difficulties with the information processing approach is that it begs the very important question of what is an appropriate representation of the problem. Some of the research in the field of intelligent tutoring systems has attempted to answer this by analysing students' problem-solving procedures in comparison with expert approaches. By modelling the student's problem-solving procedure as a perturbation of the expert's, it is possible for a computer program to generate remedial teaching from the nature of the perturbation, e.g. the student can be reminded of the omission of a vital step, or if an incorrect rule has been inserted into the procedure, they can receive remedial teaching on that. However, as I have argued elsewhere, this kind of analysis locates the student error at an inappropriate level of description (Laurillard, 1988). The particular omission or incorrect rule may often arise for the student from an underlying learning problem, such as a misconception or a misrepresentation of the structure of the problem. In such a case, remedying the resultant error will not remove the underlying problem. A program can model the procedural aspects of a student's approach to a problem, but not the conceptual aspects. If the mistake in a subtraction problem is to insert the rule ' $0 - n = n$ ', for example, the program may be able to model this, and hence diagnose the error at this level, but what is the conceptual representation that allowed the student to entertain such an idea in the first place? The program has no access to that, and yet that is where the underlying learning problem probably lies.

The Gestalt theorists set out to describe the underlying structure of a problem from the expert's point of view, which can be used within instruction to direct learners towards the most appropriate form of representation of the problem. Information processing theories described how experts proceed through a problem, and more recently, student modelling studies set out to compare how novices proceed through a problem. Both theoretical frameworks analyse approaches to problem-solving, and produce complementary findings — the one on the importance of perceiving the underlying problem structure in an appropriate way, the other on the importance of following the appropriate solution procedure. We might expect that we could combine the two to give a complete picture of how students solve problems. The question is: how far does the theory apply to the practice of problem-solving?

The Application of Theory in Practice

To achieve an understanding of the students' experience of learning through any medium, it is necessary to develop rather different methodological procedures from those described in the previous section. We are no longer concerned with describing the general processes of human psychology, nor with the computational modelling of procedures, but with the personal reality experienced by students as they learn. In order to understand learning from the learner's perspective, we need to use investigative methods that are capable of probing the students' learning experiences, and of eliciting data that will give us some insight into the full complexity of the learning process as practised by students.

A study of how students learn from problem-solving was carried out with a group of 12 students studying the second year of a combined science course at a British university. The aim of the study was to investigate how students approach and carry out problem-solving tasks set as part of their coursework. The course chosen was a course on micro-electronics, and the study focused on three of the problems set. For each problem, the student was asked to complete a short open-ended questionnaire, including such questions as 'how did you start the exercise?', 'were there any points you found difficult — what did you do about that?' and so on. Questionnaires were completed soon after the problem task had been finished so that students were able to remember what they did in some detail.

The questionnaire data were analysed by searching for students' descriptions of the kinds of heuristic activities defined by Newell and Simon. Several such heuristic devices were apparent, but they did not operate in quite the way we might have expected.

Data of this kind necessarily give us a different perspective on the process of learning. They cannot tell us what cognitive processes are involved and how they operate, but instead they can tell us, for example, how the student perceives the given problem-solving task. Consider these quotes from students, explaining their initial approach to a problem which involved writing a device control program for a given microprocessor. The quotes record the important first step of making sure they understand the problem.

> I read through the question to see what was familiar from the lecture, i.e. phrases or specific words that were repeated.

> I have to sort through the wording very slowly to understand what he wants us to do.

> I read through with reference to the class notes making sure I understand the sequence.

> First I thought: the drawn circuit was incorrect: experimented with the current version (in the) notes.

The students' descriptions of their initial approach to the problem vary in the degree of activity involved; the first one is clearly taking a 'surface approach' (as described in Chapter 3), and the last is active to the point of being critical of the question. But what is common to all these students is the focus of their attention, not on the problem itself, but on the problem as set by a teacher in the context of a particular course. We might expect that the first stages in solving such a problem would be to consider what kind of microprocessor it is, what kinds of control would be needed, which instructions are relevant etc. But the students' attention is focused not on the program to be written, but rather on what they think the teacher requires. The domain of the students' problem is not the world of microprocessors but the world of the teacher setting this question. Each student, in different ways, relates the problem to its educational context: the lecture, the lecturer, the lecture notes.

The same tendency can be found in students' descriptions of how they carry out the problem task; again, they may be working not just on the content of the problem in isolation, but on the problem in context:

> I thought of a diagram drawn in a lecture and immediately referred back to it. Then I decided which components were wanted and which were not and started to draw it out, more or less copying without really thinking.

> I just looked back at the class example and tried to think of how it was similar and how it differed and where I would fit in the new stages of 'initialisation' and 'recovery'.

> I decided since X was setting the question, block diagrams were needed.

Each step, and each strategic decision made, refer to the immediate context of the problem as it occurs in that course. The criterion is not "is that what this type of microcomputer needs?", but "is this what this teacher is looking for?".

For these students, the problem situation is quite different from those featured in experimental studies. The problem is not an isolated event; as Wertheimer said, it occurs "within the social situation" (op cit.); it comes after a certain lecture and is likely to relate to it. It will also be marked by a particular lecturer, and the solution should take that into account as well.

The final stage of any problem-solving process involves checking back and examining the solution. And again, some students evaluate their solution not within the terms of the problem alone, but in relation to other aspects of its context, such as their own level of commitment to the task.

> I don't think the finished product was right, but I decided it would do.

> I drew what I thought seemed logical although [I] was not satisfied as I couldn't really see how it fitted in ... I didn't really do this exercise with a view to getting anything out of it. I felt it was something to copy down and nothing to understand really.

> I went back to re-check again the answer, not only to make sure that it was correct but to make sure that I had understood what I had written.

These illustrative quotes show that it is possible for the student to be so concerned to solve the problem *in its educational context* that they pay little attention to the problem itself or its inherent subject matter content. Teachers should always be aware that the student's perception of a problem is likely to be different from their own in this respect, and that this difference may have an undesirable effect on the problem-solving heuristics the students adopt. These heuristics, as illustrated above, are perfectly reasonable and reflect the rational procedures outlined by the information processing theorists, but if the content of the students' problem is this curious 'problem-in-context', then the content of their heuristic thinking will have less to do with microelectronics or whatever the subject matter is, and more to do with the requirements of their course. So the problem-solving task may fail to ensure that the student learns about the subject matter. They do learn something about the 'problem-in-context', but that includes knowing about how to get good coursework marks, about reading between the lines, about interpreting the lecturer's behaviour, and so on. This will no doubt be of some value to them, but it will not satisfy the teacher who intends them to learn about microelectronics. This is a serious difficulty in making sure that a problem-solving task evokes successful learning.

We have seen that students pay considerable attention to peripheral aspects of the problem, but students do also have to consider the problem itself. In the next section, we consider alternative ways of approaching a problem-solving task and attempt to determine the origins and consequences of these.

Students' Approaches to Problem-Solving

A more wide-ranging study of students' problem-solving activities was carried out on a group of 31 university students studying a range of science and engineering courses (Laurillard, 1978). The primary aim of this study was to find out how far existing descriptions of the learning process, such as the deep/surface approach, were applicable to students taking these courses. Each student was interviewed on at least three occasions about a coursework problem task they had been set. The interview lasted one hour and included three stages:

Teachback	the student 'teaches' the problem situation to the interviewer, who interposes no substantive questions (based on the work of Pask, discussed later).
Stimulated recall	the students are interviewed about how they worked on the task in detail, using the problem statement and their written work to stimulate recall.
Questions on context	the students are interviewed about why they did what they did, relating this activity to other aspects of the learning context such as the relevant lecture, tutorial, assessment etc.

Transcripts of the interviews were analysed by searching for descriptions of, for example, a deep or surface level approach, and their interpretations were then independently checked by two other judges. Such data are rich not only in confirmation of the existing descriptions of learning, but also in insights into how the students experience these particular learning tasks. In Chapter 3 the students' approaches to reading were discussed in terms of the deep and surface approach, and it was demonstrated that the two forms of activity led to different learning outcomes for the students. It was also indicated there that these descriptions of the learning process do not apply only to reading. And here we find similar activities in students' approaches to problem-solving. The deep approach is <u>active</u>, with students looking for the <u>meaning</u> of what they are doing. The following quotes are taken from interview protocols of students describing their approach to various coursework problems in science and engineering. Each one illustrates the student's concern to focus on the meaning of the problem:

> What I'm trying to do is picture what's going on and see the model they're using.

> I was trying to work out what's happening to this point moving on a surface.

> First I read the introduction to see what they had to say about it, why it gives a reasonable approximation and what it neglects, because you have to realise the limitations of the method.

> Looking at the system, I was thinking of what is actually happening, relating numbers to features.

It is therefore possible to show that there are circumstances in which student's attention is focused fully on the subject matter content of the problem, and thus that the 'deep approach' describes one aspect of how students learn from problem-solving. Similarly, the alternative 'surface approach' can also be found. This is more passive, with the student content to treat the elements of the task in a purely mechanical way, not considering their meaning, merely their form:

I didn't really look at my notes because you don't have to actually look at the system, you don't have to interpret it in terms of its application.

I just copy from last year's notes ...

You can't really go wrong, it's all done on the diagrams for you, you can go through without thinking at all.

The key to the deep/surface dichotomy, as found in reading tasks, is the focus of the student's attention; whether it is the meaning behind the words, or the words themselves. In applying the dichotomy to problem-solving tasks, we find an exact parallel, with students focusing either on the meaning, or on the words, numbers and diagrams themselves. The deep and surface approaches to learning can therefore be seen as characterising a fundamental aspect of how students learn, applicable in different types of learning task.

The origin of a student's approach to a particular problem is not apparent from their descriptions of how they work it out, but the interview questions about their perception of the educational context within which they are doing it, indicate that the approach derives from their intention — why they are doing it and what they expect to get out of it. Students who describe a deep approach in carrying out the tasks, respond to those questions with descriptions such as the following:

I want to understand the theory of what I'm doing to do a good write-up and get the results.

I have to use this for my project. I want to do as much of the steps as I can, to understand what's going on.

These quotes illustrate the students' intention to understand the meaning. In contrast, the surface approach derives from an intention merely to memorise or to reproduce:

These are general notes. It's an easy way of putting down principles so you can revise it.

I tend to write down certain things I rely on myself remembering for the next year or two ... you can remember it that way.

If the origin of the approach is the student's intention, then as the student may have different intentions within different learning situations, the same student may use either approach, on different occasions. In this study 19 out of the 31 students exhibited both types of approach (Laurillard, 1979). The internal consistency between intention and approach is illustrated by the following quotes from the same student talking about two different learning tasks:

Deep Approach

This has to be handed in — it's an operation research exercise, a program to find a minimum point on a curve. First I had to decide on the criteria of how to approach it, then drew a flow diagram, and checked through each stage. You have to think about it and understand it first. I used my knowledge of O.R. design of starting with one point, testing it and judging the next move. I try to work through logically. Putting in diagrams helps you think clearly and follow through step by step. I chose this problem because it was more applied, more realistic. You can learn how to go about O.R. You get an idea of the different types of problem that exist from reading.

Surface Approach

This problem is not to be handed in, but it will be discussed in the lecture because the rest of the course depends on this kind of thing. I knew how I'd do it from looking at it; it practically tells you what equation to use. You just have to bash the numbers out. I knew how to do it before I started so I didn't get anything out of it. There's not really any thinking. You just need to know what you need to solve the problem. I read through the relevant notes, but not much because you don't need to look at the system. It's really just a case of knowing what's in the notes and choosing which block of notes to use. You don't have to interpret it in terms of the system. It's only when things go wrong, you have to think about it then. In this sort of situation you've got to get through to the answer.

Thus the deep/surface dichotomy does not characterise a stable characteristic of the student, but rather describes a relation between the student's perception of a task and his approach to it. The student's perception of a learning task encompasses a multitude of things: it depends on its form and content, on its relation to other tasks, on the student's previous experience, on the student's perception of the teacher who marked it and of how it will be assessed. But the operational outcome of this combination of judgements and perceptions is an intention either to understand or to memorise, and thereby to use either a deep or surface approach.

Thus the referential character of the deep/surface dichotomy — its description of what the student attends to — has been shown to be relevant to how students learn from problem-solving. The dichotomy has implications, however, for the way the student engages with the subject matter, and this is of crucial importance in problem-solving. This relational aspect of the dichotomy was described in Chapters 3 and 4 in terms of the distinction between 'holistic' and 'atomistic'. The terms define students' activities in carrying out the task. As we saw the 'holistic' approach involves students in attempts to "search for the author's intention to relate the message to a wider context and/or to identify the main parts of the author's argument and supporting facts" (Svensson, 1977). The 'atomistic' approach involves students in "focusing on specific comparisons", focusing on the parts of a text in a sequence (rather than the more important parts), memorising details and direct information indicating a lack of orientation towards the message as a whole" (Ibid.) The holistic/atomistic dichotomy focuses on the way students manipulate the structure of the text they are reading, and thus makes clear how the differences in outcome arise: the difference in approach constitutes a difference in outcome by virtue of the fact that the students are interacting with the subject matter in a different way.

The holistic/atomistic dichotomy is again mirrored in students' descriptions of their approach to problem-solving tasks. The parallel to the holistic approach is manifested when students describe ways of dealing with the problem content that preserve the structure and meaning of each part and its relation to the whole.

> I started by (deciding) what I needed to prove. I tried to set up in my mind how I was going to do it.

> You do it by putting things in boxes, forget what's inside them and look at the whole picture.

> You're told so much, you need to find some kind of relationship.

Contrast these statements with those that illustrate an 'atomistic' approach which ignores the structure of the problem and concentrates on cobbling together a solution by manipulating the elements rather than understanding the whole.

> First, you have to isolate what one knows, or what facts are known. Then, consider what expressions to use.

> I started by writing down equations, but you should start by thinking of what you need.

> I looked up the formulae and made calculations from those.

The essential difference between a holistic and atomistic approach is that whereas the former preserves the underlying structure of the subject matter content, the latter effectively distorts it, because the students pay no attention to the structure and concentrate only on juggling the elements together until they fashion a solution.

This structural aspect of approaches to problem-solving, which the holistic/atomistic dichotomy emphasises, is crucially important. The whole point of problem-solving as a learning task is that it should engage the students actively in thinking about the subject matter, and in operating on the relations within it, so that personal meaning can be created. The evidence from these interviews demonstrates that the two alternative approaches to problem-solving do exist, and clearly one is desirable and the other less so, at least if students are to be effective problem-solvers outside the narrow educational context. But we need a full understanding of how deep and holist approaches lead to a higher level of learning outcome if we are to make use of this finding in designing problem-solving tasks. What does it mean for a student to understand a topic, and how do different approaches to learning relate to understanding? The next section introduces a theoretical analysis of these questions from which we can derive a further way of describing how students learn from problem-solving.

Problem-Solving Tasks and their Relation to Understanding

The studies reported in this book deal mainly with studies of the learning process as seen from the student's point of view. The power of this type of research is that it allows us to investigate a process that is essentially internal by obtaining

the domain itself — the external representation of the subject. As an example, take Pythagoras' theorem as the theoretical framework, techniques such as constructing a square on a line as the manipulative procedure, and geometric triangles as the domain.

From this purely theoretical account, Pask derived two styles of learning, both of which are necessary for understanding, i.e. the proper development of the theoretical framework. 'Operation learning' refers to the vertical pathways: the construction of hypotheses, the use of rules, techniques, procedures, the manipulation of entities in the subject matter domain. 'Comprehension learning' refers to the horizontal pathways: the description of the construction at both levels, global and local, the interpretation of their meaning, the search for analogies with other similar constructions.

These are theoretical descriptions of learning, but they may nonetheless be applicable to the reality of student learning. In the research study already described (Laurillard, 1978), the students' work on their coursework assignments was also used to investigate the applicability of operation and comprehension learning in this kind of learning situation. Ten of the students were interviewed about three of their assignments, each one a problem-solving task — in chemistry (reaction kinetics), crystallography (stereographic projection) and metallurgy (equilibrium diagrams). The students were interviewed individually, and at the start of the session they were asked to do a 'teachback' (Pask's term), i.e. to teach back to the researcher what they had learned about the subject matter of the problem-solving task. Each teachback lasted 5–10 minutes and was recorded and transcribed for later analysis. The analysis was done by inspection, looking for examples of statements that described either operation learning (statements of rules or procedures) or comprehension learning (descriptions of concepts or interpretation of operational constructions). The analysis was checked by two judges who achieved an average of 82 per cent agreement in assigning these categories.

Given this form of analysis, the presence of operation and comprehension learning within students' normal academic work can be demonstrated by selecting quotes from protocols which have been classified according to the two styles. The following quotes, where each student is describing how to work out a problem on an equilibrium diagram, illustrate how they employ the lower, localised level of operation learning in the form of standard techniques in working out the solution. An equilibrium diagram represents the structural phases that metal alloys go through as they cool. The students were asked to work out the sequence of phases for particular alloys using the diagram. This involves them also in interpreting shapes and sections of the graph.

> If we're at a certain point, we can find out the proportions of the length of the line.

> You work from this side of the graph, you get 12.5°A; as temperature is raised, solubility is increased.

> Now, bring in that rule, anything between those two single phases, you've got a double phase, so that's a double phase.

> Now then, you've got a straight line. Now then, another rule is that if
> you've got a straight line . . that is a compound.

These students are clearly using operations — procedures and rules — but
they are not operating at the level of the theoretical framework of equilibrium
diagrams. The focus of their attention is on isolated details of the subject matter,
and operations are carried out on the basis of selection from a standard repertory
of techniques rather than by recourse to theory. Similarly, we can find evidence
of comprehension learning at the lower level, where descriptions of concepts
are local, and there is no attempt to integrate concepts or establish relations
between them.

> This is eutectoid reaction here. This is your a phase. This is a two-phase
> region, which is a mixture of the a and carbon compound.

> ... this line ... is called the liquidus, and by liquidus, it means everything
> above it is liquid.

> If you've got pure iron and you elevate its temperature you get structured
> changes with increasing temperature, at 90° you start off with the first
> structure you call.

These students are focusing on the meaning or interpretation of the
diagrammatic representation, but they are not descriptions of a theoretical
framework, rather they are descriptions of its detail in isolation. Quotes of
this sort indicate the presence of comprehension learning, but only at the
lower, localised level. Evidence of learning at the more theoretical level can
be found but in this study it was rare. One such example is still a description
of structural changes, but here the meaning of the diagram is related to the
theoretical concept of the crystal pattern. It is thus not simply a description
of the existence of the phases as areas on the diagram, it places that
interpretation in its theoretical context.

> In some types of material, a lot of them when they freeze, metals that is,
> you get two distinct crystal patterns. In a particular metal you could end up
> with one phase with dendrites in it ... they're two completely different
> phases and so, because a lot of metals aren't completely soluble when
> they start to freeze, you get these two phases out.

This student is offering an explanation of the theory to support his identification
of the two phases of the diagram, and this is a form of high level comprehension
learning, i.e. the student is building descriptions of the theoretical framework
underlying the problem. Thirty such protocols were analysed in this way. All
students were found to use both styles of learning, but in varying proportions
and, more strikingly, in varying proportions depending on the task. For example,
on the stereographic projection task, all the students showed a high incidence
of operation learning, whereas on the Equilibrium Diagram task, only half the
students did so, with half biased more towards comprehension learning. This
unequal distribution of styles among different problem-solving tasks is strongly
indicative of a task effect on choice of learning style, and this will be discussed
further in the next section.

This research had thus demonstrated that the theoretical constructs of *operation learning* and *comprehension learning* also help to describe problem-solving tasks in everyday studying. An obvious question is, how are these constructs related to the descriptions of 'approaches to learning' we have already encountered?

We can begin to make sense of the relations between these constructs if we consider again their definitions. Operation learning concerns the manipulation of the concepts and objects in the subject matter domain. Comprehension learning concerns their meaning, or description. The global level involves integration of the descriptions into a theoretical framework: the local level does not. The descriptions of deep/holistic or surface/atomistic approaches do not involve a separation into procedures and descriptions. Thus the only parallel that can be drawn between the two sets of categories would suggest at least a tentative correspondence between deep/holistic approaches and both comprehension and operation learning at the global level, and between surface/atomistic approaches and both comprehension and operation learning at the local level.

If we consider approach, with its intentional component, as a preliminary to style, it is then possible to suggest that the choice of approach affords the opportunity for one or other level of style to be implemented. For any particular problem, a student who is thinking deeply and holistically will be looking for meaning and will be able to attend to the global level of descriptions, whereas the student who is thinking atomistically will consider only the local components of the problem without seeking to integrate them meaningfully. The effects of a surface approach, insofar as it involves the intention to reproduce, will be to produce low-level descriptions or unintegrated sets of operations.

A deep approach may go through the initial stages of low-level operation learning, but only as a preliminary to the high-level integration of descriptions and operations into a full understanding of the subject matter domain.

What Pask's theory tells us is that for any problem, there are global and localised forms of description of its domain, and the student has to be able both to manipulate the concepts and the relations between them and to interpret the meaning of those manipulations. What Svensson and Marton tell us is that the global forms of description will not be considered by those students who take a surface/atomist approach, and they will achieve a full understanding of the problem only if they take a deep/holist approach.

It has been possible to show that the two forms of descriptions of learning, the one derived empirically, the other theoretically, are applicable to a wide range of normal academic tasks, and are compatible with each other. These descriptions give us a way of simplifying the complexity of students' experiences of learning from problem-solving so that the task of trying to understand how students deal with this form of learning becomes more manageable. But how does this help us to use problem-solving more effectively as a form of learning?

Implications for Teachers

The student's choice of operation or comprehension learning may depend as much on the nature of the task as on the student's own personal characteristics.

Some tasks necessitate operation learning e.g. the stereographic projection problem required students to do considerable manipulation of mathematical objects, but did not require them to do any interpretation of the objects or the manipulations. Similarly, the Equilibrium Diagram task required students to interpret a diagram to give an account of what was happening to a cooling metal alloy, and this required some manipulation of objects and concepts as well. The empirical results confirmed that the requirements of the task, in each case, matched the predominant style of learning exhibited in students' protocols (Laurillard, 1979). A similar result was reported by Taylor (1990), from an observational study of students solving problems in programming Prolog. Those teachers who took the declarative approach to teaching Prolog, which emphasises the logical rather than the computational representation of a problem, created a task that led students to embark on:

> a simple surface 'translation' exercise when writing programs, rather than a transformation of the problem statement. (Taylor, 1990, p. 307).

Here again, the teaching essentially *required* students to focus on a logical representation of the problem. This emphasis to a failure to focus on the computational structure of the problem which they had to do if they were to construct a satisfactory solution. The process of 'translation' using operation learning was adopted, whereas a reinterpretation or 'transformation' using comprehension learning was actually necessary for success.

The choice of learning style has also been related to the student's intention, as characterised by his approach to the task. But we must take care with the deductions we make here, because the categories of 'approach' have been derived from a reading task. There is an important difference between the two: a reading task does not itself make demands on the student — the text is there to be read as the student chooses, with some purpose in mind certainly, but the text itself does not state the purpose. A problem-solving task, on the other hand, explicitly requires the student to solve it. As in reading tasks, the student may approach the task with an intention to learn meaningfully or superficially and may choose how he carries it out, but the crucial point about a problem-solving task is that it may itself make very minimal demands. For many such tasks, there is a standard procedure which students are wise to adopt, but which need not engage them in thinking about the subject at a deeper level. Few such tasks really deserve the name 'problem-solving', and it is hard to find examples of genuine problem-solving in many degree courses. The students' comments on their problem-solving strategies reveal how minimal some of these task demands can be. Thus the choice of approach may not derive wholly from the student's intention.

We can see, therefore, that the student's choice of approach and style is dependent to some extent on the nature of the problem-solving task itself, and also on how the requirements are perceived. Both of these influences are in the control of the teacher. If teachers wish the tasks set to be effective in improving students' understanding of the subject, if they are meant to be more than purely mechanical exercises in rehearsing some standard procedures, then the design of those tasks is crucial. They must be complex enough to demand hypothesis-testing or explanations of theory. The design process must take into account the various descriptions of learning we have discussed, and ensure that the problem requires the student to engage in the appropriate kind of thinking. It must also be considered in relation to assessment procedures and the whole educational context, as we shall see later in Chapter 13. After that, the responsibility for learning lies with the student.

Students take a largely rational approach to learning. They consider what is required of them, they decide on priorities, and they act accordingly. The teacher plays an important part in forming their perceptions of what is required and what is important, and it is this, as much as their style of presenting the subject matter, which influences what and how their students learn.

CHAPTER NINE

Revision and the Experience of Understanding

NOEL ENTWISTLE AND ABIGAIL ENTWISTLE

Approaches, Conceptions, and Understandings

The idea of a deep approach to learning was introduced in Chapter 1 and its meaning should have become clearer through discussions in several subsequent chapters. Its essential defining feature is the intention to understand, and that intention evokes the processes of learning which allow deep levels of understanding to be reached. The deep approach involves relating new information to prior knowledge and experience in ways which transform the information and create personal meaning. But what, exactly, is produced by these processes? What is understanding? In spite of its centrality in descriptions of approaches to learning, its meaning has been rather taken for granted. Students presumably develop conceptions or understandings of the topics they study, but how stable are they? Does their form vary, depending on the situation in which the understanding is evoked? Svensson (1989) argued that the conceptions which students held in solving physics problems were dependent on the particular problem they were examining at that time. On that basis, he expressed doubts about the stability of conceptions. In Chapter 14 we shall see that students' conceptions of learning develop as they progress through their courses, confirming that conceptions change over time. But how much do they change, and in what ways?

The most usual way of judging someone's understanding is through the way that understanding is demonstrated — what Perkins and his colleagues at Harvard have recently described as *understanding performances* (Perkins and Blythe, 1994). In exploring students' conceptions, evidence can only be derived from the expression of a conception through the explanations students give of the target concept or through their performance in solving problems related to it. On any one occasion, the explanation or performance will have elements which are specific to that particular occasion, but the understanding might also be expected to have a certain stability, in the short term, over a series of explanations or performances.

The importance of understanding in the literature on student learning, and the paucity of work looking directly at its nature, suggested that further work was required. The research reported in this chapter explores the nature of academic understanding through the experience of students. As in previous chapters, relevant data was obtained through interviews with students about a particular study task — in this instance, the intensive revision process involved in preparing for final examinations.

Interviews on Revision Strategies

In traditional degree courses in Britain, substantial weight is still put on final examinations in determining the class of degree to be awarded. In the final year, teaching usually finishes before the Easter vacation, leaving students with up to ten weeks in which to prepare for some six three-hour essay examinations intended to test their conceptual understanding of each course. For the purposes of this investigation, this context was ideal to explore students' experiences of developing conceptual understanding and of explaining their understandings in the examinations.

The empirical analyses presented here are derived mainly from an interview study of eleven final year students, nine of whom were taking final examinations in psychology. Two of these psychologists were taking a year out of medicine, while two additional students included in the sample were studying zoology. The analyses of these data have been supplemented by the written comments of a further eleven final year psychologists, and by a preliminary analysis of interviews with fifteen students taking social and economic history.

Interviews were based on a set of broad issues which were arranged in a logical progression, starting from past experiences of revision and leading up to revision for Finals. The interviews concentrated mainly on concrete events and strategies during revision, but all the students were also asked about feelings and experiences connected with the development of understanding. Interviews were tape recorded and transcribed in full. The qualitative analyses carried out on the data were of two kinds. First, all aspects of the phenomenon experienced by the respondents were identified. While logic is used in separating out these aspects into a coherent pattern, no relationships between the categories are necessarily expected. The other form of analysis was essentially phenomenographic, with logical relationships between the categories being fully explored (see Marton,1994).

Here, four separate analyses are summarised: the revision strategies adopted by students (for additional details, see Entwistle, N. and Entwistle, 1991); the nature of academic understanding as generally experienced by the students (Entwistle, A. and Entwistle, 1992); differences between students in their *forms of understanding* (Entwistle, N. and Entwistle, 1991); and, finally, the way students had experienced the understandings as quasi-sensory *knowledge objects* (Entwistle and Marton, 1994; Entwistle, 1995).

Revision Strategies

The interviews all began by asking about revision strategies — how students had revised in the past and how their strategies had changed during the degree course. This initial focus was deliberately 'concrete', allowing students to describe their actual study behaviour before asking them to consider less tangible aspects of their experience.

Students described revision strategies which had certain elements in common, although they differed considerably in the extent to which these strategies were used. Essentially, students had accumulated during each course sets of notes and reports from lectures, from books and articles, and also from projects and practical work. Of course, the volume of notes each student had produced varied considerably, depending on the amount of independent reading undertaken. Even so, all students in their final year were faced with such a substantial pile of material that most of them tried to make sense of it through condensation into revision notes. The volume of notes was progressively reduced, step by step, often finishing with a single sheet of notes for each topic. This final condensed revision sheet usually contained a set of headings and very brief indications of related ideas, and was used as a mnemonic through which to retain more detailed information. Some students organised the main headings on this sheet in the form of a patterned note or concept map, the structure of which was more easily remembered in the examination.

Students reported that they revised in a succession of phases. Realising that understanding was required, they started their revision by trying to make sense their notes as a whole, reading them through several times. The process of 'concising' then began and summary notes were usually written at each stage of revision. Understandings were rehearsed, either by talking the ideas through with other students, or by constructing explanations for themselves on paper or out loud. Once understandings were established, students became more strategic, although to varying degrees. They looked at previous examination papers and began to consider the amount of information needed and also to think how best to structure typical answers. Finally, students rote learned the details necessary to support their explanations in the exams, and the summary sheets were used to see to what extent the structure of answers and the supportive details could be remembered. As one student said:

> I designed a sort of check-list system which I used to cross off what I knew ... going from many to few. ... Basically it went from going through the whole lot of notes ... and making condensed notes. (Then as I went through those) I would ask myself if I remembered (each bit), and if I could (explain) it, then that went off the list... Under (various) headings I would have the important points which showed the understanding,...(although) it was basically names, experiments and important examples, which triggered off the understanding by reading it through.

The Nature of Academic Understanding

The analysis, so far, has been derived from students' comments on their revision strategies. The next section of the interview moved on to the students' experiences of understanding — how they knew when something was understood, what it felt like when they did not understand, and what they did to develop their understanding further.

In the interviews, students tended to describe similar components within their experiences of reaching understanding. There was a *feeling of satisfaction*, although that feeling varied in its expression from the sudden 'aha', as confusion on a particular topic was replaced by insight, to a less dramatic feeling associated either with being able to follow a lecture or with an emerging appreciation of the nature of the discipline itself. This feeling was derived from a recognition of the *meaning and significance* of the material learned. The feeling of understanding also included a recognition of *coherence and connectedness*. The idea of 'things clicking into place' or 'locking into a pattern' was frequently mentioned, and this conveyed an implication of completeness. However, students often commented that their understanding might well develop further, which seemed to imply *provisional wholeness*. The students seemed to be experiencing 'closure' — feeling that the current understanding was satisfactory — and yet also anticipating from their previous experience that their current understanding might well be adapted and extended in the future. This almost paradoxical combination of completeness and potential for further development does seem to be an important aspect of the concept of understanding which contributes to it being both stable and changeable.

Associated with wholeness, was a recognition of the *irreversibility* of the understanding achieved — at least once it had been thoroughly established. The feeling of coherence and connectness led students to express *confidence about explaining* — a belief that they could provide a convincing explanation of what they had come to understand, either to themselves or to others. They also recognised that understanding provided them with *flexibility in adapting and applying* ideas and information effectively. It was this confidence, both in being able to provide a convincing explanation and in adapting ideas flexibly for use in varying and novel contexts, which distinguished 'understanding' from 'knowledge' in the students' descriptions.

Bringing together typical comments from several students, the following composite description of the experience of understanding can be presented.

> Understanding is the interconnection of lots of disparate things,… the feeling that you understand how the whole thing is connected up — you can make sense of it internally… If I don't understand, it's just everything floating about and you can't quite get everything into place — like jigsaw pieces, you know, suddenly connect and you can see the whole picture… But there is always the feeling you can add more and more and more… (Really understanding), well, for me, it's when I … could explain it so that I felt satisfied with the explanation… (When you understand like that)… you can't not understand it (afterwards). You can't 'de-understand' it!

Individual Forms of Understanding

While the experience of understanding seemed to be described in similar ways by most students, there were marked differences in the *forms of understanding* which students sought. These forms of understanding appeared to differ in the three main ways — *breadth, depth,* and various types of *structure* — summarised in Table 9.1 below.

The idea of breadth of understanding was made explicit in the following comments:

> I think there is more than one type of understanding — understanding of a specific paper or point or experiment, and then a further understanding of how these relate within the whole topic.

> It's a nice feeling when everything begins to click into a wider picture and you can see, like Art History clicks into History, which clicks into Anthropology, and what was happening in Psychology, and the whole thing

across the board... It's all coming together and you can locate things on the picture.

TABLE 9.1

Individual Forms of Understanding

Breadth of understanding
Depth or level of understanding
Structure used to organise the material being learned
1. little or no structure being imposed on the facts learned
2. relying exclusively on the lecturer's structures
3. producing prepared answers to previous years' questions
4. adapting own understanding to expected question types
5. relying on an individual conception of the topic

'Breadth' described the amount of material which students sought to integrate during revision. This breadth depended partly on the extent of additional reading carried out during the course, and partly on the willingness to look for connections across more than one topic or course. Students also recognised that understanding could be developed to different levels, which can be seen as variations in the 'depth' of understanding. Initial understanding was successively deepened from the initial understanding by actively seeking links between ideas.

When you're coming up to Finals (you ask) — "Do I really understand it ? "... I think your understanding increases gradually on each topic. You think you understand something (in first year), but you don't really understand it until you really understand the whole subject. There's never a moment of (total) enlightenment. As you gradually build up knowledge, the understanding comes with it.

Finally, individual forms of understanding differed in terms of how the understanding was structured. A hierarchy could be detected in the different types of structure identified among the students' contrasting descriptions of their revision. At the lowest level of the hierarchy there was little or no structure, with the students seeking to understand only the content of the notes, so as to obtain the information they would then rote learn. This category was found only in the comments of the two students taking psychology as an interlude in their medical studies. They were describing, not Finals, but the way they had revised for their pre-clinical examinations. As one of them said:

One thing I do is, at the beginning of every course, I read the past papers on the day I start the course, and ... get orientated towards the exams. I don't like to waste my time... Well, medicine is different, I think, from other subjects... The facts ... you just have to learn them... Sometimes, I would ... get up at 5 am and read a few subjects the morning before and use (that, and pass)... But then I would forget it very quickly after the exam, which isn't much good for the patients in the future...

The second category of understanding was in some ways particularly worrying. Students had simply adopted the structure provided by the lecturer and were seeking to reproduce it in the exam answer. It was worrying because the answer might appear to represent thorough, well-structured understanding, and yet that understanding derived wholly from the lecturer, not the student. There was, of course, a sense in which the student had understood the topic, but it represented a narrow and rather inflexible form of understanding — understanding at a surface level, as it were. Students with this form of understanding seemed to have difficulty in explaining what they had understood. They tended to rely on paraphrasing their notes, and looked out for questions in the exam which allowed them to do just that.

> Some questions are basically asking you to discuss (a topic), and if that comes up, it's just remembering my lecture notes and putting down what they said.

> Sometimes I was lucky, when the question said (in) effect " Re-write your mind map in prose". (Well) the mind maps were, to a large extent, based on past exam questions. ... But other times I had to make connections which weren't there in the first place, by extending them (as I went)... By and large, those were worse essays than ... I would have written, had the question been more favourable.

In the remaining three categories, the students had all made some effort to reorganise their revision notes so as to understand the material for themselves. They differed mainly in the breadth and depth of the understanding they had sought, and the extent to which they were being strategic — gearing their learning directly to the form and content of the examination questions they anticipated from looking at previous papers. In the third category, students revised mainly by writing out answers, or structures for answers, to specific questions or question types, showing little evidence of wide independent reading during the course. In the fourth category, the independent reading and thinking was much more extensive, and the initial studying seemed to have developed structures which implied a thorough, personal understanding of the material. In the revision process, these students were quite strategic, relating their revision notes to anticipated question types and thinking about the time constraints in the examination.

> The main thing that I really relied on during revision ... involved going through all the past papers and identifying all the questions on certain topics (the ones I had chosen to revise) and doing short essay plans for each question I had found on that topic.

> The more I have done exams, the more I'd liken them to a performance, like being on a stage; ... having not so much to present the fact that you know a vast amount, but having to perform well with what you do know. ... Sort of, playing to the gallery. ... I was very conscious of being outside what I was writing.

Students in the final category had also read widely and developed their own structures of understanding, but were less strategic in revision. Their focus seemed to be directed towards developing an effective and independent understanding of the discipline as a whole, within which the structure of individual answers could be subsumed. However, this strategy sometimes led to problems in the examinations. As one student commented:

> Well, there were cases where I knew too much... I had to go through all the stages of working through (the topic) and showing that I had understood it. I couldn't gloss over the surface. And once I started writing, it all just 'welled up'. I felt that I couldn't interrupt the argument half-way as it was developing... Half an understanding doesn't make sense!... It's essential to demonstrate your understanding of the whole, and its implications and limitations... You could say I shouldn't be (doing) that in an exam, but basically I have to do it that way, because that's me. Gearing your learning too closely just to previous exam papers seems a bit like a form of cheating.

In preparing for Finals, all the students had to be strategic, to some extent. Yet, there were marked differences in the balance between focusing on the academic content and on the assessment procedure. In lectures, the strategic approach involves a conscious awareness of two focuses of attention — the content of the lecture and what the lecturer considered to be important. In an earlier study at Edinburgh, a politics student had stated:

> I play the examination game. The examiners play it too. ... The technique involves knowing what is going to be in the exam and how it's going to be marked. You can acquire these techniques from sitting in the lecturer's class, getting ideas from his point of view, the form of the notes, and the books he has written — and this is separate to picking up the actual work content. (Miller and Parlett,1974)

This same divided attention was also found during revision — between understanding the content and preparing to answer questions — and the balance and tension between these affected the form of understanding the students sought and reached.

Experiencing the Structure of Understanding

The final analysis was carried out jointly with Ference Marton. The form of that analysis was triggered by one particular extract and led to a reanalysis which concentrated on the experiences of the understandings themselves, rather than on the processes preceding them (Entwistle and Marton, 1994). This extract came from a student who was able to reflect particularly clearly on how she used the structures in her revision notes and brought them to mind on demand within the examination.

> (From my experience) there's no differentiation between things that have been learnt visually, mechanically, or (through hearing); they feel exactly the same... (In exams), I just clear my mind and something comes... You

know it's visual in some ways, but it's also just there without necessarily being visual... (It's not as if) you remember a page, and the page is locked in your memory. What I'm saying is that the ideas are locked in your memory and they display as a page when you're thinking about it, but not necessarily when you're putting it down... I think, in a stress situation like an examination, you don't actually (have to) reach for it, it comes out automatically. That may show that it's not actually a visual memory as such, but a visual expression of 'central memory'.

The subsequent analysis of the whole set of interviews suggested that this experience was not uncommon, although the majority of students found difficulty in articulating it. The experience was related to the way in which revision had been carried out. As we have already seen, students seek to understand their notes first, and subsequently rote learn details needed for examination purposes. During the exam, students relied on recalling the structure of their understanding; concentrating on that structure then 'pulled in' the details as they were needed. In the words of one student, describing his ability to visualise a diagram he had been revising:

I can see that virtually as a picture, and I can review it, and bring in more facts about each part... Looking at a particular part of the diagram sort of triggers off other thoughts. I find schematics, in flow diagrams and the like, very useful because a schematic acts a bit like a syllabus; it tells you what you should know, without actually telling you what it is. I think the facts are stored separately, ... and the schematic is like an index, I suppose.

Piecing together the range of incomplete descriptions, we concluded that students were experiencing their understandings as having some internal form and structure — almost as independent entities which came to control their thinking paths (Entwistle and Marton, 1994). The term *knowledge object* was used to describe the essence of these experiences. Its defining features involve an awareness of a tightly integrated body of knowledge, the ability to visualise the structure in a 'quasi-sensory' way, an awareness of unfocused aspects of knowledge, and recognition of its use in controlling explanations during the exams (Entwistle, 1995).

The control of explanations through the knowledge object can be seen in the following extract.

This (way of revising) gave you quite a broad base from which to answer any question that came up on that topic, so you were used to being flexible in the way that you answered the question — it allowed you to adapt to different ways in which the question could be worded, and it also organised in your mind the relationships between different aspects of, and approaches to, a question.

Another student talked about her knowledge object in ways which seemed to give it an almost independent existence, as it was used to monitor the adequacy of the developing explanation.

Following that logic through, it pulls in pictures and facts as it needs them... Each time I describe (a particular topic), it's likely to be different... Well, you start with evolution, say,... and suddenly you know where you're going next. Then, you might have a choice ... to go in that direction or that direction... and follow it through various options it's offering... Hopefully, you'll make the right choice, and so this goes to this, goes to this — and you've explained it to the level you've got to. Then, it says "Okay, you can go on to talk about further criticisms in the time you've got left".

The knowledge object is used to provide flexible control of an examination answer as it develops. There is a dynamic interplay between the knowledge object and the demands of the question and this produces an essentially unique answer. However, the knowledge object also seems to produce a generic structure for a topic which is likely to remain consistent, and would presumably lead to recognisable similarities in the way the topic is explained on different occasions. This conclusion might explain the suggestion made earlier that conceptions or understandings are to some extent stable, and yet the expression of those conceptions must necessarily depend on the specific context and on the particular problem set.

The introduction of the term 'knowledge object' has provoked a variety of reactions. Some people accept the concept as describing a 'recognisable reality', but others have challenged the use of the term 'object', its generality, and its stability. 'Object' might suggest blocks of knowledge, but in our work the term is not intended to suggest that knowledge is a commodity which can be transferred from teacher to student. Far from it. The knowledge object is essentially a personal construction providing a memorable framework which holds together and summarises complex interconnections created in the process of developing conceptual understanding.

Doubts about the general value of the term stem from its link to the intensive revision demanded for Finals. What happens in everyday studying? In a more recent study, students have been asked about how they research coursework essays (term papers). Our preliminary conclusion is that the knowledge objects formed in essay writing are much less firmly established than through extensive revision, and occur only when the students engage actively and personally with the topic (Entwistle, 1995a). In coursework, students probably have to be far too strategic in their approaches to essay writing and time management for personal engagement to occur on a regular basis.

Other recent evidence about the existence of knowledge objects is anecdotal. It appears that part of the process of preparing a formal presentation or lecture may involve the production of a knowledge object which is then used to control the structure of the explanations provided to the audience. And there is evidence from one student that a knowledge object, created during revision five years previously, could be recalled and used to remember the structure of an explanation (Entwistle, in press). In this instance, the knowledge object involved enduring visual images and these had been accidentally triggered in a specific task. This experience invites further consideration of the role of metaphor and imagery in teaching and learning.

Implications for Education

There has been increasing criticism of the use of formal examinations in higher education. Some of the experiences of the students interviewed in this study add to these criticisms by highlighting negative effects on learning, and showing how the format of many examinations may induce superficial forms of understanding. But where individual forms of understanding have been actively sought, they suggest the importance of providing opportunities for bodies of knowledge to be integrated into personally meaningful, and enduring, patterns of understanding.

The negative experiences were mentioned by several students who resented a distortion of their learning activities. They distinguished sharply between the understanding which they sought initially in their studying and the learning they had to do afterwards to cope with the examinations. The comments of two of the students illustrate this point well.

> After I'd been reading all the books for three or four weeks, ... I understood things perfectly well... But I knew that understanding wouldn't help me in the exam. When you're under pressure, you've got to remember things quickly and get the facts down... I could discuss books with people, but if it actually came to an exam and writing an essay, I would have been hopeless. So, I took my lecture notes and actually memorised them, not verbatim, but memorised the themes and the questions brought up.

> The problem at university is that there is just this immense pressure to learn everything, because you're going to have to do exams at the end of the year... I'm quite resentful in a way, ... because I feel I understand so much more than I can put down in exams... You've got to learn this for exams, so you're always trying to structure it in a way that you know you're going to have to write in this essay question... It's an immense release, now that I've finished university, to know that I can read books without having to learn them, because there's definitely a different way of reading them if you just read it for messages and understanding, whereas for part of the course it's learning it.

Most students had recognised that they would have to fit their answers into a restricted time period, while others had also tailored the form of their understanding to the type of examination questions anticipated. Where the questions were more demanding — requiring individual answers or solutions to problems — students realised that they would need a more flexible structure to respond to the specific question set. Such a flexible approach was easier to achieve where understanding had been developed within a personal structure, particularly if it followed the fundamental principles of the discipline. Moreover, open questions elicit answers which allow conceptual understanding to be assessed with more confidence.

There is already convincing evidence that the general approach to studying can be affected by examination format, with fact-orientated multiple-choice or short-answer questions encouraging surface approaches and essay questions evoking deep approaches (Thomas and Bain, 1984). However, this present study indicates that essay questions also differ in their effects on revising. Narrowly technical questions, or those closely aligned to the taught course, allow weaknesses in understanding to be disguised — the crucial connections on which understanding rests will not have been tested.

Thus, degree examinations at apparently the same level may be making very different intellectual demands on students. What external examiners may judge to be conceptual understanding, may be no more than a close match between the content of the lecture course and narrowly based examination questions. The nature and format of assessment procedures will affect their level of difficulty, creating formidable difficulties in making convincing comparisons between standards.

The present small scale study can do no more than draw attention to the possible effects of questions of different kinds, but it does seem to be an important area for future work. More research is also required into the ways in which understanding is demonstrated — either through applying knowledge within novel contexts or through providing convincing individual explanations. And, to make progress in this direction, the nature of understanding across a variety of topics, disciplines, and professional areas would have to be systematically explored.

Part III

Teaching and the Learning Environment

CHAPTER TEN

Lectures and the Experience of Relevance

VIVIEN HODGSON

Introduction

Despite the development of new approaches to teaching and learning in higher education, lectures remain a prominent feature of many courses. Whilst research carried out on lecture methods is not as common-place in the 1990s as it was one or two decades ago, there remains nonetheless a steady output of research which continues to examine and question the effectiveness of lectures. The emphasis is probably less on the identification of teaching skills and teacher characteristics than it was, and more obviously on the lecture methods compared to other methods. Research has also focused more on the merits of combining the lecture method with other methods, for greater effectiveness.

There are very few studies which attempt to look at lectures as they are experienced by students. The study described in this chapter looks at how students experience and interpret the meaning of what is being said in a particular lecture. And since the study took place in the natural setting of the students' undergraduate courses, it also explored the influence of the course context upon learning from lectures.

Existing Studies

That the lecture remains a dominant method of teaching in higher education continues to be regularly confirmed (see, for example, Collier, 1985; Shore *et al.*, 1990; and Butler, 1992). And the prominence of the lecture in undergraduate teaching has stimulated considerable research and discussion (see, for example, Bligh, 1972; Brown, 1978). In the earlier research, empirical studies shared the single aim of assessing the relative effectiveness of lectures as a teaching method. In his review of this research, Bligh (1972) distinguishes between three main objectives for which the lecture method may be used: acquiring information; promoting thought; and changing attitudes. His conclusion from the available evidence, however, is that while the lecture is as effective as other methods for transmitting information, it is not as effective as more active methods for the promotion of thought, and should not normally be used when changing students' attitudes is the objective .

If Bligh's conclusion seems fairly clear-cut, we should recognise the limitations of the research from which it stems. One limitation is that the focus of investigations of teaching has been virtually exclusively on method, in isolation from setting. As McKeachie (1978) observes, a college course cannot be divorced from the total college culture: a method of teaching greeted enthusiastically by students in one institution may be less than warmly received in another. Linked to this is the problem that research has for the most part concentrated on trying to measure the impact of lectures by testing students' knowledge before and after they have been exposed to lectures and other methods of teaching. The fact that the findings of a large number of these studies have been inconclusive can be seen as a consequence of their narrowness of approach. There has been little attempt to look at lectures from the standpoint of the lecturer, or to explore what students' experiences of lectures have been. Where the attempt has been made, however, the picture presented is a rather different one. Method looms less large, and instead the focus shifts towards factors such as attitude, enthusiasm, involvement and the qualities of the relationship between lecturers and students.

If we look at more recent research on lectures, there seems to be a general acceptance of the conclusions reached by Bligh (1972), which has led to a shift in focus towards exploring the effectiveness either of modifications of the lecture method, using various techniques such as 'buzz groups', or of alternative methods of teaching. Effectiveness is usually measured in these studies in terms of student preference and such studies generally conclude that the 'straight didactic format' is the least preferred method (see, for example, Butler, 1992; and Grieve, 1992).

These studies do not, however, seem to take account of the many studies in the 1970s which raised doubts about the appropriateness of relying on student preference as measures of effectiveness (for example, Ware and Williams, 1975; Coats *et al.*, 1972; and Sherman, 1976). Indeed,

> consistency of response (in such studies) can be attributed just as legitimately to a collective student mythology of teaching, as to any rigorously conceived model of teaching behaviour (Johnson, Rhodes and Rummery,1975).

A more worrying study, from the point of view of the recent research work, was perhaps that of Zelby (1974) who found that students gave high evaluations of lectures deliberately aimed at the level of "information, storage, and retrieval". Lectures aimed at the development of an ability to learn independently and cope with novel situations received the lowest evaluation. It could be argued, however, that today's students are more favourably inclined towards independent learning than were previous generations of students. Certainly, Williams (1992) recently reported that the majority of students, in a study she had conducted, prefer more responsibility, and would take on more active roles if they were allowed to. On the other hand, Entwistle and Tait (1990) reported that preferences for these contrasting types of teaching and learning contexts depended on the approach to studying adopted by the student in that particular course. Students with a deep approach preferred stimulating and challenging teaching, while students opting for a surface approach looked for teaching which was less demanding. Thus, we should expect students to vary quite considerably in their reactions to the same teaching methods.

A rare glimpse of lecturers' experiences is given in a study by Sheffield (1974), who invited twenty-three Canadian lecturers (identified as excellent teachers by a sample of their former students) to write about their teaching. All twenty-three used the lecture as the chief vehicle of their teaching and were broadly in agreement that the most important role of the teacher is "to stimulate students to become active learners in their own right" (p. 199). Other areas of agreement included the belief that there is no one way to teach; the general acceptance that students are important, or are liked, respected or cared for; enthusiasm and love for their subjects; and lastly, a stress upon the importance of preparing properly and on conveying general ideas rather than details. One of Sheffield's own conclusions, based on his examination of both the essays and students' descriptions of the 23 lecturers is that "attitudes towards students and teaching are more important than methods and technique" (p. 215). To this statement, however, he adds the rider that "little is known about how attitudes are formed, less about how they may be changed" (p. 215).

The Students' Perspective

One pathway towards a change in attitudes may well lie in helping lecturers to gain a greater understanding and awareness of the lecture situation as experienced by students. In fact there are a small number of studies concerned with a student perspective and though none of these deals intensively with students' experience of lectures, each does include lectures within a more widely based investigation into students' experiences.

An early study by Marris (1964), for example, involved "discursive interviews in which students were encouraged to talk freely" (p. 2). Its aim was to examine "how the experience (of higher education) appears to the students who go through it" (p. 2). One of the many questions Marris put to students was what they wanted from lectures and what in their experience distinguished good lectures from bad. Whilst Marris's questioning was generalised rather than specific and likely to elicit students perceptions of their 'ideal' lecturer or lecture, he found that "after techniques of presentation, and clarity of arrangement, the students most often mentioned the importance of a lecturer's interest in his subject, and his ability to make it interesting to his audience, so that they were stimulated to pursue it further" (p. 49). In the light of the students' comments, Marris concluded that:

> The essential function of lectures is to place knowledge in a meaningful context. By his synthesis of different points of view, or textbook treatments; by his emphasis on essentials, and the extrapolation of basic principles; by the clarity with which he relates the parts of his exposition, a lecturer can enable the student to perceive the subject coherently. But, perhaps even more usefully, he can provide a more personal context, showing why the subject interests and excites him, how he has used it in his own experience, how it relates to problems whose importance his audience already understands. From this, the student can more easily imagine how he himself could use it: he develops his own context of motives for mastering a problem. (Marris, 1964, p. 53)

A more recent study by Parlett and others parallels Marris's' investigation in its concern to examine and discuss "the experience of academic life more directly from the point of view of its principal consumers, undergraduate students" (Parlett *et al.*, 1977, p. 2). Again, like Marris, Parlett and his colleagues tried,

especially at the beginning, (to) let the students talk freely about their
courses, the way they were taught, the way they learned, the staff they
knew, the problems they encountered, and the hopes and disappointments
they privately harboured (p. 3).

The interviews were deliberately informal and relatively unstructured, and
although the aim was to look at university experience as a whole, many of the
students' comments were about lectures. These were mostly made in response
to the question: 'What are the hallmarks of good teaching?'. This question
again is a rather general one likely to invite perceptions which are directed
towards an 'ideal' lecturer rather than ones grounded in specific experiences.
Nonetheless, a significant difference was found between teachers who were
'interesting and enthusiastic' and those who were 'boring and lifeless'. The
concluding observation again puts emphasis upon attitudes towards students
and teaching:

The important point was that teachers should demonstrate their
commitment and their 'interest in communicating the subject'. Students
want to be stimulated and enlivened by lectures (p. 5).

A study by Bliss and Ogborn (1977), *Students' Reactions to Undergraduate
Science*, takes a somewhat different approach. Students were asked to recount
'good' and 'bad' stories about learning. As the authors comment:

Lectures form a great part of the normal work of science students, indeed
it is no accident that nearly half of all the stories were about them. This
makes it particularly important to understand a little better what makes a
good, and what makes a bad, lecture experience. (Bliss and Ogborn,
1977)

Where the students' stories were concerned with lecturing, therefore, the
question was not how 'good' and 'bad' lecturers differed but what distinguished
a 'good' from a 'bad' lecturing experience. In several stories, Bliss and Ogborn
found "a strong element of reacting well to the personal human qualities of the
teacher as well as his teaching ability as such" (p. 114). In good lecture stories
typical feelings were interest and increased involvement in the subject; while
conversely, a lack of involvement was apparently the most common feeling in
'bad' stories. Indeed, Bliss and Ogborn observe that:

Running like a thread through both 'good' and 'bad' lecture stories are both
involvement and understanding. Essentially all 'good' stories mention
interest, enthusiasm, and so on, if they mention nothing else. Essentially
all 'bad' stories mention their gloomy opposites. Again, both kinds stress
understanding or not understanding as the single most frequent reason for
feeling 'good' or 'bad' (p. 114).

Bliss and Ogborn also examine the reasons students give for characterising
their experiences as 'good' or 'bad' ones. They conclude that:

In 'good' stories, reasons to do with the emotional aspect of the teacher-
student relationship are more prominent than in 'bad' stories, where the

emphasis is heavily on ideas. It shows also how in 'good' stories, reasons to do with human interaction come more to the fore (p.116).

In all three of these studies, therefore, as in Sheffield's study too, the traditionally narrow focus on the effectiveness of methods and techniques has given way to a wider concern with the teacher-student relationship. As attention has shifted, therefore, towards the experiences of the participants themselves, the teacher-student relationship has begun to occupy the foreground of discussion. Yet each of the three studies of students' experience we have looked at has examined lectures only incidentally, as part of the general pattern of undergraduate teaching. A fuller understanding of student learning from lectures requires a more tightly focused investigation, and we turn now to our own study of students' experience of the relevance of lecture content.

Background to the Study

The students who took part in the study were taking one of three different undergraduate courses: a second-year social science research methods course, a final-year microbiology course, and a first-year applied physics and energy course. Each of the courses was a component in the students' degree schemes, and it was the relevance of the content of the lectures given on these courses, as experienced by the students, that formed the main focus of the investigation. As the lectures occurred as an integral part of the students' degree programmes, it was possible to take into account the influence of the students' experience of the teaching and learning context of the three different courses. Information on the perceptions of the different groups of students was collected by informal interviewing throughout each course together with an end-of-course questionnaire designed to tap into comments and concerns expressed during the interviews.

Because of the numbers of students involved, a sample was selected from each of the courses. The students were chosen on the basis of their response to a questionnaire which sought to identify students who thought that interpersonal qualities of the lecturer (for example, whether or not the lecturer had good student-lecturer rapport), influenced their opinion of the lectures more than impersonal perceptions (for example, whether or not the lecturer had a wide knowledge of the subject). For each course, between two and six students were chosen from those who were apparently most or least influenced by personal factors, together with a further two or three students who seemed to be mid-way on that particular dimension. Altogether, a total of 31 students was selected.

These students' experiences of the relevance of their lectures were in the main studied through the use of a technique known as stimulated recall. Stimulated recall was originally developed by Bloom (1953) to compare students' thought processes in lectures and discussion groups. It involves audio-taping a teaching situation and then, within two days playing back to individual students extracts from the session. The students are then asked to recall the thoughts they had during the original situation. As Bloom himself explains:

The basic idea underlying the method of stimulated recall is that a subject may be enabled to relive an original situation with vividness and accuracy if he is presented with a large number of cues or stimuli which occurred during the original stimuli (Bloom, 1953).

In the current study lectures were recorded and extracts played back to students within 24 hours. Recall sessions took place with individual students, so that the replies given could be probed in depth. The main criteria used in choosing extracts to play back was whether or not they seemed to reflect aspects of what had been observed, over time, to be each lecturer's characteristic style of lecturing. On average eight extracts from a fifty-minute lecture were chosen and these were each played to the students who were then asked to recall their thoughts or feelings at the time of the extract. Students replies were then recorded. In total, 48 recall sessions were carried out with the 31 students.

In the recall sessions students both described what they were doing and thinking at the time of the extract and explained why they thought they had responded in the way they had. The example below shows how students can respond in markedly different ways to the same lecture extract.

Lecture extract
The thing to underline I think, here, is it's not always the organism in maximum numbers which can cause the spoilage. So, if you've got 100 organisms in your sample, it's often only 1 to 2 per cent of the organisms present which can actually cause the spoilage that is significant.

> *Student 1 recall*: Now here I had a definite thought, "Yes, what I haven't done in my essay", because I think she was giving that as a particular reference to all of us because we'd all done the essay. What some of us, or most of us, had missed out and I was thinking, "Ah, perhaps I should have done that in my essay". Ah, I was going, just thinking that's a good point, and I should have actually done that... Actually throughout the whole of that part, I think she, there was a lot of information there that I think most of us would probably have missed in our essays.

> *Student 2 recall*: Yeah, yeah, I remember thinking what a hell of a lot of work there'd be to do because she mentioned there could be about 100 colonies but yet only 1 to 2 per cent causes spoilage. So I was thinking, if you've got a plate with 100 colonies, how many you'd have to pick up before you'd pick up a spoilage organism. That was the main thing, but other than that, but you know it's a pretty standard point really, but it would involve a lot of work to get that.

It can be seen from the above example that the two students are each experiencing the relevance of the lecture content in different ways. The first student is thinking about the lecture content in terms of assessment, in relation to an essay that he had done and whether or not he had included the particular point being made by the lecturer. The second student is thinking more about the meaning of the content, and what the implication might be of what the lecturer is saying. This second student seems to be thinking about the lecture content in terms of his own understanding of it and the meaning it has for him. He is therefore experiencing the relevance of the content in an *intrinsic* way, whilst the experience of the first student, whose thoughts are directed towards assessment, is by contrast *extrinsic*. Systematic analysis of students' responses to the lecture extracts showed that many responses could be identified as reflecting either extrinsic or intrinsic experience of relevance.

Extrinsic Experience of Relevance

There were essentially two kinds of *extrinsic* experience of relevance. The first was specific in nature, as in the following example:

> When I checked on to it being experimental design—the next piece of work is on that—we have to design something, design a piece of research work, and I kept — all the way through — I kept asking, how am I going to use this in my work?

Thus the student is thinking about the next piece of work she has to do. In both this and the earlier example, where the student was thinking about an essay he had recently completed, the students have a specific extrinsic demand in mind and consider how they have tackled or might tackle the task set.

In other cases, the students seem to have no particular demand in mind, nor are they thinking about the content in a way meaningful to themselves. For example:

> You expect what the lecturer writes on the board to be the important things, so whatever you write you get that down.

Here, the student seems only to think or recognise that what was being said might <u>potentially</u> be useful or relevant. The experience is much more general in nature. The sole reason, apparently, for writing something down is because the lecturer has written it on the board and it must therefore be important. And it is important, one must presume, as something students may subsequently be assessed or examined on.

As just described, an extrinsic experience of relevance, with its emphasis on external demands is, of course, reminiscent of the descriptions given in earlier chapters of a surface approach. Moreover, as we shall see, an intrinsic experience of relevance is qualitatively very similar if not precisely the same as a deep approach. These similarities will be further discussed at the end of the chapter.

Intrinsic Experience of Relevance

In the 'spoilage' example given above, the student realises that one implication of what the lecturer was saying about the number of organisms that can cause spoilage is that picking up the spoilage organism would entail considerable effort. The student thus seems to be thinking more about the meaning of what was being said, and how it relates to his own understanding and framework of thinking. The student is drawing upon his existing knowledge and fitting this new information into his own framework. He is therefore experiencing the relevance of the content intrinsically. A second example of intrinsic experience parallels the first:

> I had two thought, "Yes, it does happen in the hospital situation, where they tend, because staff just forget this person, um, that it's this person's private life: it becomes part of their form-filling". And my other thought was: "I don't think it happened where I worked".

Here again the student seems to be relating the content to her own framework of thinking and experience in a way that is personally meaningful.

In both examples the students actively relate the content to their own understanding in a specific way. In some cases, however, the students are more passive. They appear to acknowledge that the material has some sort of relevance to their understanding, but they do not go further and actively think this through. For example:

> I understood it and I found the content interesting, so I didn't stray, my mind didn't wander.

Influence upon Intrinsic and Extrinsic Experience of Relevance

It was possible to identify three sources of influence upon whether different students experienced the relevance of their lectures as extrinsic or intrinsic: students' general orientation towards the course; the teaching and learning context; and students' background knowledge and familiarity with the subject.

(i) Students' general orientations

Students' orientations towards the lecture courses differed, and the differences were particularly marked in the case of the research method students, some of whom were following a degree scheme in home economics rather than in human science. For these home economics students, the predominant concern was with assessment demands and how these could be met rather than with what might be learnt from the course. As a consequence, many of these students' statements reflected extrinsic experiences of the lecture content.

For the human science students, on the other hand, the research methods course was more generally accepted as being an important and relevant subject: they were able to recognise the significance of it to themselves and to what they were doing. Of the five human science students studied in depth, three were predominantly intrinsic in their experience, and the whole group of five had a relatively high level of intrinsic experience.

One might expect to find similar contrasts among students following a final year option which they themselves had chosen (as was the case for the microbiology students) and those who, like the applied physics and energy students, were following a compulsory first-year foundation course. And indeed, analysis of the microbiology students' accounts displayed a relatively high incidence of intrinsic experiences of relevance.

(ii) The teaching and learning context

Of the three groups of students taking the research methods course, the home economics students, as we have already noted, were the only group not from the Department of Human Sciences. Their perceptions of the teaching and learning context were as a consequence distinctly different from the other students on the course, and displayed substantially less certainty about the relevance of the course to themselves. It was, however, the norm rather than the exception for home economics students to take courses outside their own department and to cope with unfamiliar subjects, the relevance of which they could not always see. In such circumstances therefore, one might expect that extrinsic experiences of the relevance of their courses would be frequent and that consequently the most 'successful' students might be those who had best developed work styles tailored to extrinsic experiences. The findings seemed to bear this out, for the home economics students with the highest levels of extrinsic experience of relevance were also those who obtained the highest grades on the course. This finding is all the more striking because, while it could be anticipated in this specific context, it is still at odds with the pattern for the study as a whole. Generally speaking, the students who were predominantly intrinsic in their experience achieved the highest grades.

The context of the applied physics and energy course was also quite interesting. Amongst the students there was, on the one hand, a feeling of uncertainty about the usefulness and specific relevance of the course and, on the other, a high acceptance of the general relevance and interest in the energy component (rather than the physics component) of the course, together with a belief that the course was not so important from an extrinsic, assessment, perspective. These last two factors may have counter-balanced any negative effects of the first. An alternative interpretation is that there were other factors, beyond those associated with the teaching and learning context, which were strong enough to overcome any negative effects of uncertainty and so help to sustain the high degree of intrinsic experience characteristic of this course.

(iii) Students' background knowledge and familiarity

Another important influence upon intrinsic and extrinsic experience of relevance was the students' background knowledge and familiarity with the subject. Here again the home economics students, who professed to have a poor knowledge of research methods, were a distinctive sub-group. As the course progressed, however, this obviously changed, since the high incidence of extrinsic experiences recorded in the early stages of the course declined as the course progressed. Other students, such as the final-year microbiology students and the human science students taking the research methods course, were obviously more familiar with their subject and their recall statements reflected comparatively greater degrees of intrinsic experience. Again the first-year applied physics and energy students were interesting because they had an unusually high perception of their background knowledge, and they displayed an unusually high level of intrinsic experiences despite the doubts they expressed about the usefulness and specific relevance of the course. One student, for example, commented that he could not altogether see how the course fitted in with his other courses. However, he felt very familiar with the course content and to a large extent experienced its relevance intrinsically. Moreover, it was on the apparently more familiar material of the physics component of the course that the highest levels of intrinsic experience were recorded, in spite of the fact that it was the energy component of the course that was perceived as the more relevant one.

Vicarious Experience of Relevance

In analysing the students' experiences of relevance, it was evident that some experiences were closely related to or linked to the lecturer's presentation and were best described not as extrinsic or intrinsic but as vicarious. Students who experienced the relevance of the lecture content vicariously seemed to do so essentially in one of two different ways. Either they took over the lecturer's perceived interest or enthusiasm for the material, for example:

> ... but the energy is obviously very interesting to him, and of course to us, so the way he puts it over is much more interesting.

or, alternatively, the lecturer seemed, in discussing a particular point, to provide an illustration, and example or a description of his or her own experience which students were able to identify with and take on board as something recognisable and interesting. Thus it was the illustration or the example that the student could relate to rather than the underlying issue being discussed, as in the following instance:

> It was interesting, wasn't it? Interesting to see what — just the information — her explaining her work in another country, what the attitudes are like. It was interesting.

The vicarious experience of relevance is therefore qualitatively distinct. It differs from an extrinsic experience in that it does not seem to be associated with external demands and it differs from an intrinsic experience in that students do not quite seem to see the content in terms of their own view of the world and their understanding of it. Instead the students seem to relate more to something the lecturer offers, whether that takes the form of enthusiasm or an interesting and recognisable illustration or example. Vicarious experience is thus very closely linked to the lecturer, perceptions of the lecturer, and the lecturer's presentation. Interestingly, amongst students who had closer contact with the lecturer (for example, because the lecturer was also their tutor) there was a stronger likelihood of vicarious experience. Furthermore, the students who apparently knew their lecturers best tended to record the highest incidence of vicarious experience, as did those students with the most positive perceptions of their lecturers.

Vicarious experience is arguably the most significant level of experience identified because it brings to the fore an important potential role of lecturers as facilitators of intrinsic experience of relevance where that might not otherwise have occurred. Indeed, in many cases it was very difficult to differentiate rich vicarious experiences from intrinsic ones and there was every reason to believe that the former could easily lead to the latter. There was, for example, one lecturer whose style of lecturing was such that a great deal of vicarious experience seemed likely to be associated with her lectures. She made extensive use of vivid examples and illustrations, tried hard to bring the subject alive and spoke in an enthusiastic manner. This can be illustrated to some extent by comparing an extract from her lecture notes with the transcript from her actual lecture.

Extract from lecture notes:
Commercial process; that they are loaded on the deck of the fishing vessel, may be tumbled, gutted and often contaminated with bacteria.

What the lecturer actually said:
I'm sure you have seen pictures, on television and things, of what happens to the poor old fish, they are tumbled on deck, they are trodden on, they are handled, they are gutted, and they are washed and all these operations add enormous other organisms to them.

And yet, despite this lecturer's style of lecturing, the level of vicarious experience associated with her lectures was not exceptionally high. There was evidence, however, of considerable intrinsic experience which frequently seemed closely related to vicarious experience. For example, in response to the above extract one student recalled:

> It sort of flashed through my mind, actually picturing what happens because I've seen them pulling their catch in, the trawl. It was just like that, they sort of tread all over them, I thought goodness me, how do they ever get back, if they're not in one piece are they fairly fresh?... Imagining all the bacteria on their boots coming off on to them ... I was just imagining it.

It could be argued that this student not only accepts the vivid picture offered by the lecturer (which would make the experience a vicarious one) but goes beyond it in picturing it for himself: 'How do they ever get back, if they're not in one piece are they fairly fresh?'. The student therefore experiences the content intrinsically rather than simply vicariously. Further evidence that many of the intrinsic experiences of this lecturer's students were closely related to vicarious experience of her 'vicarious' style came from analysis of three other students. For one lecture recalled by all three it seemed the lecturer did not achieve her usual level of vicarious projection. The students' experiences of the lecture were mostly extrinsic with apparently hardly any vicarious experience. In the case of a later lecture, however, two of the students' statements reflected greater degrees both of vicarious and of intrinsic experience of relevance. Similarly, the third student recorded more vicarious and more intrinsic experiences for an earlier lecture. In other words, in those lectures where the three students recalled higher levels of vicarious experience, all three also recalled higher levels of intrinsic experience. And conversely, when the incidence of vicarious experience was low, all three recalled high levels of extrinsic and low levels of intrinsic experience. As far as this lecturer was concerned, therefore, there was an evident relationship between the levels of vicarious and intrinsic experience associated with her lectures.

There was other evidence too, from this and from the other two courses studied, which indicated that vicarious experience could be seen as pivotal and transitional. Where vicarious experiences were few in number, extrinsic experiences tended to be frequent, and where vicarious experiences were abundant, there was also greater numbers of intrinsic experiences, suggesting strongly that vicarious experiences could serve as a bridge towards experiences of an intrinsic kind. The implication of this finding for teaching is clear-cut, especially when seen alongside the earlier finding that vicarious experiences were highest amongst students who knew the lecturer best and who were the most positive in their perceptions of that lecturer. By seeking to heighten vicarious experiences amongst their students, lecturers may help to bring about the personal understanding which is the hallmark both of intrinsic experience of relevance and of a deep approach to learning.

Experience of Relevance and Student Learning

As the study we have just described has shown, students seem to experience the relevance of lecture content in three ways, intrinsically, extrinsically or vicariously. And as we suggested earlier, intrinsic and extrinsic experiences can be related to deep and surface approaches to learning. Where an experience is intrinsic or an approach deep, students perceive learning as bound up with themselves as individuals. As Marton observes, when students adopt a deep approach:

> They grasp the fact that the university subjects they are reading have to do with the same reality as that of their daily lives. This means they make use of their knowledge and skills. (Marton, 1975a, p. 131).

As described in this chapter, intrinsic experience is very much about students making use of their knowledge and skills. Similarly, there is a strong link between extrinsic experience and some of the characteristics of a surface approach as Marton describes it:

> Learning does not take place in a vacuum, but in various social contexts. Learning situations are characterised by the demands they make, primarily in the form of exams, grades, etc. Thus it is a matter of external demands, to some extent inescapable: one must try to learn certain things not because one wants to find out something, but because someone else thinks that one ought to learn them for the future (Marton et al., 1977).

Marton suggests that in a surface approach, the aim is not to find something out but to be able to reproduce a text or to answer specific questions. Students who experience relevance extrinsically similarly focus on what is necessary to fulfil external demands such as these.

It is the vicarious experience of relevance, however, which is potentially the most important result of this study. This finding is especially interesting in relation to traditional research on lectures, a striking feature of which is the frequency with which characteristics or skills of the lecturer such as 'maintenance of student interest', 'lecturer enthusiasm', and 'lecturer-student rapport' have been identified as 'effective' (see, for example, Cohen *et al.*, 1973; Wimberly and Faulkner, 1978; and Hildebrand, 1973). What that research fails to do, however, is to clarify the relation between those characteristics and skills and student learning.

Vicarious experience establishes the nature of this relationship. In the course of a lecture, students whose experiences might normally be largely extrinsic may find their interest in the subject matter itself kindled by the lecturer's enthusiasm or, through the medium of a vivid example or illustration, see the content of the lecture as having meaning in the real world. Vicarious experience of relevance can thus be viewed as transitional, providing a bridge between extrinsic experience or a surface approach and intrinsic experience or a deep approach. Through vicarious experience of relevance, therefore, it becomes possible for the lecturer to help students to go beyond the outward demands of a learning situation and make connections between the content of the lecture and their understanding of the world around them.

CHAPTER ELEVEN

Learning Formal Representations through Multimedia

DIANA LAURILLARD

Introduction

It is a universal feature of academic discourse, no matter what the discipline, that it represents ideas using a particular formalism. Most subjects use a special language, often using everyday words but with specific connotations and precise definitions that are importantly different from the normal meanings. Many subjects also make use of formal representations such as symbolism, notation, diagrams, graphics, and all of these require mastery of their interpretation and implementation for the subject to be properly understood.

It is also a universal characteristic of student learning that students find it difficult to master the interpretation and implementation of formal representations. What heightens the difficulty is that the content of a subject is usually articulated through its formal representational devices, which hinders the student trying to find a toe-hold on which to build a sure-footed route to understanding. The formal representation is meant to act as a vehicle for mediating the teacher's knowledge, whereas in reality it is itself an impediment. A straight-line graph is a beautiful representation of a linear relationship, but it is only interpretable by someone who already understands that a linear relationship concerns the form of the mapping of the domain of one variable onto the domain of another — which gobbledygook is also only interpretable by someone who already understands the concept of a linear relationship. There is a circularity of language and ideas.

The difficulty for the student is that academic knowledge is necessarily mediated through some form of representation — at least a specialist language —and it cannot be experienced directly as most of our knowledge is. Academic knowledge is essentially a second-order phenomenon, the description of someone else's experience of the world (Laurillard, 1993). This is the principal reason for the primacy of discussion as a medium of teaching and learning. Through debate and discussion with the teacher, or at least vicarious experience of it in tutorials, the student can begin to see how the specialist language works, how the discourse proceeds in a particular discipline. The task of learning this 'second language' mirrors all the difficulties of learning a second national language: immersion in the target language is usually the most efficient method.

It is not given to many students to spend their days in research labs, or in conversation with their teachers. Our typical instructional style requires a different approach. If we are to help students gain access to the 'precepts' of a subject we must determine their affordances.

Affordance as an Aspect of Learning Activity.

The idea of 'affordance' originated with the psychology of perception. The 'affordances' of an object are what we perceive, and from which we infer its properties. We perceive a dumb-bell made of metallic-painted balsa-wood as heavy because it affords the perception of 'heaviness', although its actual property is 'lightness'. Mostly, affordances do not deceive us of an object's true qualities: thus 'percepts', the content of our perceptions, are reasonably unproblematic.

By contrast, most 'concepts' must be acquired over time: we need to process a series of experiences in order to distil concepts such as 'redness' or 'table manners' or 'length'. The affordances of these concepts concern not just immediate perception , but longer-term analysis and interaction with the environment over time. It would be quite possible for a series of experiences to fail to reveal a particular concept. The sequence and frequency of instances of a concept affect its learnability, which is why primary school curricula must be carefully structured and sequenced to allow students to apprehend the fundamental concepts of the physical environment, such as conservation, equality, etc. The affordances of concepts, therefore, go beyond the immediate perceptual properties, their percepts, and include also the timing of the presentation of instances. Of course the processing of that information is a further stage that must be carried out by the learner, and is independent of the affordances. The sequence and timing may be perfectly optimised, but individuals may approach the processing of that information differently: for example, one study showed that students using a 'focusing' strategy on the instances presented were better able to discern a concept than those using a 'scanning' strategy (Bruner, Goodenough and Austin, 1956).

The term 'concepts' is widely used in the student learning literature, to refer to the theoretical ideas covered in academic study. We talk of the concept of 'force', of a 'vector', of 'short-term-memory' — and of students' conceptual understanding. The term was already being used by psychologists, however, to refer to abstractions from everyday experience. This wide-ranging usage overworks the term. The apprehension of Bruner's 'red circles' is fundamentally different from the apprehension of Newtonian 'force', which is itself very different from the apprehension of the normal meaning of 'force'. In the context of this kind of discussion, the terminology needs to be differentiated more precisely. This is why here, and elsewhere, I have coined the term 'precepts' for academic ideas expressed as theoretical constructs (Laurillard, 1987).

They are 'precepts' because they are defined givens, they cannot be experienced, as percepts can, nor can they be acquired through experience, as concepts can. They are the personal constructs of the scholars in an academic field, whose ideas are the content of academic discourse. 'Precepts' can only be known through formal representation, therefore, such as a specialist language, or some other kind of symbol system. In order to learn and understand these ideas, students can only have access to them through some form of mediation — they cannot be experienced directly because they are someone else's ideas. As I have already argued, the mastery of formal representation is itself problematic for the newcomer to a field of study. The interlinking problems of mastering the formal representation, and mastering the precept to which it provides the only access, make academic study the province of those who can tolerate both complexity and uncertainty. In many areas, of course, the ideas are sufficiently simple, and the formal representations sufficiently transparent that this is a surmountable difficulty. But every subject discipline has some topics which remain opaque and inaccessible for many students, for precisely these reasons. When that is so, how do we best support the student?

The different kinds of affordances I have identified for percepts and concepts will have their parallel also for precepts. If we can establish the affordances of precepts, then we shall begin to see what must be done to help students acquire them. 'Percepts' are directly perceived, and their affordances are those perceptual properties that match the physical properties; 'concepts' are directly experienced, and their affordances combine their perceptual properties and the pattern of their occurrence over time; 'precepts' require interaction with both the content and its representation, and their affordances are therefore the opportunities available to the student to link these two together.

This is expressible in terms of the 'conversational framework' for the academic learning process (Laurillard, 1993). This identifies four kinds of activity for learning to take place: 'discursive' — the discussion between teacher and student, 'interactive' — the task/action/feedback cycle operating in the world of the content, 'adaptation' — of description and task by teacher, and of description and action by student, and 'reflection' — on student performance by the teacher, and on experience by the student. The framework is represented in Figure 11.1. To achieve full understanding of the ideas being put across by the teacher, the student must be able to experience them through interactive operation on the real world, and use reflection on this experience to inform their dialogue with the teacher, and use this dialogue to adapt the way they operate on the world. This dual-level processing is necessary for the student to be able to capture both the content and the representation of the ideas.

Thus, in borrowing the idea of 'affordance' from the psychology of perception, we can see an analogy with what we must provide in the teaching context if students are to apprehend academic knowledge. The affordances of precepts are quite complex, they involve the combination of all those aspects of the learning process, and if we do not provide for them, we cannot always expect the student to achieve a sound understanding.

The Role of Multimedia in the Provision of Affordances

Traditional teaching methods can support the learning process in the full complexity outlined in Figure 11.1, through a combination of lectures, reading, tutorials, supervised practical work and assessed assignments. Such a combination allows tutor and student to discuss and debate the ideas in the lecture, allows the student to operate on tasks set by the tutor in the practical, and to relate the results of their actions to the theoretical ideas in some form of independent expression — usually an essay — on which they receive further critical feedback. This combination addresses the full conversational framework, which is why these traditions have been established in university teaching. It can work well in the context of small group tutorials and regularly assessed assignments, where the iterative loops in the framework have short time-spans. However, these traditions are being drastically undermined in universities as numbers increase and resources decrease, and even where the traditions worked well, their effectiveness is now under threat. Large classes and more so-called 'independent learning' address only the input to the student, and not the interaction with the teacher.

FIGURE 11.1

Conversational framework for academic learning

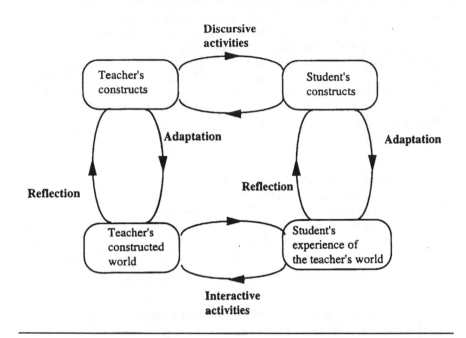

There is no substitute for personal contact with a human tutor, but there are ways in which multimedia technologies can address aspects of the conversational framework that cannot be easily done by other independent learning methods. These are essentially interactive media, incapable of providing genuine discussion with the student, but certainly capable of providing interaction and a degree of adaptive feedback to students on their performance. How well they do this depends on the extent to which the instructional design incorporates the affordances needed for precepts.

This chapter began with reference to a particular instructional problem, namely the problem of the interpretation and implementation of formal representations. This can be used to illustrate the role that multimedia can play in supporting learning if the capabilities of the medium are fully exploited to incorporate the necessary affordances of these particular precepts. The peculiar characteristic of multimedia that is so valuable here, is that it can offer both interaction with a formal system, expressed as a computer model, and a description of that system at any level of sophistication, from the formal to introductory natural language. More than any other medium, therefore, it can address many aspects of the conversational framework, and thereby provide the affordances students need for mastery. Three case studies will serve to illustrate the point.

Case studies of Learning Formal Representations

The three case studies are taken from three different disciplines: earth science, physics, art history. All three use data from studies on student learning which have attempted to document students' misconceptions for a particular topic. In each case, the clear analysis of students' learning needs enables us to derive, almost logically, the instructional design they need.

These cases concern three different kinds of formal representation: geological maps, equations and definitions, and specialist language. In each case, students typically find themselves operating within the formal representation as a vehicle for understanding the content before they have fully understood the representation itself.

(i) Geology

In the case of geological maps, students have to interpret complex maps that represent the geological formations underlying an area of terrain in order to produce a cross-sectional drawing of the formation of the strata beneath. The drawings they produce may be so bizarre that the teacher has great difficulty in knowing how to help them. Students are well aware of their difficulties. They try to use the rules they have been given, but do not understand them:

> This my big problem. I can put marks on the topography, but I can't tell what to do next.

> My difficulty is this river — it is going down and then climbing up again... Rivers don't do that.

> The way the streams are running gives you the topographic layout, and that's what I'm more familiar with, and I seem to be overly influenced by it.

> I have to be careful since sometimes I confuse myself with the dip of the rock and the gradients of the ground. (McCracken and Laurillard, 1994)

These quotes contain the germ of the difficulty. The geological maps in question look very similar to topographical maps, and it is easy for students to interpret the curving boundaries of rock strata as contour lines. Even when that problem is overcome, there is still the difficulty of being able to use a 2-dimensional representation to determine the 4-dimensional story of how the geological events led to this resulting formation. The content is not difficult — the ideas of sedimentation, of folding, faulting and erosion, are not conceptually difficult. But the formal representation of all that information in one 2-dimensional diagram is difficult, and needs special care in its presentation.

(ii) Physics

Newton's Laws of Motion have been extensively researched in an attempt to articulate why students find the idea of force so difficult. It has been studied often in relation to the Second Law, which expresses force as a function of acceleration and mass. Interpretations of situations where the law applies often result in students expressing force as varying with velocity. The mathematical expression may be used in a procedurally correct way, but verbal interpretations may still be incorrect. The normal experience of the use of the word 'force', where it appears to relate to giving some motive impulse to an object, or to define a property of an object, is hard to overcome.

In a study which looked at interpretations of the Third Law, another kind of difficulty emerged. The law, in its simplest form, states that any force has an equal and opposite reaction. Students asked to apply this to an object in free fall reveal another kind of misconception. They believe it concerns equilibrium, and they identify the paired force incorrectly, which makes it difficult to apply the law to this case:

> Air hasn't got the capability to hold something stationary. So there's an unbalanced force down... the force upwards is far less than the force downwards, so it's unbalanced. [Pause]... I'd say that the law does apply but there must be some more to it that I haven't thought of yet.

> This case isn't applicable because the body is moving, and it's not constant velocity...Um... you can't sort of say the law only exists for certain bodies... Um...It applies to when they're in equilibrium and at rest, but when the actual system is trying to reach equilibrium, it doesn't apply.

By identifying the paired force with air resistance, and by trying to find two equal forces acting on the object, the law becomes unintelligible. The correct interpretation emphasises the fact, stated in the original version of the law but not always repeated, that the two forces act on different bodies. The forces that should be paired in this system are 'the earth acting on the object', and 'the object acting on the earth'. By the second law, the very small mass and very large acceleration of the object matches the very large mass and the very small acceleration of the earth. It has nothing to do with equilibrium, which balances forces on a single object.

The combination of mathematical symbolism, static diagrams, and specialist language here creates a formal representation that bears little relation to the student's normal experience of the idea of 'force', and the confusion apparent in these quotes is often maintained over years of study of physics.

(iii) Art History

Students of art history, coming to the subject for the first time, may find that their expectations of the subject are at odds with the way it is taught. Academics see the subject as highly theoretical — "art history is about the made image as a register of broad social, ideological and psychological structures", "art history is an academic discipline conducted like other arts disciplines entirely through reading, writing and verbal discourse" (quoted in Durbridge, 1995). By contrast, students come to the subject because they want to know more about paintings.

I really don't know where to begin to study a painting. I'd latch onto something striking, like it was very splodgy, or in vivid colours, perhaps... I don't know how to do more than that.. what else to say, or what else matters.

How can people possibly do this stuff until they've learned how to look? What they need is practice.

If there was more enjoyment, a sense of exploration and discovery in the beginning, it might encourage us. [Durbridge, 1995].

There is a striking contrast between what the students expect of the subject and what the academics seek to provide them with. For the students, the immersion in theory and description occurs before they feel properly grounded in the experience of the phenomena being described. As Durbridge points out, the students need to have more experience of looking at paintings, and considering their own reactions to them before they can realistically confront the experts' theoretical constructs. The precepts bear no relation to any concepts, or even percepts, for students who are novices in the study of art. It is like trying to describe geological formations to someone who has never seen a hill. If they have little experience of the phenomena, then students have no access to the affordances of the precepts that describe them. As Durbridge argues, they must be given the chance to 'play' first.

The argument is identical for the two previous case studies as well. Formal representations formalise a way of describing our experience of phenomena, whether the phenomena be objects falling, or the earth moving, or cultural artefacts. Students need access to the affordances of these precepts, and our traditional mode of teaching frequently fails to do this. For many topics this may not matter, as the complexity is not so great that students need additional help. However, as in the examples of the case studies quoted here, there are many topics in higher education that occasion considerable and continuing difficulty for students because the precepts are sufficiently complex, and because we pay sufficiently little attention to providing their affordances.

In the next section the particular role that multimedia can play in providing affordances for academic ideas is illustrated with respect to the three case studies.

Instructional Design in Multimedia

The preceding sections have suggested that the affordances of academic ideas, or precepts, will be given through both interactive experience of the phenomenon, and a correlated discussion of the formal description of that phenomenon. Multimedia, uniquely of any of the teaching media, can offer something close to this. A computer model of the phenomenon can be controlled by the student through parameter manipulation, or commands. This process can simulate experience in the real world, but has the advantage that it is more focused and creates the particular experiences the teacher requires. The same is true of a laboratory practical, of course, except that a computer model typically behaves more reliably than a practical. The multimedia program can also represent the phenomenon in a variety of ways — iconically, graphically, symbolically, linguistically — and the descriptions given can be under the control of the model, so that the two are indeed correlated.

In addition, the program can interrogate the student for their description of what has been produced. The student may communicate their description in two ways: by selecting from a given set of alternatives, or by typing in their own answer which is then pattern-matched with a pre-defined list of possibilities. It is an imperfect form of communication, but for many purposes may suffice as a reasonable approximation to allowing the student to communicate their idea to the program. It is then possible for the program to compare the student's idea with the pre-defined correct answer and provide feedback either through control of the model, or through pre-programmed text associated with that answer.

With these two levels of processing, the interactive and the discursive, linked by adaptation of the task set, and analysis of the student's performance, the computer-based program can achieve an approximation to coverage of all the affordances necessary for apprehension of certain kinds of precept. Not all precepts could be adequately modelled in a computer program, but when that is possible, then something like this is achievable.

In the three case studies above, we have seen that students need a certain kind of experience before understanding is likely.

(i) Geology

Students in this case study need to see how the experiential relates to the formal in a much more direct way than most media allow. The interpretation of very complex maps is particularly difficult when both the representation and the content are unfamiliar. If students can focus on one aspect to begin with, they can begin to build a surer understanding.

Figure 11.2 shows how an interactive tutorial could provide the affordances students need to make the connection between geological formations and their representation in two-dimensional maps. If students are initially given control over the development of the formation, then they are in a position to know what is being mapped. The program can interpret their commands to generate both an iconic representation of the geology and the corresponding formal representation in the form of a map, since there is a logical relationship.

As students input successive commands to the system, the computer model generates the successive geological forms and their corresponding maps. Student are able to make sense of the link between the two because they know what is being mapped, and because the complex map is built up in stages. Their control of the geological system provides a form of experiential learning, showing the effects of combinations of erosion, sedimentation, folding etc., generating different formations according to the students' input. However, this system does not yet provide the affordances for making the connection between the experiential and the formal — the opportunity is there, but they may not take it. An affordance worthy of the term makes it inevitable that they make the connection. To do that, the program must require of students that they make the connection. One way to do this is to set them a task to find a set of commands that will generate a given map. This requires students to attend to the relationship between the formation they generate, and its formal representation. Similarly, once the generation of the map is understood, it is possible to move to the next stage of asking students to interpret a given map in terms of the successive formations that would have generated it. This is now close to the original task.

FIGURE 11.2

Mapping Geological Formations

As the student creates the geographical structure through successive geological events, the corresponding map is displayed.

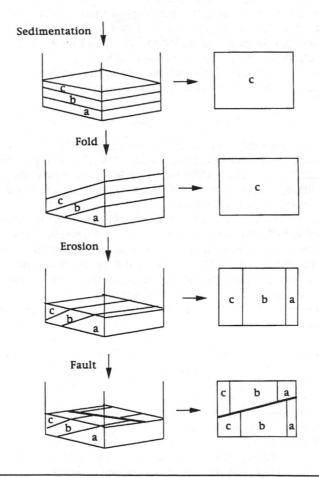

(ii) Physics

In this case, students need to see that the Third Law relates to a two-body system in which the forces acting on the two bodies are equal, no matter what the respective sizes. The force between them is a property of the system, not of a body; it is analogous to a mirror image, which necessarily requires an equal and opposite image. It is difficult to experience the Newtonian idea in the real world because it is idealised and theoretical: you cannot experience the earth accelerating towards a falling object. But in a multimedia world, where the computer models the system and its behaviour, this becomes possible. Figure 11.3 illustrates how a program might construct the control of the two-body system in such a way that it provides the affordances of this precept.

FIGURE 11.3

Computer Representation of a Two-body System in Physics

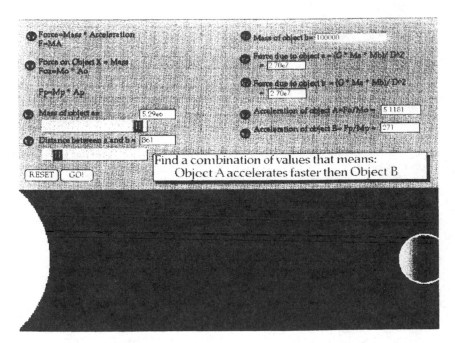

Students can control the behaviour of object A, by changing its mass. As they do so, the model shows how the objects move, with the two accelerating together if their masses are similar, object A as moving much faster if it is much smaller, and vice versa. Students can therefore experience the phenomenon much more directly than is possible anywhere else, other than a ice-rink, perhaps. Moreover, the program can display the related formal description, showing how the equations in the model determine the resulting force and acceleration, using the parameters input by the student. Buttons on each formal statement expand to an elaborated description of what it means in normal English. Moreover, the student has their attention focused on a specific goal — a combination of parameters that makes the system behave in a certain way — so that they attend to what results from their actions, rather than merely playing. Such an interaction, with the simulated system and with its formal description, gives the student better access to the affordances of this precept than any other medium, apart from the dedicated teacher.

The task-setting in both these cases is an essential aspect of the instructional design because it is this that creates the affordances for making the link between experiential and formal representations. Without it, we provide a mere simulation of the experiential, where students may merely 'see what happens', and not make the vital cognitive link. The task-setting requires that they both reflect on the representation of the interaction with the model, and adapt their actions in that model in the light of what the formal representation tells them. Thus both levels of the conversational framework are served, together with the reflective and adaptive links between them.

(iii) Art history

In this case study the formal representation being targeted is language — the specialist language of the academic. The expert writes about paintings in terms such as 'genre', 'period', 'tonality', etc., but what experience of paintings can students bring to the interpretation and application of this language? They have very little to draw on. They need to begin by extending their experience, and generating their own language with which to confront the experts.

Figure 11.4 shows how this was done in a design followed through from the original research with students (Durbridge, 1995). Students can examine some 20 paintings in close-up, and decide how they would like to sort them.

FIGURE 11.4

Mutimedia program to allow individual categorising of paintings

In a task similar to construct elicitation techniques, the program invites students first to generate their own categories, then sort the paintings according to those which fit a category and those which do not (e.g. the category 'lots of sky'). They are also asked to generate a category that will discriminate between two given paintings. Thus they begin to look closely at paintings in a way that helps to develop their own language of description. At later stages they are shown which of their categories produce similar 'sorts', so that they can gradually refine their use of language as they develop their own descriptive system. Once this is established, they are then shown how others have sorted the paintings, both students and experts, and again they can refine their own categories.

Stand-alone multimedia systems cannot set up a debate and discussion between student and tutor, but this design comes very close to enabling students to establish their own linguistic constructs and then test these against those of the expert. The task set requires them to look closely at the paintings, in a variety of combinations, and to reflect on their own categorisations, compare them with others', and adapt accordingly. The program affords practice in the interpretation and application of the expert's constructs. When the students now confront precepts concerning the evidence of 'tonality' or 'texture' of a painting, they have some experiences and formal descriptions of their own against which to test these new ideas. They have some ground on which to build. And once again, the nature of the task set is the key to providing the affordances they need.

Concluding points

In all three case studies, I have tried to show that (a) students have considerable conceptual difficulties in mastering precepts given through formal representations of experiential phenomena, especially when the phenomena are scarcely experienced by students, and the formal representation is complex; and (b) interactive multimedia programs can provide the affordances they need for understanding such precepts because they can combine so many aspects of the conversational framework necessary for academic learning.

Instructional design should proceed from a detailed understanding of students' needs, especially for the traditionally difficult topics in a subject. A needs analysis will not always lead to a requirement for interactive multimedia, but where a topic requires that kind of extensive support, then we must also attend to the construction of the affordances for understanding the topic, making full use of the characteristics the medium can offer.

CHAPTER TWELVE

Enabling and Shaping Understanding through Tutorials

CHARLES ANDERSON

Introduction

The accent in many of the earlier chapters has been on the purposes in studying and processes of learning of individual learners. This present chapter reports a study of the student experience of tutorials — of discussion groups led by a lecturer — and so has a somewhat wider focus, looking at perceptions of learning-and-teaching. It describes types of teaching interactions during these discussion groups which students identified as valuable, and discusses learning as a joint activity by students and academic staff. It also examines students' expectations concerning the nature of the relationship that should exist between a tutor and students, how tutors should and should not exercise their authority, and the *moral order* that ought to prevail within tutorials. Students talked of marked changes in the nature and quality of their experience of tutor-led discussion groups as they became acculturated into the ways of the 'academic tribe' in the course of their undergraduate career. It is argued that this distinct developmental progression in reported experience of tutorials has important implications for tutoring practice.

Background

Tutorials, small group discussions that focus on some aspect of an academic discipline and which are customarily led by a lecturer, form an important part of the teaching which undergraduate students receive in most British institutions of higher education. These tutorials usually take place every week during term time in each of a student's courses and may take a number of different forms. Some centre around the discussion of a particular topic, and students are asked to read around this topic in the week preceding the tutorial. In others, an individual student, or a subgroup of students within the tutorial, may make a short presentation which is followed by wider discussion. In science based subjects, and also in some social science subjects, discussion usually centres around the solution of problems and the wider points of theory that are raised by specific problems. Particularly in the first year of undergraduate study, tutorials may be used to pass on advice concerning essay writing, examinations and other academic tasks. They may also serve as a forum where individual students are able to raise difficulties that they are experiencing in understanding aspects of a course.

Advocates of university discussion groups have claimed that they provide an arena where 'active' learning can take place and where critical thinking and the development of communication skills can be encouraged. It has also been claimed that 'democratically' run discussion groups can encourage students to think more independently and gain confidence in their own abilities.

Abercrombie, for example, who was a leading exponent of the benefits of tutorial group work, claimed that:

> The group system aims to emancipate the student from the authority-dependency relationship and to help him develop intellectual independence and maturity through interaction with peers, by glimpsing not only the context in which a more experienced scholar sees his problem, but the various contexts in which several equals see the problem. (Abercrombie, 1974)

To further the aims of developing clear perceptions, objective judgement, critical thinking and autonomy in learning, Abercrombie argued that the tutor's main task was "to establish a climate in which all participants can listen and speak" (Nias, 1993, p.117). The tutor should also be socially reassuring and encourage spontaneous expression by the students (Abercrombie, 1960, p.70). This view of student-centred discussion groups, with the tutor setting up a climate in which understanding could be clarified and deepened, was consonant with wider developments in educational thinking at that time. The years which saw the advocacy of student discussion groups with this kind of 'permissive' atmosphere, also saw a 'child-centred' view of education come into prominence, and a belief in the power of 'discovery learning'.

The conception of the role of the tutor established by Abercrombie and others has, by and large, informed all subsequent writing on small group teaching. It also had a very influential effect on shaping the nature of much of the research that has been conducted on small group teaching, and led to a 'deficit model' view of tutor actions (e.g., Crick and Ralph, 1980; Luker, 1989). Guided by the assumption that small group teaching should be characterised by a 'hands-off' style of tutor facilitation and high levels of student participation, researchers have tended to see situations where tutors spend a lot of time talking, or where they play too 'active' a role — such as in paraphrasing or controlling a student's language — as evidence of deficiencies and the need for reform.

In the study that is reported here, no prescriptive stance has been taken on the nature of the relationships that should obtain within tutorials or the actions that a tutor ought, and ought not, to be pursuing. The intention, rather, was to gain a clear sense of the *students' perceptions* of what were appropriate, or inappropriate, teaching actions for a tutor to pursue.

Methods

The interviews with students concerning their experience of tutorials formed part of a wider study of tutorials, which was conducted within the Faculty of Social Sciences in the University of Edinburgh. This study of university tutorials involved:

- non-participant observation of fourteen tutorial groups drawn from different social science departments and different years of study,
- analysis of audio-recordings of the discussion,
- interviews with a sample of students (52) who took part in the observed tutorials, and

interviews with ten tutors concerning their aims for, beliefs and feelings about tutorials.

The sample of 52 students was drawn from eleven of the fourteen tutorial groups which had been observed, and included individuals from each of the four years of undergraduate study. The style of the interviews was *focused* and *interactive*. A full account of the research stance adopted in this study, the content and style of the interviews, the process of analysis, and the approach taken towards questions of validation, can be found in Anderson (1995).

Two important cautionary observations need to be made concerning the context and content of the tutorials observed. Within the faculty, considerable emphasis is placed on students acting in a co-operative, collaborative fashion within tutorials. Other institutions might be marked by a somewhat different ethos and promote a more competitive form of interaction in small groups. It is recognised that variations in practices and values in differing institutional contexts will lead to differing sets of perceptions of small group teaching.

The nature of the content discussed within tutorial groups may also have a considerable effect on students' experience of this form of teaching and learning. In the majority of social science subjects there is much 'unsettled territory' where debate is vigorously engaged between the advocates of different perspectives. Early in their academic career, undergraduates are typically introduced to the debates that shape their discipline, and helped to appreciate that there may be a number of competing 'expert' positions on the same topic, all of which possess both strengths and weaknesses. To some extent at least students can engage, within discussion groups, in the argument between stance and counter stance. The content of most social science subjects thus seems to be particularly well suited to discussion by undergraduate students. By contrast, in disciplines where the content taught to undergraduates is more 'settled', less marked by continuing, active debate, discussion may be different in nature. Given the potential importance of these disciplinary differences, caution will have to be exercised in considering the potential generalisability of our findings to contrasting disciplinary backgrounds.

In the space of a chapter it is not possible to present a fine-grained analysis of the wide-ranging accounts which the students provided of their experience of tutorial groups. That has been provided elsewhere (Anderson, 1995). Here, the strategy for reporting and examining the students' comments on their experiences is to concentrate on a few principal matters. Accordingly, an overview is initially presented of the features which were identified as important for active discussion and listening by most of the students. Then, differences between students in their *preferences for how debate is structured* are reviewed, and their implications for tutoring practice are considered.

Much of the previous work on small group teaching has had a fairly narrow focus, concentrating on aspects of the process of discussion and group dynamics, with little attention being given to the tutor's role as subject expert and teacher. In an attempt to redress the balance, the next section of the chapter — *talk on teaching* — presents and discusses accounts of teaching actions that students valued. A key finding of this study was that a distinct developmental progression can be discerned in students' reported experience of small group teaching.

This developmental progression is detailed in the section, *change in the experience of tutorials over time*, and is followed by a consideration of the *moral order* that students believed ought to prevail within tutorial groups.

Features that Promote Active Participation and Listening

Table 1, below, lists what students saw as the key features in promoting active participation and listening within a tutorial, including *tutor actions* and *group dynamics, student characteristics and actions*, and the *content* of the discussion. While many of the features mentioned by students are unsurprising, and fit closely with what has previously been reported both in research findings and staff development handbooks (e.g. Brown and Atkins, 1988, Ch. 4), this study moves away from a narrow focus on the *processes* of discussion to consider, in addition, the purposes and content of tutorial discussion.

TABLE 12.1

Features promoting active participation and listening

- informal group atmosphere
- tutor's skill in facilitating debate in an authentic, engaged manner
- not too large a group

- students themselves investing effort in discussion and
  creating a good group atmosphere
- students' own self-esteem and confidence

- the nature of the subject matter being discussed
- personal interest in the specific subject matter being discussed
- personal knowledge of the topic and of the discipline as a whole

- appropriate preparation by the students
- clear focus for preparation provided by the tutor
- not too much pressure from other coursework

The first set of features to be discussed relate to the context of the tutorial discussion. As in previous studies, students identified the existence of an *informal group atmosphere* as a key determinant of the quantity of participation and the quality of discussion and listening. They not only appreciated the more comfortable, relaxed social atmosphere that prevailed in groups with an informal character, but also had a strong belief that such groups functioned more effectively, reducing anxiety and so increasing the willingness to participate. Informality was also viewed as creating a secure climate within which it was easier to raise difficulties and to explore problems in understanding. For example, one third-year Accountancy student commented that:

I find that tutorials are at their best when there is a very, very informal nature about the class... Because if you can feel as if you can open up, right, ask questions without either fears of being stupid.

There was a general expectation that tutors would *energetically apply the skills appropriate for facilitating debate*. One of the facilitating skills that students particularly commented on was the tutor's expertise in ensuring that all members of the group were involved in the discussion, at least to some extent. Students also expected that tutors would act to moderate students' contributions to prevent the 'floor' being monopolised by a few 'dominant' members of the group. In addition to facilitating debate, tutors were very much expected to *tutor*, in the older sense of the term meaning to teach. Students appreciated tutors who engaged in one-to-one teaching interactions with individuals to enable them, and the group as a whole, to gain new knowledge and perspectives and to refine or to construct new understandings of particular topics. The specific teaching actions felt to be helpful will be discussed in a subsequent section.

The *manner* in which tutors applied the skills of facilitating debate was seen as contributing markedly to the success or failure of a tutorial. Several students contrasted tutors regarded as unsatisfactory, who were merely going through the motions of their job, with those who displayed real interest, enthusiasm and engagement with their students. It was generally expected that tutors would perform their role in an *authentic, engaged* manner.

The quality of the tutorial experience was seen to depend on the size of the group, which also affected willingness to interact. There was a strong consensus that tutorials ran much better when there was *not too large a group*. Group functioning, participation, listening and intellectual benefits were all seen to be advanced by a smaller group size.

Although students' comments revealed that they saw the tutor's actions as the key determinant of the success or failure of a tutorial, they also recognised their own responsibilities, in terms of the students *themselves investing effort in discussion and creating a good group atmosphere*.

A large number of informants explained active participation or lack of engagement, by themselves or others, partly in terms of individual characteristics such as *self-esteem* and *confidence*. A lack of confidence was not, however, considered immutable. As we shall see later on, students in the senior, final two years of their degree course recognised that their confidence in taking part within tutorials had increased over time.

The remaining set of features listed in Table 1 relate mainly to the content of discussion. Although this aspect was clearly seen as very important in facilitating both engagement in the discussion and reflective listening, it has attracted rather little attention in previous studies. Quite a number of students drew attention to *the nature of the subject matter being discussed*, recognising that some subject areas were much more amenable to active debate than others. Some informants drew contrasts between disciplines, while others observed that even within a particular discipline some subjects were more likely to spark lively discussion than others. *Personal interest*, or lack of interest, in a particular topic within the overall content of a course was generally described as a very important influence on how students prepared, took part and listened within individual tutorials. It was also felt that the manner in which lecturers and tutors dealt with a subject could either increase or diminish their interest. Several students recounted instances of tutors arousing their enthusiasm for topics they had previously had no curiosity about. Their comments on how tutors had awakened their interest in a topic resonate with the account presented in Chapter 10 of how certain students gained a "vicarious experience of relevance" from some lectures.

Personal knowledge of the specific topic being discussed, together with their general background of *knowledge of the discipline* which increased over the course of their undergraduate career also allowed individuals to contribute more to the discussion. But such knowledge could, of course, only be achieved by investing time and effort in studying. The students described the importance of *appropriate preparation*, in terms of reading relevant literature or becoming familiar with solving a particular class of problems. They recognised that achieving a good, and highly interactive, discussion was dependent on students coming along to a tutorial with the requisite knowledge. Strong disapproval was expressed of peers who came along to tutorials unprepared and therefore unable to make an appropriate contribution.

Preparing effectively for tutorials was also regarded by some students as a matter which depended not only on their own investment of time and effort, but also on the actions of the tutors. Preparation was seen as easier to achieve when tutors provided *a clear focus for preparation* through well focused reading and a clearly defined topic for the next tutorial. However, the amount of preparation that could be done was constrained by competing *pressure from other coursework*, such as essays, that had to be completed. As this other work, unlike tutorial work, was usually formally assessed, it tended to take precedence. This finding fits into a range of other examples, provided in Chapter 13, where assessment has been found to have profound influences on the quality of studying.

Contrasting Ways of Structuring Debate

The preceding section has outlined the key features that students agreed encouraged active participation and listening. However, there were distinct differences in perspective among the informants on how debate should be structured. Tutors can vary considerably in the way they conduct tutorials, some preferring a style which keeps discussion clearly and fairly tightly focused on a topic, or set of topics, while others prefer to have a rather more wide-ranging discussion. When the students were questioned on whether they preferred a more free-ranging or a more focused discussion, the differences of opinion revealed were wide and fairly evenly distributed. Responses to this question could be categorised for 51 of the 52 interviews. Sixteen students preferred more focused discussions, while eighteen would rather have more wide-ranging discussions, leaving nine adopting a 'middle-of-the road' position. Seven students did not indicate an overall preference, saying that a desirable and appropriate style of structuring talk would vary according to the subject area, or even the individual topic, being discussed. One mature student firmly believed that in the first two years of the undergraduate degree discussion should be clearly focused, becoming more wide-ranging only in the third and fourth years.

The following two quotations provide some sense of how participants' preferences concerning the structuring of discussion were described. The comments come from two third year women students from the same Economic and Social History tutorial group.

> I want it to be always very focused. I want it. I don't like them to be just [unfocused]. They are a waste of time if you just sit there and everyone just talks about what they feel like talking about.

> I don't like when tutors focus all the time because I think that's wrong, ... it is to me very important to understand the relationship between two things which maybe initially you don't think of relating but as you go to discussion you think, "Oh, maybe they are"; and I think that's very important ...

These differences in stylistic preferences suggest a need to rethink the prescriptions that Abercrombie, and other pioneers of the use of small group teaching, provided for the structuring of discussion. Such writers had placed great stress on the tutor facilitating a free-ranging discussion (Nias, 1993). A wide-ranging discussion of that type may well be of very considerable value to some students, yet create a sense of frustration among other students who want a clearer and tighter structure. It thus seems unwise to make any firm, unqualified prescription of wide-ranging, open discussion as the ideal way to assist students' intellectual and personal development. Rather, good tutoring practice should include the ability to vary the structure of discussion to take account of the stage of the course, the differing stylistic preferences of students, and the content and specific aims of the tutorial.

Specific pedagogic skills shown by tutors

Besides facilitating debate, whether in a free-ranging or a tightly-focused fashion, tutors were expected to teach. A considerable number of students commented approvingly on specific questioning strategies, or teaching tactics, which tutors had employed. Two main themes covered teaching actions which were perceived to be of considerable value. One was an appreciation of the shaping and direction of understanding provided by the tutor's actions, while the other reflected the motivating effects of this supportive shaping of understanding by the tutor. For example, the following quotation indicates a welcome from the student not only for the intellectual direction provided by the tutor's 'lead questions', but also for the way the tutor supported her efforts to contribute to the discussion – in her own words "backing her up".

> Normally the tutor will back you up, follow up and say, "Yes, but do you not …?" You know, he can sort of ask little questions, little lead questions (such as): "Would you not think it's more this —", and you think, "Oh, yeah, well", and go on like this.

> *Interviewer*: Is that useful?

> Yeah, that's useful. [laughs] Puts you on the right track.

Another second-year student drew attention to the benefits that came from tutors being able to imagine how students might be interpreting a topic and also engaging them in an interactive process of 'clarifying' their understanding of a particular topic. The following two extracts from his interview illustrate how he described both of these benefits.

> Having an encouraging tutor helps, rather than someone who is obviously very clever, but so clever that they can't see your problem, because they understand it. It's nice having someone that can see why you've got a problem...

> Often you sort of say something and it's a bit unclear. So, it's nice for them to sort of help *them* sort out what you mean, and help yourself sort out what *you* mean.

The latter comment contains an interesting observation on the way in which the 'diagnosis' by a tutor of a student's difficulties, and the construction by a student of a new personal understanding of a topic, may be intimately connected. The following short quotation from another part of the same interview demonstrates even more clearly his appreciation for tutors whose talk *constructs a space within which students can think*.

> It's nice when it's .. , it is built upon and twisted around and things. It gives you room for thought.

A third year Accountancy student gave an account of actions which clearly revealed the tutor's *scaffolding* (Wood, Bruner and Ross, 1976) of the student's problem-solving. It is interesting to note how this student distinguishes between the direct transmission of information, which is seen as not being useful, and the beneficial effects of the tutor guiding and structuring the student's own exploration of a problem. The tutor's scaffolding activities are seen not only as compatible with, but indeed as a strong aid in, *thinking for yourself*. The statement seems to provide a valuable insight into how learners may view their own agency in 'thinking' and conceive of the practice of thinking.

> Yeah, he won't tell you the answer, he makes you think for yourself, but he sort of prompts you along the lines. I mean he won't come out and say what the answer is, but if you don't get it somebody else might be thinking along the same lines.

> *Interviewer*: So you are quite happy with that?

> That is a good way. I mean there's no point of being spoon fed all the time, and if somebody tells you the answers even you'll see. That's not doing you any good. You're not thinking for yourself. And in the way he does that it, sort of, it does make you think. It structures your — your thoughts.

In a somewhat similar manner, another third year student described how certain tutors are skilled at 'correcting' students' statements, at *drawing in* students' understandings towards expert positions in the discipline. His words also express an appreciation of the fact that this process of "bring[ing] it round" is accomplished in a *sensitive manner which is not at all face-threatening*.

You normally find tutors that can sort of like, they don't say you're wrong, but they can sort of work, work it round so that you realise that you were wrong. Yeah, I mean, so you agree with [them] eventually... You know, they never say, "Oh, you're wrong", put it that way, sort of laugh at you or whatever. It's the way they do it, sort of, getting you to bring it round.

The very interactive shaping of students' understanding of a topic described in the preceding extracts was indeed a common occurrence in the groups led by the ten skilled tutors observed in the current study. Examination of the transcripts of tutorial talk reveals that these shaping, and scaffolding, actions were also achieved in a socially sensitive manner.

While some students stressed the value of tutors insisting on the very clear and precise formulation of statements, including the exact use of technical terms, others commented favourably on tutors who widened out and enriched discussion, introducing new aspects to debate and encouraging a more differentiated view of topics which had surfaced in discussion.

Tutors were also expected to act as mentors to studying, and tutorials are generally seen as providing an opportunity to provide advice on essay writing and other academic tasks. In this study, students stressed the importance of tutors making explicit to them their expectations of how they ought to be engaging with their studies, and also making clear the criteria used in their discipline to judge the quality of course work.

On the evidence of the interviews with students (and of the transcripts of talk in tutorials), tutoring involved an interplay between *taking out* an expert's view of a subject to students, in terms that novices are likely to understand, and *drawing in* students' more common-sense understandings towards expert positions within the discipline.

Change in the Experience of Tutorials over Time

Comments from students make clear the need for tutors to adjust their teaching and facilitation actions to the level of knowledge and academic stage of the students in a particular tutorial. Students reported marked changes over time in their experience of tutorial groups, as they became accustomed to the social and intellectual practices of small-group discussion in particular, and of university life in general. These changes involved two stages. At first, students are faced with the transition from school to university and making an adjustment to the social and intellectual demands of small group teaching. Then, there follows a slow process of long-term change in the quality of the students' experience of tutorials and of their assimilation of the practice of academic discussion.

Many students described how, at the beginning of their undergraduate career, they were faced not only with the uncertainties involved in meeting new people in their tutorials, but also with the need to make sense of a new *type* of social context and to act appropriately within it. Their comments drew attention to a number of specific adaptations that students may need to make in this initial period at university. They may have to get used to tutors taking a less directive, authoritative, stance than their teachers did at school, and realise that they themselves are expected to show more initiative and take more responsibility for their own learning. Students coming from schools with an individualistic, competitive ethos may also have to adjust to the norms of co-operation which prevail in university discussion groups.

Some students described tutorials in the early part of their degree course, not only as a novel social situation in which they were somewhat uncertain about how to act, but also as a source of considerable anxiety. This concern about the social and intellectual challenges was, however, counter-balanced by a recognition of the potential benefits of establishing new social contacts and friendships. The value of having a sense of personal contact with a member of academic staff within the tutorial was also recognised. This personal contact with tutor and peers was particularly appreciated by those students who, at the beginning of their academic career, saw university life as rather impersonal or 'faceless' in character.

Entering fully into the practice of academic discussion involved more than making an initial set of adjustments to the values, and ways of acting, within a novel social situation. It required a much longer, slower process of acquiring knowledge in a discipline and of fuller acculturation to the ways of academic work and the forms of academic discourse. Student participants in the later years of study identified a progression in their experience of tutorials in terms of:

- *greater demands;*
- *an increase in confidence;*
- *changes in the quality of social atmosphere and interaction;*
- *the benefits of experience, including the understanding of expectations;* and
- *subject knowledge and the quality of discussion.*

In brief, students talked of how, over the years, there had been an increase in the intellectual demands that were placed on them, and in the requirement to demonstrate rather more independence and personal initiative in their studying. This increase in intellectual demands over time was accompanied by a decrease in the perception of tutorials as *socially* demanding. Students noted a distinct increase in confidence in participation within tutorials as they progressed through their undergraduate career. They also identified a marked change in the quality of discussion between first year, and third or fourth year, tutorials, which was linked to an increase in the knowledge of specific disciplines and knowledge of how to engage appropriately with academic tasks. For example, a fourth year Psychology student gave a very clear account of the effects of differing levels of subject knowledge on the nature of tutorial discussion. He talked in the following terms of the problems which can arise when first year students are not given sufficiently focused advice on tutorial preparation, and have insufficient background knowledge of the subject on which to draw.

I dislike tutorials where we haven't been – I mean, it happened a lot in first year — we weren't told "Right, prepare something" – and I suppose in any given area, particularly in first year, if you're not given any kind of instructions to go and do some reading beforehand, then people have much the same view, ... the sort of layman's view of the subject, and there's no discussion at all.

He then went on to draw a contrast between first and later years of study:

It's more difficult in the lower years – I mean a lot of the stuff in the higher years, the discussion arises from people's own views anyway that they've acquired through the years. There's a lot more general knowledge obviously in the subjects that you've picked up.

This increase in knowledge, the building up of experience in taking part in tutorials, and the clearer understanding of the expectations governing debate, changed the value some students attributed to tutorials. These students described how the benefits of tutorials had become more salient as they had gained experience in the ways of academic life.

This reported increase in the quality of discussion in the later years of study was accompanied by a qualitative change in the social atmosphere of tutorials, and in interaction with peers. Informants also pointed up a certain change in the nature of the relationship between tutor and students. As the intellectual distance between students and staff diminished, the social relationship between them was perceived as becoming somewhat more equal.

Implications for practice of changes over time

In a real sense, the first and fourth year tutorials observed within the current research project were somewhat different phenomena. Therefore, there can be no single, ideal way to proceed, appropriate for both first year and fourth year groups. Indeed, the tutors in the present study reported marked differences in the way that they conducted first year, as opposed to final year, tutorials commenting that they needed "to do less" when they were leading fourth year groups. In contrast to the fourth year groups which could be run in a more "hands-off" fashion, some tutors described how with a first year group they needed to give direction to the discussion and to take a very active part in shaping the content of the talk. Analysis of the talk that was recorded within tutorials also reveals striking differences between first and fourth year tutorials. The adjustments in style that tutors described themselves making could indeed be observed happening in practice. Rather than seeking to define a single, invariant set of features associated with success in tutoring, it would appear more sensible to view good tutoring as requiring flexibility of response – an ability to tailor actions sensitively to the characteristics and needs of individual groups of students.

The Moral Order of Tutorials

So far, we have reported the conditions and actions seen to affect active participation, listening, and learning in tutorials. However, the student's talk on many of these features, such as maintaining a safe, informal group atmosphere, can be seen to have a dual aspect. Students saw direct benefits from an informal climate which encouraged engaged participation and attentive listening. But their comments also suggested that an atmosphere where individuals could feel that they were safe from threat *ought* to be provided — there was a moral obligation for such a group climate to be created. Students were thus saying what *did work well*; but they were also concerned with *how things should work*.

In the interviews, students and staff described in similar ways the *moral order* that they believed ought to prevail within tutorials. Tutors and students alike were expected to avoid treating individuals in a threatening way; and to contribute to a friendly, co-operative ethos. Students viewed their peers as having to make an effort for the common good by preparing for tutorials; and expressed strong disapproval of 'dominant' students who took an unfairly large share of the 'floor'. A democratic form of discourse was expected within tutorials, with students agreeing on what constituted legitimate and unacceptable displays of tutor authority.

Unacceptable displays of tutor authority included the overt display of power, or actions which highlighted the differences in social status between students and the tutor. Such actions clashed with the expectations that status differences would be minimised – expectations established by the informal atmosphere and 'democratic' forms of address which usually prevailed in tutorials. It was also regarded as unacceptable for tutors to use their authority to moralise about the shortcomings of students or to scrutinise students' statements in a way which made them feel ill at ease. Actions of this type were viewed as conflicting with the students' rights to certain forms of respect.

There was also a feeling that undue pressure should not be placed on individuals to participate – what one informant described as "being put on the spot". At the same time, the participants viewed the tutor as having a responsibility to involve everyone in the discussion — a duty to be active in soliciting contributions, particularly from the quieter members. In effect then, the tutor was asked to walk a fine line between observing a student's positive freedom — to be drawn into the discussion — and negative freedom, to be safe from undue pressure to participate.

There were, as we have already seen, acceptable displays of tutor power. There was a clear expectation that tutors would make appropriate use of their authority as subject experts to *tutor* — that is to engage in teaching interactions. In particular, it was anticipated that tutors, in their role as subject experts and teachers, would act to re-direct a discussion which had gone "a bit astray". Informants talked of the need for the tutor "to correct", or "to clarify", student contributions to the discussion where necessary. At the same time, it was assumed that any 'corrective' teaching actions would be carried out in a socially sensitive manner which would not threaten the student's public face of competence. Thus, the disparity in knowledge between tutors and students was not viewed as inherently problematic. Key matters for the participants were the *manner* in which this knowledge was put to use, and that it should be displayed solely for the *purpose* of enhancing students' understanding of a subject (see Anderson, in press, b).

Constraining or Enabling Understanding?

Different interpretative stances can be taken towards the practice of shaping and directing students' understanding towards appropriate positions within a discipline. One could, for example, follow the line of argument pursued by Valerie Walkerdine in her radical deconstruction of the discursive practices of child-centred primary education (Walkerdine, 1988). Walkerdine notes how the practices of child-centred primary education render the power relations between teacher and children invisible, and how "the *illusion* of choice, of security and safety, are key features of what is taken to be correct classroom life." (p. 211, italics added). She claims that:

> The child is so positioned within the practice as to have not 'seen' power, and believes itself the originator of its actions, its choice. It is a powerful illusion, an illusion of choice and control over one's destiny taken to be centrally implicated in producing the possibility of 'rational argument'
> (p. 210).

A similar position could be advanced with respect to the discursive practices that prevail in university small group teaching. It could be claimed that the informal social atmosphere and the democratic forms of address which characterise such groups provide a false front of agency that disguises the real power of social discourses to shape the minds and actions of individuals. Such a radical critique, however, would appear to put into too sharp a contrast the nature of the relationship between university teachers and students, and of the purposes of teaching. Other publications stemming from this present study (Anderson, 1995; Anderson, in press, a, b) have depicted the complexity of the relationships of power and of consent that exist between tutors and students, and have argued that this complexity is not captured by an interpretative position which focuses solely on constraint and the imposition of power.

Students' experience of learning and teaching within tutorial groups is more appropriately represented by recognising the way in which their understanding of a discipline is both simultaneously *enabled* and *constrained* by their tutors. Tutors in their dual roles as 'gatekeepers' for a discipline and guides to the less expert have to lead students towards ways of construing particular topics or problem situations in an appropriate fashion. This might be perceived as a *constraining* function. Yet, tutors are, at the same time, *enabling* novices to gain new framing perspectives on topics and so develop their abilities. They are assisting students to gain the knowledge and ways of acting needed for them to participate more fully in academic life, for example, by taking part in the debates which enliven and sustain many disciplines.

Shotter (1993a, 1993b, 1993c) has recently argued that gaining 'agency' within a particular culture is dependent on learning the appropriate performance of the practices of that culture. He suggests that:

> ... our own task in learning how to act personally, as an autonomous member of our culture, is in learning how *to do* all the things in our culture, like measuring, inferring, remembering, perceiving, listening, speaking, etc., we must learn how to do them as the others around us do them – we must learn how *to be* as they are. Indeed, if we do not, then they will sanction us and not accord us the right to act freely. (Shotter, 1993a, p.70)

The *enabling* and *constraining* functions of teaching can thus be seen to be necessarily interlinked rather than opposed.

Shotter also draws attention in this quotation to the intersubjective and interpersonal nature of learning and teaching – a theme which has featured strongly in the examination of students' reported experience of tutorials within this chapter, and which appears again in the final chapter of the book, *Understanding Teaching and Teaching for Understanding*. There, implications for day-to-day teaching practice are explored in ways which are consonant with the findings of this study of tutorials, and of other research which looks at learning from a similar sociocultural perspective.

Chapter Thirteen

The Context of Learning in Academic Departments

PAUL RAMSDEN

Introduction

Previous chapters have already indicated ways in which the educational context is bound up with students' approaches to learning. The framework of institution, department and courses, affects students' perceptions of reading, listening to lectures, writing essays and solving problems. Students do not, for example, simply read an article. They read it for a purpose connected with a course of study and in response to the requirements of those who teach the course. It is a central theme of this book that a student's perception of the learning context is an integral part of his or her experience of learning. The special concern of this chapter is with how students' *perceptions* of teaching, assessment, and course content and structure within the natural setting of academic departments may influence how students learn. The focus is thus not on the framework of courses and assessment itself, but rather on what the students *construct* out of this framework. How do students experience the effects of the context of learning at university? The following three extracts from research interviews serve to illustrate the pervasive influences of teaching and assessment on students' attitudes towards studying and on their approaches to learning.

I certainly don't like it if you get tutorials where the guy just comes along and sits down and makes you stand up and do the work on the blackboard. Usually he picks on people that can't do it, which I think is terrible because you get stuck up at the blackboard and made to look a fool, and it switches you right off… I think I'm not going to do that if this guy's going to do that to me, because I don't learn anything; nobody else learns anything because it takes you so long to do the question; and it makes you very unhappy with that particular course, so I lose interest in the course. (Student taking Physics)

I hate to say it, but what you've got to do is have a list of the "facts"; you write down ten important points and memorise those, then you'll do all right in the test …. If you can give a bit of factual information—so and so did that, and concluded that—for two sides of writing, then you'll get a good mark. (Psychology)

Recently we were doing Fourier analysis, and the lecturer mentioned in passing that it was something which they used when they transmit moon pictures back to earth … that makes a lot of difference, you can see it being used … Another example he quoted was about why when you bang a drum you get lots of different sounds rather than when you say, play a violin you just get the one note … he said, if you look at this you can see why—and he was right, you could see why; it did make sense. (Physics)

198

At first these perceived effects may seem commonplace enough, and yet it is very important that we do not exclude them on that account. We saw in Chapter 1 how general principles of learning derived from controlled experiments— experiments which, by definition, exclude the sort of "background noise" illustrated in the examples given above —have often failed to help students and teachers to deal with the everyday problems they face. In contrast, this chapter will argue that recent research looking at students' own descriptions of their experiences of the learning context has crucial implications for improving the quality of teaching and learning in higher education.

Effects of the Learning Context in Historical Perspective

There is nothing new about the idea that learning in educational institutions is related to the environment in which it takes place. One of the dominant features of undergraduate education in universities is that it is usually confined within one subject area and often, especially in Britain, to one discipline. At least since Aristotle, men have commented on the differing demands made on the learner by different bodies of knowledge, and a complicated set of culturally defined norms and rituals has come to be associated with the process of learning and teaching in different disciplines. We shall look in more detail at differences in students' approaches, and in the contexts of learning provided in different subject areas, later in this chapter.

But the context of learning is not defined solely by the type of subject being taught and researched in an academic department. Teaching and assessment procedures vary between different academic units, although the effects of these differences on student learning are poorly understood. The realisation that university teaching contexts might have unintended consequences for learning— that they might discourage students from coming to grips with the fundamentals of their subject and encourage them to use tricks and stratagems to pass examinations—is certainly not a recent one. At least by the mid-nineteenth century the relationship between teaching and assessment methods and the quality of student learning was recognised. Cardinal Newman, for example, advocated "self-education" as "preferable to a system of (university) teaching which, professing so much, really does so little for the mind". Students who did without contact with what Newman (1852) held to be inappropriate teaching methods were more likely

> to have more thought, more mind, more philosophy, more true enlargement, than those earnest but ill-used persons who are forced to load their minds with a score of subjects against an examination, who have too much on their hands to indulge themselves in thinking or investigation, who devour premiss and conclusion together with indiscriminate greediness, who hold whole sciences on faith, and commit demonstrations to memory.

A little later in the century, Pattison (1876) rounded on the Oxford assessment system in equally uncompromising terms.

> [The examination papers] could not be answered by a mere knowledge of the subject ... Quite another way must be taken in the preparation of the

candidate. For two years the pupil is thus forced along a false road of study in which neither science nor philosophy encounter him. Memory is really almost the only faculty called into play.

The examples could be multiplied. Thorsten Veblen (1918) wrote a bitter and sardonic critique of the American academic establishment in The Higher Learning in America, arguing that impersonal staff-student relationships and rigid assessment systems had destroyed scholarship and understanding in the process of increasing the apparent efficiency of universities. Whitehead (1932) described an "evil path" in education along which easy texts enabled answers to be learnt by heart and reproduced in the examination, and worthless teaching churned out the same knowledge time and time again, unleavened by a spark of imagination.

More recent research work, such as the studies by Snyder, Becker, and Miller and Parlett described in Chapter 1, unfortunately seems to confirm the potentially debilitating effect of the academic environment on student learning. Students may often respond to the "hidden curriculum" whose intentions run counter to those of the teaching staff. Instead of developing independence in judgement, problem-solving and analytic skills, they are obliged to devote their attentions to the narrow requirements of assessment, including the memorisation of ideas and facts.

Yet the picture is not uniformly gloomy. There is evidence to suggest that there is another side to the academic context. Good teaching and student control over pace and subject matter may facilitate understanding. Links between effective learning, satisfaction with studying, choice over topics of study, and positive evaluations of teaching have been discovered in a number of investigations (see, for example, Centra, 1976; Brennan and Percy, 1977; Fearn-Wannan, 1980) — although it is still unclear whether we can regard these as causal relationships. The arguments of a number of educational theorists, however, do indicate a functional link between the context and students' intentions to understand. Whitehead (1932) and Rogers (1969; see also Chapter 1), among others, argue that an appropriate mixture of imaginative teaching, choice and structure in the curriculum, and fitting assessment methods, can help students towards personal meaning in learning.

A Framework for Understanding the Effects of the Learning Context

Let us now turn to the more recent findings concerning the effects of the context of learning on students' approaches to studying. It is worth re-emphasising that our concern here is with the ways in which students' *perceptions* of assessment, teaching, and courses may influence their attitudes and approaches to studying, and not with apparently objective characteristics of the context such as continuous assessment methods, the use of learning packages and aids, and the division of teaching methods into lectures, tutorials and other techniques.

We can best try to understand the effects of the context of learning by examining the relationship between students' approaches and their perceptions of learning tasks at a number of separate but interconnected levels. Students' approaches depend on their interest in the task and their previous experience of the area to which it relates; these influences are themselves associated with their perceptions of how the work will be assessed and with the degree of choice over content and method of learning available to the student. The perceived demands and support of teachers, and the content of the subject, also influence the students' approaches. At the most general level, the atmosphere of the academic department affects students' study orientations and ultimately their approaches to specific academic tasks.

The Student's Interest and Experience

The student's intention to understand or to reproduce material is very clearly related to his or her interest in carrying out the learning task, either for its own sake or in response to external requirements. Chapter 3 reported the work of Fransson (1977), for example, who showed how a lack of interest in the material studied, or a failure to perceive relevance in it, was associated with a surface approach, while interest was related to a deep approach. Here a British student identifies a similar contrast in the natural setting of her courses; having described a deep approach to essay-writing in one part of her Literature course, she compares this with her approach in a subject in which she is less interested.

> It's a bit confusing, [this subject]. When it comes to writing essays, because I'm not very interested in it, I tend to rush through the books I'm reading for the essays, so I don't really understand it when I've finished reading. And because there's such a lot of information I think you can either oversimplify or get into too much detail. I think I tend to oversimplify.

Attempts to understand the material being studied may also be frustrated by inadequate background knowledge of the relevant field. This is especially the case where the learning task demands that the student has grasped a fundamental concept. To the extent that this kind of task is more commonly set in scientific subjects, background knowledge is more frequently related to the approach a student takes to a task in science than in arts and social science disciplines. Conversely, students tend to mention the effects of interest (or lack of interest) more often in arts subjects than in science ones (Ramsden, 1979). Here a physics student describes how his previous knowledge of a type of problem helps him to take a deep approach, while his weakness in a basic mathematical concept makes his approach to another part of the same question anxious, passive and superficial.

> It was like one of the questions from a previous course, which I could relate. It was a Schrödinger equation for a particle in a box, which we'd solved generally before in chemistry, so I could relate it, I could see a picture of what I wanted. I knew basically what sort of answer I should get, and from that I could work my way through it... The other bit was different; I couldn't do it. Basically I gave up with it, because it was a function, which I've never really understood... I looked at it and I thought "That looks complicated"... It was very short, it looked like it would need a lot of rearranging.

It is not surprising to find that interest and background knowledge are related to each other in the natural setting of student learning.

I think if I already know something about the subject about which I want to write, it helps. Because then I can write something out without having to refer to the books first, sketch something out in much more detail rather than just skeletal ... This question was about popular recreations, and were attitudes to them changing. Well, having been grounded in Folklore— a consuming passion for the last eight years—I knew quite a lot about that already. So I just kind of wrote out three or four hundred words which gave a basis for it ... mentally I was much more aware of accomplishing something useful.

Effects of Assessment

Even if they accept that interest and background knowledge influence a student's approaches to learning (and thereby the level of understanding reached), lecturers in higher education may attribute these effects to differences in students rather than to the effects of their teaching. Lecturers often argue that it is not their business to motivate students; poor academic progress, as we saw in Chapter 1, is typically explained in terms of low ability or of a lack of interest or motivation on the student's part — but these are seen as faults in the student (see also Entwistle and Percy, 1974). The first thing to say about these arguments is that they are at variance with the results of the recent research. It is clear that students take different approaches to different tasks: more precisely, the *same* student takes different approaches in different circumstances. The second point is that evidence now exists to show that students' interests, attitudes to studying, and approaches to academic tasks are strongly related to their experiences of teaching and assessment. In other words, lack of interest or motivation can be seen as arising from a context, rather than being fixed attributes which a student brings to a situation—although past experiences (at school, for example) clearly affect current perceptions.

The study from which these findings were mainly derived was carried out at Lancaster University from 1978 to 1981. The research involved both an intensive interview study and a large scale questionnaire survey. Let us look first at the interviews. A group of 57 students in six university departments (physics, engineering, independent studies, psychology, English literature and history) formed the sample. The students were interviewed about their methods of tackling recent academic tasks set as part of their normal studies. The range of tasks included problem-solving, reading, essay-writing and report-writing. This focus on specific tasks avoided too ready generalisations and provided more detailed information about the strategies used. Students were also asked about what they thought "typical" ways of studying were in their own and in a contrasting subject area, and were encouraged to relate their approach to the particular task they had described to their experiences of the learning context. They were asked, finally, to say something about the "good" and "bad" aspects of the main department in which they worked. Transcripts of the interviews were analysed in a similar way to that described in other chapters; categories of descriptions for approaches and contexts and the relationships between them were identified, and later checked by other judges. Only a small part of the data is presented in this chapter; the extracts given are no more than illustrations of the categories and functional relationships revealed in the complete analysis (see Ramsden 1981; Entwistle and Ramsden, 1983).

We have seen throughout this book, in experiments and in everyday studying, that perceived assessment requirements are strong influences on the approach to learning a student adopts when tackling an academic task. For example, questions designed to encourage a surface approach to reading succeed in their intention (see Chapter 3), assessment of an overwhelming amount of curricular material pushes students into surface approaches and an incomplete understanding of the subject matter (Chapter 2); and the approach to problem-solving is related to the student's perception of marking (Chapter 8). Expectations about examinations influenced the forms of understanding students sought during revision (Chapter 9), while the anxiety experienced adversely affected the approach to learning in a learning experiment (Chapter 3). Where students *felt* that the assessment situation was threatening (whether the threat was objectively present in the experimental design or not), they were more likely to adopt a mechanical, rote learning approach to the learning tasks. Similar findings emerged from the Lancaster investigation in relation to a whole series of academic tasks and also to students' general attitudes towards studying. Students often explained surface approaches or negative attitudes in terms of their experiences of excessive workloads or inappropriate forms of assessment.

> I look at [the topic] and I think to myself, "Well, I can do that if I can be bothered to hunt through hundreds of textbooks and do the work"—and you sort of relate that to the value of the work in the course, which is virtually zero because it's so much exam assessment ... I just don't bother with it until the exams come around ... my revision is basically for the exams, purely and simply aimed at passing the exams without bothering too much about studying the subject. (Physics)

> In very few of the lectures was I picking [the principles] up as we did them. It took me all my time to get the notes down. So, and this in a way, the pace is so fast that you get the notes down and that's it. You don't really follow what's going on. You can't do two things at once. You can't sit back and listen to what's being said. You spend an hour taking notes down ... I put this down to this very keen desire to cover that much work. (Engineering)

> It seems that if you follow a sort of straight line you seem to do better than if you, you want to pass any ideas of your own. You see, this essay I got back—which was a B—I wouldn't have thought I'd have got a B for that because I'd really got it all, out of a book, sort of thing, I'd just put it down in my own words ... when I've put my own stuff down, it's all wrong. So, much more than I thought, they are, I suppose, looking for a reproduction of what's written elsewhere. (Psychology)

Taken together, these findings show that overloading of syllabuses and inappropriate assessment questions or techniques may force students into taking reproductive approaches. The factual overburdening of syllabuses may explain why students display such a poor level of understanding in assessments which demand something more than the reproduction of well-rehearsed answers. What still remains unclear, however, is how to encourage deep approaches by attention to assessment methods. The attempts reported in Chapter 3 showed how difficult it is to induce deep approaches, at least by simple techniques of asking different types of questions.

Of course not every student responds to assessment pressures in the same way. But the range of responses itself demonstrates the powerful effects of the perceived assessment context. Some students will actively exploit the opportunities offered by assessment methods which allow good grades to be obtained without understanding or without personal commitment to what is being studied, while others will accept the system at face value (Miller and Parlett, 1974; Ramsden, 1979). Whether the response takes this "strategic" form or not, the effect on the quality of learning is still present. It is not only the lecturer's stereotypical "weak" student who resorts to surface approaches. The quotation from the interview of a psychology student at the beginning of this chapter, for example, comes from a student who obtained a first class honours degree. Some assessment procedures invite, even demand, rote learning. Another academically successful student from the same course illustrates how the form of continuous assessment he experienced discouraged him from using an approach aimed at developing personal meaning in learning.

> With that essay I was just discussing, that reference group one, I wrote for, with a, the image of a marker in mind, the personality, the person, I find that's important, to know who's going to be marking your paper ... you see an essay is an expression of thought, really, but that's not what they're after, they're after a search through the library, I think, and a cribbing of other people's ideas.

These findings suggest that the experience of learning is made less satisfactory by assessment methods perceived to be inappropriate ones. High achievement in conventional terms may mask this dissatisfaction and also hide the fact that students have not understood the material they have learnt as completely as they might appear to have done.

Effects of Teaching and Course Design

Inappropriate assessment procedures encourage surface approaches, yet varying the assessment questions may not be enough to evoke fully deep approaches. How then may the context of learning be used to help rather than hinder understanding? It is probably true that assessments which are seen to require deep approaches by the students can discourage the use of reproducing strategies (see Elton and Laurillard, 1979). But a positive influence on deep approaches seems more likely to come from two other aspects of the context of learning: good teaching and greater freedom to choose both content and ways of learning.

Although staff development efforts in higher education have typically been directed towards improving teaching techniques (lecturing, giving tutorials, using audio-visual aids), the research evidence (see, for example, Dubin and

Taveggia, 1969) suggests little direct effect of teaching on learning. What has been missing is the important *indirect* effects. How teaching and assessment affect students' individual ways of studying and, through those, what they ultimately learn has not been given enough attention. The ethos of higher education, especially in Britain, emphasises individuality and autonomy. It is very much a part of this ethos that what students do with their own time is their own responsibility: success is seen as the reward for the students' own efforts and ability. Lecturers rarely know, and perhaps feel it is not their concern, what students do in their private study time or even in lectures. Yet teaching does have important effects, in ways which we are only just beginning to recognise.

Teachers in higher education have considerable responsibility for the organisation of their own courses. Most of us have memories of an inspiring teacher at school or at university who developed in us an interest in a field of study; such recollections are frequently complemented by thoughts of a lecturer who so bored and confused us that we were put off studying a subject. Such anecdotal impressions can now be complemented by the results of rigorous analysis of interview data concerning students' experiences of learning. This research makes it clear that lecturers in higher education do have far-reaching influences on learning. The relationships identified in these studies are not direct ones between teaching methods and student achievement, but indirect ones connecting students' perceptions of what lecturers do with their approaches and orientations to studying.

These important links have already been suggested in Chapter 10. Hodgson's work shows how some lecturers' approaches to teaching, as perceived by their students, can shift students' perceptions of the subject matter from extrinsic to intrinsic. Students may begin to experience the relevance of the content of the lecture for their own understanding if the lecturer can communicate interest and enthusiasm as well as information.

The study carried out at Lancaster enlarges on these findings. Students' perceptions of the quality of teaching they experienced were found to be functionally related to their attitudes towards studying and their approaches to learning. These effects can be seen to work in a number of different ways and, as will be made clear later, have several implications for improving teaching. The influence of the teaching context is illustrated here by a series of extracts from the Lancaster interview data. The lecturer's interest in students, and helpfulness with study difficulties, are the first important qualities influencing students' attitudes and approaches.

> I find that the courses I do most work on are the courses where I get on with the tutors best ... a tutor can put you off the subject ... some of them don't like students, so they're not interested in what students have to say unless it's relevant to their approach. (English)

> Luckily I'm doing some courses with some good tutors on them—you know, they make the books come alive because they can talk about them and they can direct you to a chapter or a passage, and that's important I think ... you could spend an hour rooting through and then just come to what you think is the essence of it all ... if you get a guideline from the tutor, and I'm quite lucky in having someone who can point the way, then it's a godsend. (History)

I think a lot of the [lecturers] are just not particularly interested in you. I mean there are some who are ... but some tutors, you know, just don't really bother if you learn or not; they just prefer to sit there and wait for you to think of what you don't know—I mean, if you knew what you didn't know you'd probably learn it anyway. I've got a tutor like that at the moment ... it's no good at all. (Physics)

As long as I'm doing a subject that I'm interested in, it doesn't really matter to me how they do it ... I prefer departments to be organized and efficient, and also, more important, that's caring about their students. That to me is more important than the procedure of the coursework, you know ... (English)

Commitment to the subject area—and hence, enthusiasm on the lecturer's part—may also encourage a positive attitude in students.

If they [tutors] have enthusiasm, then they really fire their own students with the subject, and the students really pick it up ... I'm really good at and enjoy [one subject] but that's only because a particular tutor I've had has been so enthusiastic that he's given me an enthusiasm for it and now I really love the subject. But at the beginning of [another course] the tutor was ... a little bit passive for my liking ... something imaginative was lacking, there was something lacking in the seminar group ... (English)

The ability to teach at the student's own level, and lecturing ability in general, are also relevant.

We had a problem sheet to hand in for yesterday, which was really hard because the guy that's lecturing to us is really terrible ... He's given equations and in the lecture notes there's nothing about them, because he just goes on and on and mumbles to himself — nobody likes him at all ... Then you're asked questions on it, you don't know where to start. (Physics)

My criticisms will be very closely aligned to, I think, the lack of empathy that some of the staff have about the ability levels of the students relative to their subject. Not relative to being able to be good enough to be at university, if you like, but relative to the fact that the concrete knowledge that they have is virtually nil in some of the areas that we're talked at, at a very high level. So you can't attach anything that you've been told to something that you already know, which of course is a very important point in learning ... I think it's the overall problem of the experts coming in and having to give courses in a few weeks on their particular interest, and they have such a wealth of knowledge in that area that they start at too high a level. That's what I think happens. They've gone so far into their own area that they've forgotten that we know nothing, essentially, compared with them. (Psychology)

The concepts are really difficult anyway. It usually takes, I think most people like, I certainly like to sit down on my own and go at my own speed. Now the lecturers certainly assume that we know it and they just keep going. People can say, "slow down" but people of course are reluctant to say they don't understand it. So he tends to keep going, and once you get behind it, you know, you can't really get back on terms. (Engineering)

Providing useful feedback on a student's work also influences learning, in these students' experiences. Lack of information about performance makes further learning more difficult.

You give an essay in — I gave in two at the beginning of the second term and I didn't get those back till this term ... you know, it's a bit difficult when you're writing the next essay, because you want to know where you've gone wrong and the points that have been all right ... By the time you've got it back after waiting a whole term you've forgotten what it's all about and it doesn't really mean much then. (English)

Lecturers also have a great deal of say over the amount of structure, and over the balance between teacher and student direction, in their programmes of study. There is a vital connecting link here between what teachers in higher education do and how students approach learning, as the second part of the Lancaster study will show. We have already seen how interest in the learning task for its own sake tends to evoke a deep approach. Logically, interest in the task is likely to be greater if the student has a favourable attitude towards the subject-matter to which it refers and if the students perceive themselves to have choice over the content and method of study. The ideas of choice of subject-matter and freedom in pursuit of knowledge are threads running through the history of higher education (see, for example, Dewey, 1916; Whitehead, 1932) although the application of freedom in learning to undergraduate education, except in its latest stages, is unusual.

These extracts from interviews with students undertaking independent studies programmes suggest a connection between learning contexts which offer choice in both learning topics and study methods, and favourable attitudes towards studying.

If you're doing independent studies you're obviously interested in what you're doing. Therefore you're in a much more relaxed mental state for approaching work: I am, anyway, and other people I know in the course are.

In reading a particular bit of the book that I thought was relevant I was relating it to the overall arguments within the book ... and also relating it to the overall directions of the independent studies project I was doing. But that particular approach was a product of my desire to sort of do a bit of creative, original work. Had I been writing a straight essay . . I probably would have just, sort of, taken out the main points and strung them together in a typical essay form. So I think there's a definite difference between reading a book with the objective of simply summarising the argument and reading a book with the objective of using those arguments for your own ends.

On the other hand, freedom in learning brings with it greater responsibilities. Lack of structure and clarity in the goals of study may defeat the intentions behind greater choice, at any rate for some students.

You have to take responsibility for the work yourself. You're not, you don't have the advantage of a pre-existing framework of suggested reading and suggested approaches in independent studies, so you have to be damn sure that you are interested enough and confident enough to see it through those times when you come to sort of minor crises, when you realise suddenly that it's all on your shoulders and you've got no-one else to go to ... It requires commitment and personal motivation.

There is by no means a simple equation linking less structured learning contexts with more effective learning in higher education; there are likely to be particular difficulties for anxious students, as we should expect from studies of the school learning context (see, for example, Wade, 1979). But the wide variation in styles of learning preferred by students, together with the logical and empirical links between interest, approach and outcome, suggest that variety in the mix of learning tasks and some choice over subject matter is desirable.

The Context of Learning in Different Subject Areas

Even the casual observer of higher education cannot fail to notice that important differences in the context of learning are associated with different subject areas. It is clear from previous research that contrasting academic departments are inhabited by different kinds of lecturers and students. By far the most pervasive contrasts are between arts and science subjects, and between professional and non-professional courses. It appears that lecturers in science departments are more likely to prefer formal, structured approaches to teaching and assessment; in arts and social sciences, teachers endorse more flexible and individualistic methods. Not surprisingly, the students in the different types of department have complementary attitudes, while the students' perceptions of departments in the contrasting subject areas also correspond closely to the differences in lecturers' approaches to assessment and teaching (Gaff, Crombag and Chang, 1976). But are the students' approaches to studying related in some systematic way to the different attitudes and demands current in different subject areas? Whether these different demands are essentially culturally determined or in some way inherent in the subject-matter of different disciplines is not important here: our concern is with the different perceptions of students in different subject areas.

Students interviewed in the Lancaster study (Ramsden, 1981) were asked to identify possible differences in approaches to learning and learning contexts in different subject areas. Not unexpectedly, the dominant contrast made by these students was between science and arts disciplines. Their comments reveal consistent, subjectively-defined differences between the types of learning expected in the different subject areas. Science and arts students agree on what the differences are. Learning tasks in science are typically described as hierarchical, logical, heterogeneous, and rule- and procedure-governed.

They [science students] go about it more logically ... you get this impression of the history student being airy-fairy and temperamental ... scientists deal in fact, while history students and artists deal in theory—we discuss theories and opinion. (History)

It's much more—exact isn't the right word—but in Physics you're right or wrong ... here you can't think it, it happens. (Physics)

But for the sciences, they have to be more calculating, they have to know logical concepts, they have to know logical things and how an answer will come out of a calculation or a few statements which have been written down. (English)

A lot of our stuff is just sort of, you know, teaching us a logical flow of arguments, observing certain results, concepts and how they're related, whereas ... (Physics)

Arts and social science tasks are seen to require interpretation, comparison, generalisation, and to be more self-governed and easier.

[Arts students] seem to have a much easier time of it. They read a lot more, of course, they've got to read all these books, but ... it seems much easier ... it seems to be just going on and on about what you yourself think ... In these other subjects you can just sort of go on and on: "I think this, I think that". (Physics)

The work demands, in a way, a completely different intelligence. For us it's more interpretation, more analysis, more penetration into the material ... They have to look ahead to an answer: we have to look in ... For English you have to see implicit meaning. (English)

History, you can waffle, you can cover up your mistakes ... no-one can either prove you right or wrong ... you've got to take all things into account. (History)

A lot of [History] is just hypothesis, why did this guy do this? and so on—it's a lot less certain. (Physics)

The most revealing thing about these interview extracts is that they mirror with surprising accuracy the theoretical constructs we met in Chapter 8 — operation and comprehension learning (Pask, 1976). The manipulation of concepts and objects within the subject-matter domain, the emphasis on procedure-building, rules, methods, and details are characteristic of operation learning and the science approaches described by the students. The description and interpretation of the relations between topics in a more general way is the defining characteristic of comprehension learning and is related by these students to typical approaches in arts and social science disciplines.

These differences are in turn related by the students to the different demands of the context of learning in arts and science departments (see Ramsden, 1981). Formal teaching methods, limited choice of topics, clear goals for learning, and vocational relevance, are associated with operation learning and science departments; informal teaching methods, unclear goals, and so on, are related to arts and social science departments and comprehension learning styles.

It should be emphasised that we are not maintaining that these differences are immutable differences between subject areas. They are students' perceptions of differing demands and reveal a good deal about how the typical learning tasks set in arts and science departments are interpreted by students. For full understanding of any complex subject matter, according to Pask, *both* styles of learning need to be employed. Of course, the differences described above are students' stereotypes and further research is needed to discover more about how specific academic tasks are seen to be presented in different disciplines. But it may well be that differing disciplinary emphases inhibit, at least for some students, the development of a versatile style of learning in which both comprehension and operation learning are appropriately used. At its logical extreme, this perceived bias in tasks typically set could lead to science students being unable to describe the meaning of what they know, and arts students being incapable of deductive reasoning.

The next step in examining the relationship between subject area contexts and approaches to studying is to ask whether deep and surface approaches to learning reveal themselves differently in different contexts. Marton's original distinction between deep and surface approaches was derived from analysis of interview protocols in which students described how they read an academic article (see Chapter 3). Laurillard has found an equivalent distinction in approaches to problem-solving, and parallels with these categories can also be seen in relation to listening to lectures and writing essays. In normal studying the surface approach implies not only a concentration on words or details to the detriment of understanding, but also an over-awareness of assessment demands which leads to an intention to reproduce knowledge. In the Lancaster interviews both deep and surface approaches in normal studying were found clearly, but were expressed in different ways in different subject areas, because of the requirements of typical learning tasks in the different contexts.

From the interviews it emerged that even a deep approach to learning tasks in science departments often demands an initial concentration on details which is empirically hard to separate from a surface approach. This means that the descriptive category needs to be redefined somewhat in order to include this prior stage. In the humanities, in contrast, a deep approach is revealed more commonly by the student stressing, right from the start, an intention to re-interpret the material in a personal way. In describing surface approaches, science students are more likely to stress an over-concentration on techniques and procedural details, while the arts and social science students tend to report a more generalised, vague approach—oversimplifying in reading or essay-writing, or memorising unrelated generalities in their preparation for assessments. These differences in emphasis in deep and surface approaches show how the meaning of this fundamental dichotomy has itself to be understood in terms of the context in which approaches to learning are realised.

Study Orientations and Perceptions of Academic Departments

Although it is clear that the same student may use both deep and surface approaches on different occasions, there was evidence from the interviews that students also showed general orientations to studying. These general tendencies to adopt particular approaches to learning have been found to be associated with characteristic forms of motivation and attitudes to studying (Ramsden and Entwistle, 1981; Entwistle and Ramsden, 1983). Two of these orientations,

TABLE 13.1

Categories in the Approaches to Studying Inventory

Meaning orientation

Deep approach	Looks for meaning; interacts actively; links with real life.
Use of evidence	Examines evidence critically and uses it cautiously.
Relating ideas	Actively relates new information to previous knowledge.
Intrinsic motivation	Interested in learning for its own sake.

Reproducing orientation

Surface approach	Relies on rote learning; conscious of exam demands.
Syllabus-boundness	Prefers to restrict learning to defined syllabus and specified tasks.
Fear of failure	Anxious about assessment demands; lacking in self-confidence.
Improvidence	Not prepared to look for relationships between ideas; fact-bound.

Strategic orientation

Strategic approach	Tries to find out about assessment demands; seeks to impress staff.
Extrinsic motivation	Qualifications as main source of motivation for learning.
Achievement motivation	Competitive and self-confident; motivated by hope for success.

Non-academic orientation

Disorganised study methods	Organises time ineffectively; not prompt in submitting work.
Negative attitudes	Little involvement in work; cynical and disenchanted about courses
Globetrotting	Too ready to generalise and jump to conclusions without evidence.

Styles of learning

Comprehension learning	Holist strategies used to build up an overall picture, intuitively.
Operation learning	Serialist strategies used to concentrate on detail and logical analysis.

---

meaning orientation and reproducing orientation, are conceptually similar to the deep and surface approaches, even though they describe relatively consistent tendencies in individual students.

The study orientations, however, are not assumed to be unchanging characteristics of students: just as students change their conceptions of learning over time, so they may shift their study orientation during a programme of higher education. This raises an intriguing question at the most general level of the relationship between the context of learning and students' approaches to learning: is the context of learning in different academic departments systematically related to their students' study orientations? The qualitative analyses of students' approaches in relation to their perceptions of teaching and assessment suggested that it should be possible to identify such a relationship. We might expect, for example, that departments perceived to have excessive assessment and syllabus demands would create reproducing orientations (corresponding to surface approaches) in their students.

A complicating factor is the discipline taught in a department. Study orientations vary from one subject area to another, just as the meaning of the deep and surface categories differs in different subject areas. However, the teaching and assessment policies do differ between departments teaching the same discipline and so relationships with study orientations may still be observed.

Such relationships could only emerge from an analysis of a substantial number of departments and a much larger number of students. Partly as a result of earlier work at Lancaster, and partly from the research of Biggs (1978) and the ideas of the Gothenburg researchers, an inventory of approaches to studying was developed suitable for administration to large samples of students (Entwistle et al., 1979b; Entwistle and Ramsden, 1983). The inventory asks students about their general approaches to academic work in the normal context of their main courses. By item and conceptual analyses the questions can be grouped into a number of scales, and these are shown in Table 13.1. For our purposes here, the important scales are those making up the meaning and reproducing orientations.

The Lancaster research also made use of a questionnaire of course perceptions, with eight sub-scales (Table 13.2), which are the main categories used by students when they describe the context of learning in an academic department. The fact that students can respond to general questions of this sort, both in the questionnaire and in interviews, suggests that students are able to perceive general differences in teaching and assessment in departments in addition to specific differences between different lecturers within departments.

The scales of the course perceptions questionnaire divide into two main groupings. One of these — formal teaching methods, clear goals and standards, and vocational relevance — differentiates mainly between science and professional studies departments, and the rest. The second main grouping describes students' evaluations of the quality of the learning context in their department. Good teaching, freedom in learning, and staff openness to students are the defining characteristics of this evaluative dimension, with social climate and light workload playing lesser parts.

The inventory and course perceptions questionnaire are quantitative research instruments, but this does not mean that their use violates the assumptions of the perspective adopted in this book. They remain close to students' experiences of learning, as the constructs and items were derived from interviews rather than from a pre-existing body of theory. Our research strategy deliberately used an alternation of qualitative and quantitative methods. Of course the questionnaire results cannot tell us anything directly about the influence of the learning context on students' orientations: but empirical associations can be interpreted as functional relationships when seen in conjunction with the students' interview comments on what had influenced their approaches to studying.

TABLE 13.2

Categories in the course perceptions questionnaire

Evaluation of the department

Good teaching	How much help is given with study problems; how competent and well-prepared staff are perceived to be.
Freedom in learning	How much discretion students have over the choice of content and methods of studying it.
Openness to students	How friendly staff are; how prepared they are to adapt to student needs.
Workload	How heavy the pressure to fulfil the requirements of the syllabus and assessment is perceived to be.
Social climate	Quality of academic and social relationships between students.

Subject area differences

Formal teaching methods	Importance placed on lectures and classes relative to individual study.
Clear goals and standards	How clearly the standards of assessment and ends of studying are perceived to be defined.
Vocational relevance	Perceived relevance of the courses in the department to the students' future careers.

Let us now look at these results, which have been described in detail elsewhere (Ramsden, 1981; Ramsden and Entwistle, 1981; Entwistle and Ramsden, 1983). The inventory of approaches to studying and the course perceptions questionnaire were administered to 2208 students in 66 departments. The disciplines included were physics, engineering, economics, psychology, English and history. The two main study orientations (meaning and reproducing) could be identified in all the subject areas. These orientations were found to be related to students' perceptions of the context of learning in a way which was quite consistent with the interview results. Departments which were perceived to provide good teaching (and particularly help with studying) combined with freedom in learning (choice of study method and content) were more likely to have students reporting an orientation towards meaning. Reproducing orientations were more commonly found in the departments perceived to combine a heavy workload with a lack of choice over content and method. These relationships were not affected by the differences in students' entry qualifications in different departments, nor by subject area.

These results fit neatly into the findings of the experimental and interview studies which had related students' perceptions of learning contexts to their approaches to studying. Moreover, students' attitudes to studying in the departments were associated with their perceptions of the quality of the learning context. Just as students in the Lancaster interview study described relationships between effective teaching and positive attitudes to studying a topic, so the students in the survey who were working in departments that were evaluated highly were more likely to report involvement with their work. In contrast the students in the negatively evaluated departments were more likely to report cynical and disenchanted attitudes to higher education.

A second similarity in the findings from contrasting research methods is concerned with the strength of the association between students' orientations and their perceptions of the context of learning. Marton and Säljö (1976b) had showed that surface approaches to learning were relatively easy to induce in students, while deep approaches were difficult to encourage (Chapter 3). Just as we would expect from these findings, the survey analyses revealed that it was much easier to predict which departments would score highly on reproducing orientation than on meaning orientation. In other words, some departments seem to induce surface approaches in a direct way. Other departments appear to provide contexts within which students find it easier to develop an interest in the subject matter and to use approaches aimed at understanding. The influence is, however, less easy to predict, depending presumably more on the individual students. As we saw in Chapter 5, students differ greatly in what they want to achieve from their studying. If they want to make the academic content personally meaningful, these departments will facilitate such development.

Conclusions and Implications

In this chapter we have seen how important relationships between students' experiences of the learning context and their approaches to studying have been revealed by recent research. The findings have some significant implications for teaching in higher education. The detailed implications for practice are discussed in Chapter 15 in relation to the other work reported in this book; some aspects of more general relevance are considered here.

In these results are the beginnings of a model of student learning in context. The relationships are complex but should be to both teachers and students. At the most general level, we have seen how students' perceptions of assessment, choice over subject matter and methods of studying it, workload, and quality of teaching in academic departments are related to the main study orientations. The departmental context also plays a part, it would appear, in influencing students' attitudes towards studying—whether they feel that academic work is worthwhile. Previous research had shown clear links between inappropriate and excessive assessment demands and surface approaches. This effect is confirmed by the data from the departments in the survey. However it now also seems clear that some departments provide a context which facilitates the development of a meaning orientation. Further study of the detailed differences between these different types of department should reveal how changes in teaching and assessment procedures might discourage a reproducing orientation and allow deep approaches to emerge.

Students' experiences of teaching and assessment influence their approaches to learning, both directly and indirectly. Thus interest and commitment to a subject area can be fostered by certain experiences of teaching and by perceived freedom in learning, and intrinsic interest is fundamentally related to a deep approach. Inadequate previous knowledge of a topic, itself partly a consequence of inadequacies in teaching, and the anxiety created by insensitive teaching or an over-demanding syllabus, push students towards a surface approach, as a coping ploy.

This model is complicated by the need to consider subject area differences. It appears that there are systematic differences in students' perceptions of appropriate ways of learning in arts and science disciplines, and we have also seen how the meaning of the deep-surface distinction shifts in relation to students' reports of their experiences in different subject areas. The disturbing implication of this part of the research is that at least some students may be handicapped in the development and use of both operation and comprehension learning styles by the dominant culture of the discipline in which they are being trained. This is not a question of whether one style of learning is objectively more appropriate to some inherent characteristics of the subject-matter, but rather of how the tasks set in an undergraduate arts or science course may be biased towards the use of one or the other style. As both styles are characteristic of versatile and competent learners, it is important that learning tasks are seen by students in all subject areas to require the development of both styles. Scientific thinking does indeed involve much attention to details, logical analysis, and strict adherence to procedures, but it also requires students to interpret data in relation to their own experience. Similarly, personal interpretation and description certainly are important in the humanities; but so is the ability to analyse evidence rigorously. If the perceived context of learning overemphasises one style, then students may develop inadequate approaches to learning.

These arguments suggest that greater variety in learning tasks, and in forms of teaching, would probably be beneficial to students in all subject areas. One way of providing this variety is by increasing students' choice of method and content. As we have already seen, freedom in learning is valued by students in all subject areas and is related to deep approaches to learning. Freedom of choice, however, should be complemented by a provision of clear frameworks within which that choice is exercised. Unstructured freedom is unlikely to develop versatile learning skills.

The single most important message to emerge from these research findings is that intense effort must be made in course planning, and in the setting of assessment questions, to avoid presenting a learning context which is perceived by students to require, or reward, surface approaches. It is not enough to assume that course materials or assessment methods will encourage students to think deeply about the subject matter, however carefully they have been designed: it is necessary to consider the students' perspective on what is required. It is useless, for example, simply to tell students that verbatim reproduction of information in an examination is wrong, to expect this warning to discourage surface approaches, and to blame the students when it does not. If students feel that there is insufficient time to study the examined topics properly (perhaps because of the demands of other courses), or if they have experienced inadequate teaching, or if they are given high marks for reproducing lecture notes, or if their previous knowledge within the area is insufficiently developed, then they will feel constrained to use surface approaches. Only by studying the internal relationships between how students perceive course demands and how they approach studying can the complexity, and apparent paradoxes, in student learning be understood.

This indirect connection between how lecturers teach and how their students learn has a crucial implication for how we should try to develop teachers' competence in higher education. It suggests that staff development programmes should aim not only to improve teaching skills, but also to increase lecturers' awareness of their students' experiences of learning. In the last analysis, these two facets of staff development are inseparable. Good teachers have to be aware of their students' needs and purposes, sensitive to their students' perceptions of the course—and adapt their teaching and assessment methods accordingly. Our attention should be on the quality of learning, not simply on how to improve the techniques of teaching.

This emphasis on the effects of teaching is, however, not intended to remove responsibility entirely from the student. On the contrary, the decision to use different approaches to studying is largely in the student's own hands. Different students want different things from higher education and respond differently to similarly perceived conditions. Some cope better than others with adverse assessment and teaching conditions, and only part of the variation in the quality of learning is explained by contextual influences. But it would be a mistake to try to force a dichotomy between student characteristics and context in understanding how students learn. If we accept that individual students' learning skills will affect which approaches they use, and whether they achieve their goals, we should also recognise that learning skills are themselves influenced by previous experiences of learning contexts.

Acknowledgements

The research reported here was supported by a grant from the Social Science Research Council (now the Economic and Social Research Council).

Chapter Fourteen

The World of the Learner

ALISTAIR MORGAN AND LIZ BEATY

Introduction

The focus of this chapter is on what we are calling *the world of the learner*, which enables us to develop a more holistic description of students' experiences of learning. In Chapter 5 we described orientation to learning as a personal context of learning which illuminates the nature of the relationship between a student and the course of study within a particular educational institution. Orientation to learning is a 'learner's experience' seen as a relationship between a course and a learner—it is neither an aspect of the course itself or trait or personality characteristic of the learner, but rather the experience as a dynamic between the learner and a course in its institutional context. Having described the importance of this personal context for learning in Chapter 5, it is now possible to develop a fuller picture of the learner's world.

In this chapter we want to extend the discussion of the experience of learning in two ways. First, we shall bring together some of the concepts introduced in Part I and see how they appear within a holistic description of the learner's experience. A series of case studies is used to consider learners' realities through the 'conceptual lens' introduced earlier. Then, we shall discuss students' change and development as shown in a longitudinal study of student learning from foundation year through to graduation. Both parts of the chapter are taken from the research study with Open University [1] (OU) students, already mentioned in Chapter 5.

Case-studies of Student Learning

In Chapter 3, the concepts of *approaches to learning* and *conceptions of learning* were introduced and their importance for the quality of the learning outcomes has been stressed in Chapter 2. These concepts can be linked together with the concept of *orientation to learning* to provide a framework for understanding what a student gains from a course, in other words the outcomes of learning. These interrelated concepts can be seen as increasing levels of generality for describing students' experiences of learning; they describe different focuses of awareness in a learner's experience.

The two case studies that follow are extracted from a longitudinal study of 29 Open University students, and based on interviews carried out during their first year of study. They will be used to illustrate the links between these concepts which have been found in the main study, namely orientation to learning, conception of learning, and approaches to learning. The interviews focused on the experience of taking the Social Science Foundation Course and were carried out on three, occasions (i) before the course, about students' orientation to learning and conception of learning; (ii) during the course, about their approaches to studying one particular piece of teaching material and completing an essay assignment; and (iii) after the course, about what they had gained from the course (Morgan *et al.*, 1982).

The two case studies, which use pseudonyms to preserve confidentiality, have been selected to illustrate how students with different orientations go about studying in vastly different ways.

Case study 1: John Williams

John Williams is a Personnel Officer working in a London firm. He is in his early forties married with two children. He has professional qualifications, and has previously attempted a degree course on a correspondence basis but the course did not fit in with his other commitments and he completed only one year. He felt however, that to get a degree would be a 'good thing' and when he heard about the Open University he decided to try again.

> It seemed a good idea to take a degree—I'd heard of the O.U. before but I was never quite sure how it operated. I'd tried before to do a degree—an external London but it was the time keeping really—it involved evening lectures and I only did the first year. This seemed like a fairly good way to have another attempt.

His main orientation seemed to be an academic extrinsic one and he described how he hoped to do the work quickly.

> I don't really know how keen I'll get. I mean one would obviously try to do as little as possible; but obviously you're going to do a fair bit to get through it properly.—If I can get it concentrated down to as few hours as possible, commensurate with getting the degree and enjoying it, I will.

The emphasis in these statements is on efficiency and from the beginning John's concern with progress through the system was clear. There were also, however, hints of vocational intrinsic orientation where he talked about why he had chosen to study social sciences.

> I think it was possibly because the sociology ones are more related to the day to day environment things that I do—I don't think it will help me in relation to employment prospects because I think when you get to a certain age, you've either got a level of experience or you haven't. It may well help me because of a broader knowledge and applying or investigating routes in relation to personnel and industrial relations problems I hadn't thought of before, but I don't expect anything very startling, you know.

In our first interviews, besides orientation to learning, we also asked John what he thought learning consisted of. He replied as follows:

> I would say assimilation of common sense in relation to the course I was doing. Common sense which was related to sociology—as opposed to sort of parrot-fashion learning.
>
> *Interviewer*: What do you mean by common sense?

Well it seems to me there are various theories which I found when I looked at the Block [a part of the course] in relation to unemployment, crime, there are various yard sticks basic guidelines in relation to those problems and one needs to know how to apply them and what they are.

John's conception of learning appears to parallel Level 3, intermediate between reproduction and transformation, which is described in Chapter 3 as involving "the acquisition, for subsequent utilization, of facts, methods, etc.".

John's primarily academic extrinsic orientation and this procedural conception of learning links in fairly closely with his approach to learning. This was characterized by a wish to do things in the shortest possible time, using strategies of note taking that were geared to getting out the main points of the units for easy revision.

When he was interviewed again, John was half way through the course and had settled into a routine study pattern which reflected his concern with efficiency. He was enjoying the content of the course and could talk about the concepts he was learning. The overwhelming impression of his approach to learning was that it was a strategic one. He had learnt how the system operated and was working through the course in a way which was characterized by the minimum effort necessary to understand the main points. He described how he studied as follows:

I have a quick look and see how long I am going to take on it and then I just read straight through it and use the felt tip pen ... I ring various theories as I go through, I possibly go through it and I make a few notes on small cards on what the various theories are ... What I tend to put down is the main points in each block what the answers are in the main points of each block. To be quite fair about the way I am doing it, I suppose I am doing the minimal study to sort of achieve the end result and so from that point of view, my need is to have something which is more succinctly encapsulated and I use the cards in that fashion.

I've been a bit naughty on it because I've worked out that you don't need to do all the assignments and I am just doing the minimum. It really means that I have got to get reasonable mark for the ones I am doing because I'm not getting the average to bring me up.

John is clearly studying in what was described in the previous chapter as a strategic manner, and seems to be confident in what he is doing. In terms of *deep* and *surface* approaches to learning, he can be described taking a deep approach. He is attempting to identify the "main points" the Open University correspondence texts and summarize them more succinctly. However, he is doing this in a somewhat external, impersonal way or purely in a cognitive manner. This is not a deep approach in the "full sense" in that he seems to be taking short cuts to the main point without apparently considering all the evidence. This way of studying can be seen as a rational response to the distance learning system, since students study part-time at a distance and have to adapt to considerable demands of the course in terms of regular pacing of correspondence texts and assessment tasks. For John, his approach was successful in the sense that he was obtaining reasonable assessment grades, however, he was well aware the learning could be a more personal activity in other situations.

> I think on some of the essay questions you have to go deeper and beyond the definitions in the block (section of the course) and perhaps try and read a bit and become more analytical and critical but this involves time, which is a precious commodity. I tend to concentrate on the middle course of getting what's in the block.

At the end of the course, in our third interview, we again asked John what learning consisted of.

> Well it certainly doesn't mean parrot fashion, I think it's understanding it...

> *Interviewer:* What is involved in understanding something?

> Well I suppose by understanding something, it's the ability to be able to read a theory and be able to explain it to someone who hasn't read it before and doesn't understand it, to be able to relate it to someone who is unconnected with the subject.

In terms of conceptions of learning we can make a tentative interpretation that John has changed from seeing learning as making use of rules and procedures or "acquiring and using facts" to seeing it as understanding and relating ideas together, or "the abstraction of meaning" i.e. a change from Level 3 to Level 4 in terms of the framework presented in Chapter 3.

In our third interview, although John had enjoyed the course, he felt that it was really only the basis for further in-depth studying.

> I enjoyed it—it took up more time than I thought it would. I didn't have enough time to spend on it. I think you cover a lot of things reasonably superficially; you don't get into anything in any great depth and it's made me keener to get on to something at 2nd or 3rd level where you can study one subject and spend time on it.

This attitude appears to be a reflection of his predominantly academic extrinsic orientation — i.e. to continue on the educational ladder. However, his desire to study a subject "in depth" suggests a change towards an academic intrinsic orientation.

John's secondary orientation—vocational intrinsic—is also reflected in what he felt he gained from the course:

> If I hadn't done the course I think I would have missed a lot of what I've learnt in relation to my work—about the psychology of work—whereas I was inclined to take a decision fairly quickly on certain things, now I do have a certain experience having studied a bit of psychology and sociology and I do try and perhaps see how things are going to inter-relate and affect people—spend a bit more time on it and be a bit more thoughtful than I was before.

From this last quote, we can see that taking the course had affected John's approach to his work and that he was seeing the relevance of the course material to his everyday life. It would be interesting to follow this student through more years of studying to see if this personal meaning extended into his orientation and conception of learning in future years.

Integrating the concepts of orientation to learning, conceptions of learning and approach to learning provides a framework for understanding John's experience of learning. His primarily academic extrinsic orientation links to his strategic way of studying, and taking a deep-approach, although in a rather external and impersonal manner. His approach is consistent with a conception of learning based on using rules and procedures. The links between concepts exists both logically and, as this case-study shows, also empirically. By the end of the course, from his perceptions of gains from studying and how he sees studying developing in the future, we can detect some change in John's orientation. He seems to be moving towards vocational intrinsic orientation to learning with some academic intrinsic orientation. The following table summarizes these links and changes.

TABLE 14.1

John Williams: a case study

Orientation to learning (before the course)	Conception of learning (before the course)	Approach to learning (during the course)	Orientation to learning (end of the course)	Conception of learning (end of the course)
Primary - academic extrinsic, based on academic progress, looking for good grades with minimum effort Secondary - vocational intrinsic	Learning as "gaining rules and procedures" (Level 3)	Deep approach; strategic	Academic extrinsic, combined with clearly emerging vocational and academic intrinsic orientations	Learning as "understanding and relating ideas together (Level 4)

Case Study 2: Sally Brown

Sally Brown is a housewife in her mid-thirties with two children of primary school age. She had taken an 'O' Level in English at night classes some years earlier but apart from this, had no qualifications, and had not studied since leaving school. The impetus to apply to the Open University had come from her father who was half way through an OU degree and had passed on information to her.

Before the course started, Sally talked about her reasons for studying. She appeared *not* to have an intrinsic academic orientation, since she had no specific interest in the subject discipline.

It wasn't really particularly for any of the subjects, ... because I think that once you get started you can get really into doing it, hopefully.

She had vague concerns that in the future a qualification might be useful to get a job (vocational extrinsic orientation).

Apart from providing me with an interest now it might be useful, to me, sort of later on when the children get older.

There was also some indication of a personal *extrinsic* orientation.

I didn't get much academic qualification at school ... I'm testing myself to see what I can do ...I want in a way to prove to myself that I am capable of doing the work because I've never really done anything as an individual.

But the overwhelming impression Sally gave was of a strong personal *intrinsic* orientation.

I'm hoping that it will give me more confidence in myself and to actually be able to cope with different situations and life in general. I feel that I need something and hopefully this is going to broaden my outlook ... a sort of greater insight into the way other people live and the way other people think. I think one tends to be very biased. You live your own life. I'm hoping that I'll be able to see things from different points of view and lead to more tolerance really of different kinds of people and different kinds of groups ... and to play a more active role in society instead of always being the one who sits back and does nothing. I think if you could understand it more what causes some problems you could sort of perhaps react to it in a better way, and hopefully sort of perhaps help others to do the same but I don't know whether it will really make any difference.

The main reason for doing the course for Sally was to relieve the boredom of being at home all day. She also felt a lack of confidence in herself generally and hoped that the course would change her into a more accomplished and competent person. She had chosen the course, partly through a process of elimination, and partly in the hope that the content would be relevant to her own life.

I thought that, reading through the description of the course, it sounded quite interesting and would teach you more about life in general and the way that things arise. You hear about so many different things on the television but you don't seem to really understand what they are talking about. I thought this would be a very useful course to take.

At the beginning of the year Sally was very anxious about her own ability to cope with the course and although she wanted to become more competent in social situations, she was rather frightened by the prospect of tutorials and the compulsory residential Summer School. It was clear that the course was going to be a considerable challenge for her. She had no experience of post-compulsory education and appeared to have a somewhat unreflective, taken for granted conception of learning (Level 1).

Interviewer: When you say learning, what do you mean by it, what do you think of?

Um … (laughter) … Learning? Don't know really…

Interviewer: Can you describe what learning is?

Gaining new knowledge of different subjects, you know… um …

This response was quite unlike the rest of this interview where she was far more articulate. She appeared to take the question seriously and to say all she was able in response. So on the one hand, Sally had a predominantly personal intrinsic orientation which one might expect to be accompanied by an understanding of personally meaningful learning, but on the other hand she actually gave an unsophisticated response to our question about the nature of learning itself. When we interviewed Sally about her approach to studying half way through the course, she revealed a slightly confusing picture. Her way of describing her studying sometimes indicated a *surface approach.*

I have got the time, but I find it difficult to concentrate. I sit in here: and sometimes don't do anything really. I have got all the work there but it doesn't go in.…I think it is easy to do them [the multiple choice questions] as you go along, …I tended to skim rather than reading it all properly and I don't feel at all that I have taken all this block in. I just don't … I mean it shows how well I read it because I can't remember half of what it said. I read it very quickly and usually I read it maybe two or three times because I don't think you take it all in at first reading.

Similarly, her description of note taking indicated a surface-approach and can be linked to her "taken-for-granted" conception of learning.

Sometimes I underline bits—I underline things that I think are particularly important. I don't make notes very often—but because I am so bad at it, I've got this book and it's got all the bits and pieces in and various odd notes from different parts. And I decided that I wasn't doing very well at this so that is why I decided to keep it more in the Blocks themselves. I'm not very good at taking notes—they are all a bit of a muddle really.

Her problems with study techniques, note-taking for example, and dealing with the vast quantity of printed material supplied by the OU, can be seen as partly a consequence of her conception of learning and also her lack of prior experience of academic study.

In other parts of this interview, Sally seemed to be attempting to take a more active and reflective approach to study. She planned her essays, didn't like going on to new subject matter until she had completed her essay in order to avoid confusion, carefully extracted crucial points from the text, and so on. At one point in the interview she described an *outcome* of her learning which reflected her intrinsic orientations:

I think it's very interesting already when you watch the news and different things, the things they say seem more relevant now. They use the words that perhaps I wouldn't quite have understood before and having done the work, things tend to click ... whereas I used to think that inflation was inflation before, you relate it to different kinds now and the different policies that are put in. You see the differences between them better than ever I could before.

Contact with other students and the tutor at tutorials was very important for Sally and she found that just knowing that other people had the same sort of difficulties as she had, gave her the confidence to carry on. She also felt that passing the assignments had given her much needed encouragement.

I've done four essays now and I've passed them all, so I must be doing it adequately I suppose, but I don't feel awfully confident. But then, nobody else seems to either, so I don't feel too bad about it.

At the end of the foundation year Sally presented an altogether more coherent picture of her studying. She distinguished between learning and memorizing, as follows:

Interviewer: When you think of learning in general, what does learning mean to you?

Well it certainly isn't (laughs) learning everything that's in those books. I couldn't remember half... It's a hard thing to define really. I think it's understanding more than learning by heart—learning to be more critical of things — just really broadening your outlook on things. Sometimes you don't think that you've actually learnt it but all the time it keeps cropping up...you know, you're looking for more in life and you keep thinking of things like Maslow's hierarchy of needs and things like that.

After the course her conception of learning thus fitted well with her dominant personal intrinsic orientation to study. She was even using ideas from the course to explain her own attitude to learning or needs from the course. This reflexivity shows an active approach to learning. Sally felt much more confident in herself. She had passed the course and was feeling much more positive about her ability to study. When she talked about the gains from studying the course we can see how they are related to her personal intrinsic orientation—being changes in her own ability and confidence, new interests and broader knowledge.

I feel different somehow, I feel much more confident and I think I'll be much happier next year. I don't think I will worry quite as much.

She also said that the course had changed her approach to life.

Well, I think it teaches you to be more broad minded—you don't think that you are narrow minded but you realize that you are when you learn things. Well, it's difficult to think of examples, but like unemployment in the past, I was inclined to think that some people didn't want to work, they just couldn't be bothered and preferred to be on the dole. You tend to see the other side of the coin. I've learnt to be more critical, watching T.V.

programmes you learn to be more objective to look at both sides of an argument. I argue with people now, you know, I'm not afraid to come out with an alternative view.

Again, as in the previous case study, integrating the concepts of orientation to learning, conceptions of learning, and approach to learning enables us to build up a fuller picture of Sally Brown's world as a learner. There is a clear link, both logically and in terms of her own descriptions between her personal intrinsic orientation to learning and her perceptions of gains from the course— her descriptions of an increase in confidence and seeing the world differently. In commenting on the details of how she tackled particular learning tasks, she described an active and thoughtful approach—planning essays, working on one topic at once. However, many of the details of her studying, for example, note-taking, seem to be constrained by her initial conception of learning. By the end of the course she had clearly changed in her conception of learning, from seeing it as "new knowledge of different objects" to "understanding .... broadening your outlook". With this more sophisticated conception of learning, we would expect her to take a deep approach to learning more consistently. The following table summarizes Sally's experience of learning in her first year of O.U. study.

TABLE 14.2

Sally Brown: a case-study

Orientation to learning (before the course)	Conception of learning (before the course)	Approach to learning (during the course)	Orientation to learning (end of the course)	Conception of learning (end of the course)
Primary - personal intrinsic, seen in terms of self development and gain in confidence Secondary - personal extrinsic, as proof of capability	Learning as "gaining new knowledge" (Level 1)	Surface, although appeared to be attempting a more active approach	Personal intrinsic with perceptions of gains seen as changing her approach to life	Learning as "being critical and relating ideas to one's own experience" (Level 5)

Commentary

The case studies provide two examples of descriptions of the learner's world.

By relating together the concepts of orientation to learning, conceptions of learning, approaches to learning and outcomes of learning, we can develop a conceptual framework which is grounded in students' experiences of learning. The evidence is, of course, not limited to the two case studies; we are drawing on the whole sample to provide many other instances of connections between these concepts.

We have established that a *learning orientation* provides a useful construct for understanding a student's personal context for study. It encapsulates the complex nature of a student's aims, attitudes, purposes for studying. Moreover, educational orientation is not an invariable property ascribed to a student. It describes the relationship between the individual and both the course of study and the institution—it can change and develop over time. As we saw, John Williams developed, during the OU foundation course, towards a vocational intrinsic orientation with some indications of academic intrinsic orientation. Before the course, these orientations were hardly discernible.

Orientation to learning is an important construct as it contributes to our understanding of what students learn. Besides the qualitative differences in learning outcomes described by Dahlgren (Chapter 2), which focus on the variations in how students understand specific concepts, students' overall perceptions of what they had gained from studying can be understood in relation to their educational orientations. There are both logical and empirical relationships between students' perceptions and their learning orientations, which have been illustrated in the case studies of John Williams and Sally Brown. We can see how their personal context of study has a powerful influence over how they approached learning and what they gained from the course.

Students' Change and Development

How do students come to be more competent as learners? What is the nature of the changes which occur as students progress from a foundation course through to graduation? How can we, as teachers in post-compulsory education, facilitate these changes in our students? We have already seen in Chapter 4 by Lennart Svensson a discussion of 'skill in learning' as a relational concept drawing together a particular approach to learning with a related conception of learning and an associated quality of learning outcome. This part of the chapter looks at skill in learning in terms of the change and development over a six year period from foundation course through to graduation. The research presented here builds upon existing work by Perry (1970), carried out with conventional age undergraduates, and extends it for adult students studying part-time at a distance in the Open University.

In Chapter 1 we saw that Perry (1970) had explored, in a four-year longitudinal study, how students come to understand and cope with the demands of academic study. Going beyond the individuality of students' accounts of the college experience, there seemed to be a common sequence of challenges encountered by students and also a pattern to the changes they went through. Perry outlined a nine stage scheme in which there are three very clearly distinct phases. Students initially held absolutist conceptions of knowledge, where the teacher was perceived as the authority figure, 'knowing the answers'. This can be seen to correspond to the first three conceptions of learning identified by Säljö (1979) which are essentially reproductive. Then, in Perry's scheme there was a change to more relativistic conceptions of knowledge and finally some students moved to a position of having a personal commitment to a particular position within a relativistic epistemology. The later phases in this scheme clearly parallel, to some extent, Conceptions 4 and 5 from Säljö's study, but stressing the recognition of relativism rather than the the more general quality of understanding being sought.

Although Säljö's work identified these differences with different groups of subjects, there seems to be a developmental dimension in his work which is made more explicit in Perry's scheme. An important aspect of our research has been to investigate changes in conception of learning with the same group of students over six years of part-time study in the OU. The case studies discussed above suggest relationships between concepts during student's first year of study with the OU. In the next section, we shall examine students' experiences of learning over the six year period.

The case studies already discussed were drawn from the group of 29 students who were in their first year of study. After the three interviews with students in the first year (described above in the case studies), they were interviewed on one occasion during each subsequent year of study. After allowance for drop-outs and students who for a variety of personal circumstances chose to discontinue their studies after gaining a number course credits, we had a group of ten students who completed their studies to graduation.

The interviews were wide-ranging in-depth interviews designed to explore student experiences of OU study. For example, we asked students how they came to be taking their courses and what they have gained from study. In the later interviews we asked them about any changes in study habits and 'critical incidents' which stood out in their careers as students. Also to follow up the work of Säljö we asked students in each interview what they thought learning consisted of. Over a period of six years a unique rapport built up with the interviewees and the interviews became more conversational in style, covering more personal issues. Each interview was tape recorded and transcribed in full. Data analysis was carried out systematically through reading and re-reading interview transcripts to identify the 'essences' or 'significant phenomena' in the interview transcripts.

All students began their studies with the Social Science Foundation course. The structure of the degree profile allows students free choice across all the University courses, so students are undertaking a variety of course profiles. However, all the students were studying broadly within the social science, education and arts areas although a few students followed an introductory technology course. This group of students, although they have not studied at exactly the same rate, had all graduated by the sixth year.

The following analysis is derived from the experiences of these 10 students.[2] The evidence in the interviews provides very rich intensive case-studies from which patterns emerge beyond the individuality and idiosyncratic nature of the data. Over the six years of the research, students have obviously changed in the normal course of events. But in terms of their development as learners and in relation to their studies the interviews show clear developments and change.

From the interviews we can identify changes from three types of evidence, as follows: (i) there are answers in different interviews to the same question. By looking at the answers in early interviews and comparing with the answers in later interviews we can look for change and development: (ii) there are times when students are talking about the same topics in different interviews, although the context and the questions eliciting the response may not be the same. Here we can show that attitudes or understandings of concepts and subject material have changed and developed, and (iii) evidence for change and development is when students themselves are talking consciously of change and describing developments that they are aware of in themselves, sometimes specifically referring to earlier interviews; at other times talking generally about changes they perceive in themselves. These three types of evidence can be illustrated by taking examples from one student's transcripts, as follows:

Evidence of change 1: Conception of learning

One of the questions asked in each of the interviews was about the student's conception of learning. The question we asked to find out about this was "Can you tell me what exactly you mean by 'learning'?". This was asked at an appropriate time during the interviews when the students were talking about what they had learnt from their current course or when they used the word 'learning' in their response to another question. We wanted to find out if Säljö's five conceptions of learning would appear in our sample and if they would help to identify change over years of study. The examples below show extracts from the answers to this question for the same student in the first year and in the fifth year of her studies. A clear difference can be seen which indicates a growth of understanding and awareness of issues surrounding the idea of learning itself.

> Well, I don't know really. I suppose knowing things that I don't know about I'm still very much at school. I know it's a very different sort of learning and if I look through a book, it's still sort of learning facts and dates and names rather than the content. And if I have read something I'm so bothered about taking in what it said. (Year 1)

> 'Real' learning is something personal and it's also something that is continuous, once it's started, it carries on and on and it might lead to other things. So much learning is learned for a particular purpose, and when you have achieved whatever it was learned for then that's it, it can go away, it's disposable, you can get rid of it. — But with real learning hopefully the unit of work you are given is only the catalyst really it is only one hundredth of the learning and the rest goes on once you put the book down. And the next time you talk to someone or read something in the newspaper, that's when the rest happens because it's been started and you carry it on for yourself because you want to and you get something lasting from it. (Year 5)

Evidence of change 2: Using concepts from a subject

The second type of evidence comes from times in the interviews when the same topic concept or idea recurs. In the following quotations, from interviews in first and fourth year of study, we can see the difference in how 'jargon' is perceived over time.

> I was really annoyed by the word 'anomie' it didn't seem to be in any dictionary or anything and the only place I found that it was in common use was in the 1750 — well that's wonderful — if people use that sort of word, and I hate that sort of thing anyway, and I was so cross — people saying things in a way that they think sounds clever. (Year 1)

> If I am speaking to somebody either that has done the same unit or the same course or whatever, then it is really nice talking about it and I don't feel silly using the same language either. It's not a conscious effort to use it, I mean obviously it's easier using it than not, it's like speaking in shorthand in a way. (Year 4)

Evidence of change 3: Change in awareness

The third type of evidence comes from parts of the interviews when students are talking consciously about changes that they feel they have gone through or about what it feels like looking back over their years of study. Here the student is reflecting on past experience and present feelings and comparing one year with another. The change is demonstrated in one quotation as the student is reflecting on the change and developments as she has experienced them and the perception of herself in relation to the course.

> One of the things that was most significant to me was realising that it was possible to miss parts of the units or even whole blocks out and you could still pass the examination. That was really liberating. I can't remember how it happened now but it was fairly early on, maybe Year 2. Anyway, after that my whole way of working changed because suddenly I wasn't constrained by the worry of covering absolutely everything.

All the above quotations come from one student who has clearly changed in a number of ways over six years of study with the OU.

Looking at the interviews from all the students over time, there are three areas which relate to the development of the students. They are in the areas of *Confidence, Competence and Control.*

Confidence

Most of the students we interviewed had very low levels of self confidence at the start of their studies, (from their formal educational backgrounds they would have not gained university entrance). In fact, many of them were very unsure of their ability to do the course. For a few of them the effort of even applying for the course had been a great step, and they expected the course with the O.U. to help them to gain in personal confidence; it was one of their aims in studying.

> I'm hoping that it will give me more confidence in myself and to actually be able to cope with different situations in life in general. I feel that I need something and hopefully this is going to broaden my outlook.

Over their time with the OU, and with success in passing courses, they developed their confidence in a number of important areas. They began to accept that they were intelligent adults who could pass a course of study, and that feeling was important to them. They gained in self esteem. Certainly after a few courses successfully completed, they began to relax about their ability and not to feel so threatened by the exams or by the continuous assessment on the course. By the end of the first year the student quoted above could say:

I've done four essays now and I've passed them all, so I must be doing adequately I suppose, but I don't feel awfully confident. But then, nobody else seems to either, so I don't feel too bad about it.

After a time they also began to have confidence in their understanding of the system — the course and its structure. They were able to choose their own ways of working through material instead of constantly looking for guidance and examples of good practice from others; they became more self-reliant. Although at this point, students might still be unsure of their ability, they nevertheless knew how to use the course materials in a way which suited them.

I have been studying more or less the same sort of way this year. I still rely on the 'in text questions' which test for understanding. I always do them because I find I need to. If I don't do them I'm not sure that I understand what I am supposed to have done. I'm still a bit nervous about all this you see.

Students then realised that total coverage of the material was not an absolute necessity and began to have the confidence in selecting certain parts for special attention because of either inherent importance or their own particular interest.

I've got more confidence in myself now. I feel that I can afford to miss bits out that don't interest me so much. I mean I do try to do everything, I don't like missing things out. But, sometimes for time reasons I want to spend more time on one part so I miss out something else. I would never have had the confidence to do that at the beginning.

Beyond this confidence to be selective comes a confidence to question material, an ability to interact personally with the content and to engage in debate about it.

At tutorials I don't get swept along by the 'teachers talk' [O.U. students who work as teachers], if you like. I stop and say hang on a minute. It's supposed to be a course not just for teachers but there happen to be only two of us on the course that aren't teachers. I tend to feel that I'm on the parents' side or the pupils side. It's funny taking sides at all, but I feel that they are always starting from the point of view of the teacher so it needs to be more balanced.

Further still the development brings a confidence to go outside and beyond the course material on one's own.

It's difficult to pinpoint the change but it [the course] is less important to me now. I don't feel really that I learn any more now than I did a couple of years ago. I think my stage of development is the same. Maybe I should have gone on to a 3rd level course, maybe it would have been more stimulating. I don't have to work very hard to achieve a pass on an essay and because I'm not terribly keen on the particular course this year, I'm just not working very hard. — There are still courses that I'm interested in doing but right now I'm more interested in finishing and concentrating on other things for myself. I feel that I've learnt the required skills, like how to analyse and argue and in a way these courses now are just repeating what I have learnt.

The changes and development in confidence thus take students through a stage of being anxious and unsure of themselves towards a feeling of security in their own ability and also courage to become independent in their learning.

Competence

Over their time with the Open University the students developed in their ability to cope with the system and study effectively. In their first year of study all the students had to learn how the system of distance learning was organised and how to recognise and respond to different aspects of the system.

I think having done a course already you feel much more able to cope in the second year. You know what is coming and that things are going to have to fill in forms for registration and Summer School and you haven't got to worry about those things. Whereas last year those things were problems.

For some students this takes quite a long time whereas for other students this familiarity with the system takes only a few weeks. Once students feel conversant with the system and how it works, they are then able to develop their own way of working within it. They learn about how they can organise their own study in order to get the best from the system. This involves aspects of study strategy, for example, note-taking and organising study time in relation to assessment requirements. Again students varied in how long it took them to establish their study patterns and feel comfortable within the OU system. For example:

I always read the assignment question first so that while I am studying I can underline bits and make notes of things that are relevant for the assignment. And the computer marked parts of the assignment; I do those as I'm going through, because you do have to look back and I'm finding that if I've got to do it all at the end it just wastes time. I don't take notes because it all gets very 'bitty', it's better just to make notes in the margins and underline the important bits rather than making separate notes. I did try, but it wasn't terribly successful and so I gave that up.

Once the students feel they can work comfortably within the system they begin to stand back from day-to-day studying and are able to see the course as a whole. They gain an overview of the course and are able to identify the main ideas and themes in the subject area.

> I take a general look through it to see the structure of it to see what the aims of the block are and what they are expecting you to learn — so, as I'm reading it I know what is to come. I know that one part is about work and the individual and later there will be another part dealing with the economic aspects. I'm prepared for it.

Besides standing back and seeing the course as a whole, students begin to see the relevance to the outside world and to question aspects of the course in relation to their own experience. They begin to engage personally with the content of the course and to evaluate it in relation to their own lives rather than as a separate experience.

> One of the units was about education through autobiography and there was a lot about your home and school life. I really enjoyed doing that because I spent hours thinking about how my parents must have felt. I spent a lot of time thinking about me from their point of view I suppose. I really enjoyed that bit and spent more time on it. The next unit was heavily philosophical and was really quite deep and confusing and I decided to ignore most of it.

Towards the end of their student career, some students are beginning to construct their own learning environment, and so feel less ready to continue taking courses and more inclined to study on their own.

> The OU is definitely less important now, but it is only less important because I'm more important and I'm more important because of it. Because of what it has done for me or shown me — it might be just the confidence that I can look back and say well I've got through thick and thin and come out on top and pleased with myself. But, it has got a lesser place now, but only because it's given me more scope, more ammunition, more confidence. It has definitely led me to other things. It has been a self realisation I suppose of what I can do and be.

In this last quotation we can see the relationship between the two areas of confidence and competence. The two types of development move side by side and one feeds the other. We can consider the relationship not as an external correlation but as an internal logical relationship in students' experience of study. For students to become more competent in study they need to develop in confidence.

Control

Another internal relationship is a transition towards less reliance on the course and the institution to control learning and more reliance on the student to take personal responsibility for study. In many different aspects of control of learning, students demonstrated development towards independence and autonomy. Overall, they were thus showing self-regulation in studying, involving responsibility for both what is learnt and how it is learnt (Boud,1981; Morgan,1985). In the quotations above, we can see that students initially are anxious about their ability and unsure how to study. This makes them very tentative in their approach to learning. They assume they must cover everything and not question the material. Later, students begin to understand the system and learn how to exercise some control over it. They begin to take charge of their own studying and to make discriminations about the depth and breadth of their study. Later still, through a more personal orientation, they stand back from the material and begin to use it for their own aims and purposes, rather than those of the teacher or the course. They are thus beginning to take control not only of the process of learning, but of the value put on the content of learning in relation to their own needs. Quotations from the first and final interviews of two students illustrate this development.

> I don't mind what subject I study, I don't really know much about anything yet. It's all new and when I look at the titles they just say Psychology or Sociology or something I don't know what they mean yet. (Year 1)

> I suppose it's a process because whatever I am reading now, I'm not absolutely dogmatic about things but I certainly know what my position is. Whatever it is that I'm reading I know which one of the approaches is mine. I'm not thinking "Oh yes, well it could be that or I could think this way about it". My own view jumps out at me first and then I'll consider the others. Studying didn't always seem to be like that. (Year 6)

> I got worried at the tutorial because the tutor was picking the unit to bits and questioning it — I said to her, "Look, I'm a foundation student. I don't pull this unit to bits, I accept what they have told me". Sometimes I may not like something that is said, but I must accept what is there because I assume they know what they are talking about and if they are putting it to me this way — spoon feeding me, someone who is unlikely to understand any other way. (Year 1)

> I used to think that you had to use your own arguments and I found that very difficult but I know now that you use other people's arguments to build up your case. So I suppose I have learnt that there are no real right answers and if you get that in your mind to begin with then you can end up agreeing with some theory if you like, but you don't have to... It makes you realise that you can take control of your own life. I used to think that life just took hold of you and did what it wanted with you but you come to realise that you should take hold of it and make it go your way. (Year 6)

Table 13.3 summarises the points above and attempts to show how these developments are linked both logically and empirically. We are suggesting five stages from Fresher and Novice, through Intermediate and Expert to Graduate as a conceptual model for summarising our longitudinal case study data. The five discrete stages show how a progression towards independence in study is very closely linked to students' development of confidence. It appears that in order to move to a greater level of competence in studying, students first need to develop the confidence which is a prerequisite for this competence. Similarly, once the student has gained a certain level of competence in dealing with studying, this enhances the development of a greater level of confidence. So the two aspects of change develop hand-in-hand. Alongside these areas of knowledge in new contexts development, control of learning begins to shift from the system to the student. As students feel more confident and competent to make decisions for themselves, so they develop more independence from the teacher and the system.

TABLE 14.3

Stages of Development

Stage		Control of Learning	Confidence	Competence
Fresher	1	By the system and institution	To enrol	Understanding the system
Novice	2	By the system and institution	To attempt to study	Understanding about oneself in the system
Intermediate	3	By the system and institution	To select	Beginning to see a course as a whole
Expert	4	By self within a course	To question	Engaging personally with the content
Graduate	5	By self, in both in content and method of learning	To go it alone	Using skills and knowledge in new contexts

The successful students in our sample showed a development, albeit at different rates, throughout the six years of the study. Most of them had advanced through all the levels by year 6, but two were still not beyond the Intermediate stage. They were successful in accumulating course credits (and eventually a degree), but were still expecting the OU system to control their learning.

Orientation to Learning and Development

We have already described learning orientations and noted that many of the students have personal orientations, wanting to do the course for self development and/or to prove that they were capable of degree level work. When we look at the type of development and change that these students have undergone we can see that it is in line with their original reasons for studying.

This would be expected on logical grounds and is also demonstrated empirically. What we find particularly interesting is how these changes impinge on all aspects of a student's life, suggesting major steps in personal development as an adult.

It appears that some students use OU study as a vehicle for changing many aspects of their lives beyond their educational or academic levels. The interviews with students over time drew attention to the different levels of development some of the students were moving through. Although it is likely that these students would have undergone some personal change, irrespective of their OU experience, nevertheless they themselves attribute the changes to their studying. It has been, for them, the means through which they encouraged themselves to change.

Conception of Learning and Development

One of the clearest indications of change over time was in the student response to the question about their understanding of the word 'learning'. As well as being able to identify the five conceptions of learning described by Säljö (1979), we were able to trace students' development in their understanding over time. As we might have predicted, students moved from the idea of learning as memorising and additions of knowledge towards the idea of learning as understanding and as relating to life. This development was very clear for most students and in some cases went quite rapidly from Conception 1 to Conception 5. All our successful students had Conception 4 or 5 by the end of their fourth year of Open University study. In some cases the quality of student reflection on this question went beyond Säljö's scheme. Some students spoke of learning as 'changing oneself', a definition which may suggest a sixth conception of learning. In fact, a further analysis of this data by Marton, Beaty and Dall'Alba (1993) has described this further conception of learning as 'changing as a person — a fundamental change about seeing oneself and a way of seeing what is learnt'.

Intellectual Development

The changes in students towards taking responsibility for their own learning reflected a growth of awareness of the nature of knowledge and its construction. Students in their later years of study were less willing to take for granted the words written in the course units. They began to question material and to see that analysis and argument did not necessarily require right and wrong answers. Although our students are mature adults, at the beginning of their studies they were still inclined to perceive themselves as looking to the teacher (correspondence text and face-to-face tutor) for the 'right' answers.

Although our work has been concerned with adult students studying part-time at a distance, their development as learners progresses through similar stages to those identified by Perry with 18–21 year old students. This appears in part to do with the students' perceptions of themselves. At the start of their studies, they lack confidence in their ability to study. They rely on the teaching system (the OU) to control and direct their learning. Only through experience with the teaching system do they develop confidence and as a result competence in studying. These findings suggest that confidence is the key step, perhaps a limiting factor or prerequisite, in developing competence in learning. Belenky *et al.* (1986), who were interested in women students from non-traditional backgrounds, also highlighted the importance of confidence for many of the women they studied.

Developing Skill in Learning

From our research, skill in learning involves students developing confidence, competence, and autonomy in learning. By competence we refer to the specific activities a student engages in when tackling a particular learning task or a particular course. Part of this competence is concerned with the students' conceptions of learning and intellectual development. The importance of these issues is that they appear to constrain students in how they tackle a task — i.e. their approach to learning (see, for example, Morgan, Taylor and Gibbs,1982; Van Rossum, Deijkers and Hamer,1985). The importance of approach to learning is that it is directly linked to content and quality of the learning outcomes as identified by Marton and Säljö (1976).

As Svensson argued in Chapter 4, skill in learning is a relational concept. It describes the learning of particular content within a defined learning environment and in a specific institutional context. Skill also depends on other related concepts describing the individual in that context. The inter-relationship of confidence and competence in learning is, for example, closely linked to conception of learning, approach to learning, and learning outcomes. These concepts describe learning at increasing levels of generality and provide a holistic description of student experiences of learning. This relational view of skill in learning is very different to the technical notions of study skills, such as particular ways of taking notes, or the use of mnemonic devices as embodied in many manuals on study skills.

The conceptual model suggests a number stages through which students move as they develop skill in learning, with increasing independence from the teacher in terms of both the content and the process of learning. This study suggests that activities which build up confidence in learning and develop more complex conceptions of learning are likely to be the most beneficial in developing the lasting qualities of skill and self-reguzltion in learning.

Although derived from a small number of in-depth case studies, the richness of the data provide a framework from which to reflect on learning in other contexts, and to raise the level of awareness concerning students' realities of learning. We need to raise the awareness of learners' experiences of learning with teachers and staff developers (Morgan, 1993) so that the research in student learning discussed throughout the book can inform reflection on practice (Schon, 1983) and change in our practice.

Notes

1. The Open University provides degree level education for adults studying part-time at a distance. There are no formal entry qualifications. The teaching materials consist of specially prepared correspondence texts, television and

radio broadcasts, supported by face-to-face tuition at the local level. The Social Science Foundation Course is a "full credit" course extending over a nine month period. Six credits are required for a degree.

2. Some of this analysis appeared in Beaty & Morgan (1992).

CHAPTER FIFTEEN

Understanding Teaching and Teaching for Understanding

DAI HOUNSELL

Introduction

Until the early 1960s, teaching in higher education was a secret rite, taking place behind closed doors (Layton, 1968). It was little discussed and largely unstudied in any systematic way. Broadly speaking, that situation no longer obtains. The prospect of academics thinking as hard about their teaching as they do about their research may remain a distant and elusive one (Becher, 1978), but the closed doors which Layton saw have been gradually eased apart by empirical enquiry and open debate. The study of teaching has become accepted rather than exceptional, and there are fewer contemporary signs of the traditional reluctance of lecturers to engage in self-evaluation. Almost all colleges and universities nowadays mount staff development activities of some kind or other to help academics to reflect on and improve their teaching expertise. And from the 1970s onwards there has appeared a large and fast-growing array of books which deal generally with teaching in higher education, explore the potentials and limitations of particular methods, or articulate new approaches. [1]

Yet while teaching itself began to be more vigorously and openly examined, the teaching-learning process as it was experienced by students remained hidden from view. Instead, discussion was almost overwhelmingly centred around lecturers' perceptions of the teaching learning process. It derived from the vantage-points which they occupied and it was concerned in the main with the activities in which they — rather than their students — were engaged.

This 'teacher-centredness' had a number of consequences. The first of these is quite simply that while our knowledge of lecturers and of the part they play in teaching has grown substantially, students have remained shadowy and insubstantial figures, part of the background rather than the foreground of discussion and debate. Little has been known about how students respond to teaching, how they tackle the everyday demands of learning and studying, or what kinds of difficulties or problems they encounter. In short, the experience of students has been taken for granted rather than systematically explored.

As a corollary to this (and in spite of the value traditionally placed on coming to know one's students as individuals), an understanding of what it means to learn from the student's perspective has not generally been seen as an indispensable or even desirable component of accomplishment in teaching. Instead, the principal focus of discussion has been the transmission rather than the reception of subject-matter, and the formal or semi-public activities of teaching in higher education: the lectures where the lecturer introduces students to an aspect of his or her discipline in a lucid and organized way; the seminars and tutorials where students are given an opportunity to clarify and deepen their understanding in the cut-and-thrust of discussion; and the practicals where students are encouraged to work through a structured set of assigned experiments or problems. Indeed, teaching expertise has been primarily associated with accomplishment in the lecture-hall or the seminar room, and staff development initiatives have tended to be directed towards improvement of this aspect of teaching performance. The problems of how or what students are expected to learn from lectures, seminars or practicals — and more particularly, of how students might be helped to maximise what they might learn in such situations — have remained largely unexplored or unaddressed.

A further and linked consequence of an emphasis on what we might call direct teaching situations has been a corresponding lack of emphasis on learning activities in which academics are only indirectly engaged. Such activities include background reading, report and essay writing, working through set problems, note-taking and revision. Lecturers' influence on these activities is often seen as confined in the main to prescribing the kinds and amounts of work to be done and, where appropriate, assessing it. But the chief responsibility for carrying out and learning from these activities is considered to rest with students. Such activities are thus widely viewed as playing an auxiliary rather than central role in the teaching-learning process, at base reinforcing and extending what students have assimilated from more formal teaching encounters. Indeed, the custom of referring to these activities under the umbrella term 'private study' underscores their separation from the mainstream of teaching as conventionally conceived.

It is therefore important to recognise not only that a knowledge of students and of learning has been substantially lacking, but also that this has meant that assumptions about what teaching entails and what the roles and responsibilities of a teacher in higher education are have sprung from a less than complete view of the teaching-learning process. In one sense, then, the present book can help to close the gap by offering an understanding of what it means to learn in higher education. But in an equally crucial respect, the unaccustomed vantage-point which it adopts also serves to challenge prevailing assumptions about teaching and learning. Hirst's argument that a definition of teaching is contingent or 'parasitic' upon a definition of learning (Hirst, 1971) applies no less forcefully to the ways in which teaching and learning are conceptualised. If our conception of learning is transformed by new knowledge, then our conception of teaching must also undergo metamorphosis. The contribution of the findings presented here is thus not merely to extend our understanding of the teaching-learning process, but to change the ways in which that process is understood.

The purpose of this chapter is to sketch out the foundations and implications of *an experiential conception* of the teaching-learning process, i.e. a conception which is steeped in the experiences and perspectives of both academics and students. The chapter aims to highlight main themes which spring from the findings discussed in earlier chapters, to suggest what these imply for our thinking about the teaching-learning process, and to illustrate the kinds of initiatives which might follow in consequence.

Teaching for Understanding

A signal feature of higher education institutions is the great and growing diversity of undergraduate courses and of the disciplines in which these are steeped. In each discipline, distinctive conceptual frameworks and procedures of analysis are brought to bear on a specific domain of subject-matter. No analysis of learning and teaching should fail to recognise this diversity and distinctiveness: the pedagogical problems of any one discipline are in certain respects unique. Equally importantly, nonetheless, if an analysis of learning and teaching is to have any general validity, it cannot remain landlocked in a specific subject domain. A core of mutual concerns and perspectives must be sought which arch across the disciplines and are applicable, to greater or lesser degrees, to most if not all of them. Chapter 2 provides telling illustrations of this issue in its most significant form: the search for criteria which capture qualitative differences in what we have called the outcomes of learning — in other words, what it is that students have gained from the experience of higher education. On the one hand, Chapter 2 shows how the uniqueness of course content must be recognised: the precise subject-matter of a given learning task is confronted in arriving at a full description of the learning outcomes. On the other hand, differences can be identified which have wider relevance. A distinction can be drawn, for example, between outcomes which merely describe the content of a text or mention isolated parts of it, and those which are founded upon a recognition of the relationship between the evidence presented and the conclusion which the evidence was intended to support. More generally, and most fundamentally, we can differentiate between outcomes which represent understanding and those which do not.

This concern with understanding, allied to a sensitivity to subject matter, has been a thread which unites the various contributions to the present book. In different ways, each chapter has sought an overarching criterion of what students have learnt in the distinction between learning which represents the memorisation or reproduction of discrete pieces of information, and learning in which meaning has been grasped in a complete and holistic way. Equally, each chapter has shown that understanding cannot be taken for granted; it is a difficult and often elusive quarry. We saw in Chapter 10, for example, that some students may experience the relevance of the content of a lecture intrinsically, so that what they have learnt has become bound up with their own understanding of a particular subject or discipline. Others, however, may perceive the lecture content in a predominantly unreflective and extrinsic way, as something which has to be retained for assessment purposes. Similarly in Chapter 6, we saw how the meaning of a text may not be grasped because of a failure to perceive the interconnections between the specific content of the text and the overall message which its author was attempting to convey.

A concern with meaning and understanding is thus central to an experiential conception of the teaching-learning process, for the gap between reproduction and understanding represents a quantum leap in the quality of what has been learned. When the mastery of factual or procedural details — in many disciplines a vital cornerstone of understanding — becomes an end in itself, dislocated from meaning, then to have learnt is not to have partially understood but to have not understood at all. Moreover, as we have also seen, when something has been genuinely understood, it has been related by students to their prior knowledge and experience and it is perceived as helping them to make sense of the world around them. In its fullest sense, therefore, learning involves a change in the students' conception of some aspect of reality. It is an activity "through which the environment — or man himself — appears with a higher degree of meaningfulness than before" (p. 37).

This last point underlines the essentially inter-subjective and constructive character of learning and teaching. Teaching is not a hermetic problem of 'transmission', nor is it merely a 'delivery system', packaging and conveying the commodity of knowledge to those who will merely consume it. In the opening chapter of his study of college students' intellectual development, William Perry (see Chapter 1) succinctly illustrates the problem in its most general form. Let us suppose, Perry says, that a lecturer begins his lecture by stating that he will consider three theories which have been advanced to account for a specific problem or phenomenon:

> *Student A* has always taken it for granted that knowledge consists of correct answers, that there is one right answer per problem, and that teachers explain these answers for students to learn. He therefore listens for the lecturer to state which theory he is to learn.

> *Student B* makes the same general assumptions but with an elaboration to the effect that teachers sometimes present problems and procedure rather than answers, 'so that we can learn to find the right answer on our own'. He therefore perceives the lecture as a kind of guessing game in which he is to 'figure out' which theory is correct, a game that is fair enough if the lecturer does not carry it so far as to hide things too obscurely.

> *Student C* assumes that an answer can be called 'right' only in the light of its context, and that contexts or 'frames of reference' differ. He assumes that several interpretations of a poem, explanations of a historical development, or even theories of a class of events in physics may be legitimate 'depending on how you look at it'. Though he feels a little uneasy in such a kaleidoscopic world, he nonetheless supposes that the lecturer may be about to present three legitimate theories which can be examined for their internal coherence, their scope, their fit with various data, their predictive power, etc. (Perry, 1970, pp. 1–2)

These three hypothetical students, as Perry later makes clear, represent different positions in his scheme of intellectual development. The illustration thus highlights the interpenetration of learning and teaching, for whatever the lecturer then proceeds to do, Perry suggests, these three students will make meaning of the experience in quite different ways.

The teaching-learning process can thus be considered not as a matter of transmission, but rather as a meeting of minds where world-views confront and collide with one another. The success with which students are able to achieve understanding may therefore depend critically on the capacity of the higher education teacher to recognise and build from students' existing conceptions and to anchor new knowledge in a meaningful framework.

Building from existing conceptions

The challenge of orienting teaching towards the conceptions of phenomena which students bring to a course is a formidable one. Indeed, the difficulties posed are more general ones which are also confronted by, for example, historians of science. As Hans Kalmus puts it in an article on the geneticist Gregor Mendel, it is:

> the necessity to put themselves in the frame of mind of the scientist with whose achievements and ideas they are concerned. Perhaps the biggest obstacle for those entering into the thought system of a historical figure is the difficulty of "unthinking" an idea or concept which since the time of its discovery has become commonplace. (Kalmus, 1984)

For lecturers too, the central task may be to "unthink" an idea or concept and put themselves in the frame of mind of students who are encountering it for the very first time. In part, this may require the kind of empathetic understanding advocated by Carl Rogers (see Chapter 1). Yet the lecturer is not entirely in the same predicament as the historian of science. While the historian must rely upon informed and imaginative reconstruction, the lecturer has the possibility of trying to elicit and thus build from students' existing conceptions directly.

Two courses at the Open University have indicated ways in which a knowledge of students' conceptions can guide teaching strategies. One is a course in Third World Studies (U204). Members of the course team designing the unit interviewed prospective students about how they understood such terms as 'developing' and 'underdeveloped' country and what countries they would categorise as part of the 'Third World'. What the course team gleaned was therefore a more informed 'sense of audience' (Britton et al., 1975) which could underpin the design and drafting of the course unit. But there were two other consequences, reflecting the degree to which the course team was impressed by the task of examining students' conceptions directly. First, exercises were built into the start of the course which required students to articulate and analyse their own understanding of and attitudes towards the Third World. Only then were students asked to relate their own conceptions to the theoretical perspectives set out in the course materials. Second, one of the project options offered in the course unit was to carry out an interview study of the attitudes of a small social group towards the Third World. In effect, students could undertake the same task which the course team had undertaken, and so broaden their own understanding of the varying ways in which the Third World was conceptualised.

The second of the two examples stems from an Open University foundation course in the social sciences.[2] The study referred to in Chapters 5 and 14 had provided detailed evidence of how twenty key concepts were understood by mature students new to social science. Capitalism was one of the key concepts, and the students' answers in research interviews to the question "Is Britain capitalist?" were subsequently written into the course materials. In a section of the materials entitled 'Is Britain Capitalist Today?', a wide range of quotes from the interviews were followed by 'expert' comment. Students following the course unit were therefore encouraged to pursue understanding by relating their own ideas to those of the author.

A third example also grows out of research described in the present book. Chapters 2 and 4 discussed students' understanding of a physical phenomenon:

what forces act on a car which is driven along a motorway in a straight line at a high constant speed? As the analysis showed, some of the answers the students gave represented an Aristotelian conception (of movement as effect) rather than a Newtonian conception (of acceleration as effect).

This question formed part of an investigation at Gothenburg University into engineering students' thinking and problem-solving in the field of mechanics. The main focus of the project was not on the development of teaching methods as such but on establishing the foundations upon which the content and method of teaching might be more closely geared to the needs of students. While the project was still in progress, however, some of its preliminary findings on differences in students' conceptions of a range of physical phenomena were having an influence on teaching.

One of the two lecturers responsible for the courses followed by students taking part in the project used the preliminary interview findings to construct a test. The test made use of the questions asked in the interview study and concentrated on those physical phenomena where crucial differences in students' conceptions had been revealed. The purpose of the test was not to achieve a more standardised or objective way of 'measuring' the knowledge of the students, but instead to obtain an overview, however sketchy, of the conceptions held by students embarking on the courses. On the one hand, the test had a diagnostic function, alerting and sensitising the lecturer to students' conceptions. On the other, the questions it posed and the answers which the students gave could be directly incorporated into day-to-day teaching and openly discussed. The results of the test therefore became a part of the content of the courses.

The second of the two lecturers involved in the project made use of the results in a somewhat different way, by mounting group discussions which provided an introduction to central components of the course. Students were presented with the kinds of problems used in the interview study and were asked to discuss these in pairs. The students were then combined into large groups in which they presented their partner's response to a problem as they had understood it, and there was then a general discussion. In the general discussion, the teacher drew upon his awareness of differences in the students' thinking about the phenomena to identify, describe and review differences in conception.

These examples, as the discussion has indicated, have tended to rely upon a knowledge of students' conceptions already highlighted by empirical enquiries. Taken as a whole, therefore, they provide richer illustrations of ways in which courses may build upon existing conceptions than of how these conceptions might be elicited. Without this empirical starting-point, lecturers must seek pathways of their own towards a knowledge of students' conceptions. This will inevitably be a gradual process, but it need not be considered as a self-contained task. As the final example showed, structured group discussion offers a means of encouraging students to articulate and share their ways of thinking with one another and with the lecturer. Similarly, in the opening example students were given exercises which required them to make explicit and analyse their own attitudes and understandings. Eliciting and exploring students' conceptions can therefore become an integral part of the teaching-learning process. Seen from this particular perspective, to teach is to engage with students in a collaborative quest for commonality of meaning.

Anchoring knowledge in a framework of meaning

The second challenge of an inter-subjective curriculum is to set what is to be learned in a framework of meaning. This is what Marris (1964) has called placing knowledge "in a meaningful context", which he saw as the essential function of lectures. Its importance as an avenue to understanding was exemplified in Chapter 10. By means of vivid illustrations which anchored new subject-matter in a recognisable reality, or through their infectious enthusiasm and commitment to their subject, some lecturers were able to help students to experience vicariously an excitement about the content of their lectures. Such lecturing provided a bridge between extrinsic experiences and the intrinsic experiences of relevance which were associated with personal understanding. Similarly, Chapter 11 suggested how, with the aid of multi-media, carefully crafted learning tasks can provide the 'affordances' to link students' everyday understandings with the less tractable formal representations of phenomena characteristic of academic enquiry.

This kind of anchoring can equally fruitfully be attempted in a variety of teaching-learning situations, as shown in an account of efforts by a group of tutors and curriculum development specialists at Sussex University to redesign part of an introductory economics course (Eraut, MacKenzie and Papps, 1975). Their initial response to the perceived shortcomings of the existing course had been to devise self-instructional packages linked to lectures, tutorials and group discussions. But students' manifest lack of enthusiasm for the packages led to reappraisal, and so to a quite different way forward. The turning-point was the 'Demand Theory' package, an analysis of the Brighton housing market. This had been seen as a complex problem to which students could relate the basic economic concepts of supply and demand.

> Whilst students appeared to get very little out of the Demand Theory Package the members of faculty who prepared it felt that they had learnt a lot from having to sort out their ideas: and it occurred to them that the 'sorting out' process might be more important than the subsequent learning. Perhaps the students could also be involved in formulating the problems, clarifying the assumptions about the situation to be studied, choosing the analytic techniques and disentangling value judgements and empirical judgements. (Eraut *et al.*, 1975, p. 24)

The result was a series of two-hour discussions, on topical issues such as 'Should British Leyland give their workers £10 a week more?'. The discussions were deliberately open-ended and free ranging, with the tutor taking the role of chairperson rather than chief discussant. Students' reactions to the discussions were strongly enthusiastic:

> For the first time it was they who were being asked to 'sort the problem out': and the relationship between empirical judgements and value judgements could be talked out and made explicit. Moreover, they were being treated as economists rather than as novices, so it became possible for them to acquire some confidence in the value of their own personal judgement. Previously it had been assumed that the most difficult aspects of learning economics were the concepts and techniques, and that their

application would arise naturally. Now it seemed that the reverse might true. The process of analysing economic problems and deciding which techniques were relevant was the most difficult thing to acquire. Once that had begun to take root the learning of concepts and techniques became less difficult. (Eraut *et al.*, 1975,p. 25)

As the authors themselves recognise, the change of strategy had far-reaching consequences. One was to see the 'systems approach' which had been their initial guide as only spuriously student-centred. This approach, they conclude, seldom involves trying to discover what students' main concerns and problems actually are, since testing and consultation takes place only within a tightly predetermined framework. The second consequence was a recognition of the implications of inter-subjectivity. As the student pursues learning, taking part in tutorials and writing essays:

Somehow it is always the subject-matter being fed to him rather than him feeding on the subject-matter. If any real competence is to be attained it is essential for the student to construct his own personal version of the discipline. (Eraut *et al.*, 1975, p. 33)

A striking illustration of how this might be achieved through the use of multimedia was explored in Chapter 11. Students were encouraged to generate their own categories for comparing and differentiating a corpus of twenty paintings before testing their own constructs against those of recognised experts in the History of Art. In consequence, as Diana Laurillard explained:

When the students now confront precepts concerning the evidence of 'tonality' or 'texture' of a painting, they have some experiences and formal descriptions of their own against which to test these new ideas. They have some ground on which to build. And [...] the nature of the task set is the key to providing the affordances they need.

This too finds an echo elsewhere, for Chapter 12 draws attention to the pedagogical 'scaffolding' which tutors can provide to help students in thinking for themselves. Accomplished tutoring was seen as turning on the interplay between *taking out* an expert's view of a subject to students in forms that were accessible to them as novices, while also *drawing in* their more common-sense understandings towards expert positions within the discipline. Chapter 9, moreover, suggested that, in the process of revision, final-year students can forge highly distinctive 'knowledge objects' which encapsulate for them the array of complex interconnections within and across a particular body of knowledge.

Thus far we have been concerned with how tutors can foster the pursuit of understanding. Our focus of attention has been chiefly upon the content of learning and teaching, and we have stressed the importance of acknowledging its inter-subjective and interpersonal character. Yet as Bruner (1966) reminds us, a curriculum reflects the nature not only of knowledge and of the knower but also of the "knowledge-getting process":

A body of knowledge, enshrined in a university faculty and embodied in a series of authoritative volumes, is the result of much prior intellectual

> ...struct someone in these disciplines is not a matter of getting
> it results to mind. Rather, it is to teach him to participate in the
> ...makes possible the establishment of knowledge. We teach a
> ...produce little living libraries on that subject, but rather to get
> ...ink mathematically for himself, to consider matters as an
> ...an does, to take part in the process of knowledge-getting. Knowing
> is a process, not a product. (Bruner, 1966, p. 72)

In the next section of the chapter, we turn from content to process, from the 'what' to the 'how' of learning. This is a shift of emphasis rather than a substantive change. Content and process are complementary and interrelated aspects of the experience of learning and teaching.

Teaching Students How to Learn

If one thread common to the preceding chapters has been a concern with learning as understanding, a second and no less important thread has been a concern with the pathways along which understanding is pursued. In Chapter 3, a fundamental difference was described in students' approaches to learning. The distinction drawn was between a surface approach, which involved a passive and unreflective attempt to memorise and reproduce a text, and a deep approach, where there was an active effort to grasp the main point or message which the content of the text was intended to convey. In a surface approach, what was to be learned was interpreted as the text itself. In a deep approach, the text was seen as a means through which to grapple with the meaning which underlay it. These differences in approach, Chapter 3 further demonstrated, were functionally related to learning outcomes.

Although derived from studies of learning from reading, this basic distinction has been shown to have a much wider relevance as a means of identifying and describing differences in students' approaches to learning and studying. The distinction underpins the meaning and reproducing orientations to studying discussed in Chapter 13, and it is closely complemented by Svensson's parallel distinction between holistic and atomistic approaches (see Chapters 3 and 4), which places relatively greater weight on the organisational as opposed to the referential aspects of students' experiences. The deep/surface distinction is also mirrored in the intrinsic and extrinsic experiences of relevance examined in Chapter 10, and it has been a strong influence on the derivation of the conceptions of essay-writing explored in Chapter 7. And as Chapter 5 makes clear, there are evident links between students' learning orientations, their conceptions of learning, and their approaches to learning and studying. Yet despite the striking conceptual affinity between these various descriptions of how students go about learning, it should be stressed that the differences between them are not fortuitous but reflect the many-sided complexity of learning itself. One aspect of this complexity stems from the idiosyncrasy of the discipline and the course. For example, Chapter 13, "The Context of Learning in Academic Departments", shows that the distinction between deep and surface approaches is not invariant but takes on different meanings in different disciplines. A deep approach in the humanities, for instance, is typified by an intention from the outset to re-interpret the learning material in a personal way, while in the sciences, an initial concentration on details is often indispensable to a deep approach. In a similar vein, Chapter 7 presents an analytical framework through which critical differences in students' conceptions of essay-writing can be described and analysed, but the distinctive pattern and substance of the conceptions identified in this particular instance are of course functions of the discipline and course examined. In other words, these distinctions can be powerful tools in developing and supporting tutors' understandings of the learning of their own students, but they do not amount to rigid blueprints.

A second aspect of the complexity of learning is the particularity of the demands of specific tasks and activities. We have already reviewed, for example, the way in which learning from lectures can be fruitfully examined in relation to students' experiences of the relevance of lecture content, and other chapters have carried further the investigation of specific tasks. Thus Chapter 6 adopted a communication perspective to demonstrate that if the meaning of a text is to be apprehended, the learner must provisionally accept the premises of the text's author and try to reconstruct the message intended. Chapter 7 drew attention to the interplay in essay-writing procedures between a student's emergent interpretative stance and the organisation and selection of essay material. The procedures of essay-writing were thus shown to echo students' conceptions of the nature of an essay in History. And in Chapter 8, we saw how an alliance of the constructs of approach and learning style disclosed the global and localised forms of procedures and descriptions characteristic of problem-solving as a learning activity. No less tellingly, Chapter 12 revealed that entering fully into the realm of academic discussion which typifies undergraduate tutorials entailed considerably more than an initial adjustment to a novel setting. It called for "a much longer, slower process of acquiring knowledge in a discipline and of fuller acculturation to the ways of academic work and the forms of academic discourse".

These descriptions of students' experiences compel recognition of the heterogeneous and exacting requirements of learning activities. They indicate that any teaching-learning situation is as demanding of students as it is of tutors, and they serve to challenge the conventional relegation of private study to an auxiliary and reinforcing role. An experiential conception therefore in part inverts the traditionalist focus upon formal teaching situations. Instead it invites us to consider the teaching-learning process as a constellation of learning tasks, some of which take place in a classroom setting in the presence of a university teacher while others are pursued alone or in the company of peers in the university library, the study-bedroom, or even in the course of travelling to and from campus. This inversion of focus has an important consequence: the change of vantage-point prompts us to see as problematic what might formally have been taken for granted. As a research perspective, it has provided abundant evidence that many students adopt approaches which are inappropriate to the achievement of understanding. As a perspective upon teaching, it suggests strongly that lecturers should take a more active part in helping their students to learn how to learn. Before exploring possible initiatives, however, learning must also be considered in relation to the individual student or learner.

Learning and the learner

A fuller understanding of the approaches students adopt can be sought by means of a frame of reference wider than the learning task or activity: the institutional setting (which will be discussed later), or the student as an individual learner. In Chapter 3, to take one example, it was shown that five distinct conceptions of learning could be identified, ranging from a conception of learning as a quantitative increase in knowledge to one of learning as an interpretive process aimed at understanding reality. These differences in the meanings which individuals gave to learning were also found to be associated with their approaches to an experimental reading task. A second construct which focused upon the individual student was that of orientation to learning, delineated in Chapter 5. Four orientations — academic, personal, vocational and social — were distinguished. The four orientations could each take either an intrinsic or an extrinsic form, and were also an influential factor in the personal 'study contracts' which shaped how students went about their undergraduate studies. Moreover, alongside approaches and conceptions of learning, these orientations to learning provided an analytical framework through which to consider the individual student in the round, as well as the interconnections between the three sets of constructs.

These qualitative differences in conception and orientation clearly also have significant implications for attempts to help students to learn. Chapter 3 provided evidence of the difficulties of fostering a deep approach within the confines of a single experiment. Even within an everyday course setting, to restrict guidance solely to one kind of learning task or activity may be to fail to tackle the more general and perhaps more deep-seated conceptions and orientations which colour students' approaches; yet these conceptions and orientations are amenable to change, as Chapter 14 suggests. It would be erroneous to regard them as fixed traits or unyielding attributes of individual students.

Learning-to-learn

To recognise that students might need and can benefit from help with the demands of studying is not necessarily to know how one might set about helping them. There are probably many tutors who would echo the sentiments of a lecturer cited in an Australian study:

> I do have this feeling that many (students) would blossom with a bit of attention but they can't get it from me. Even my graduate students still ask me how to study — I can't tell them, but sometimes I think I should be able to. I can only pass on what worked for me and that was 30 years ago. (Frederick *et al.*, 1981, p. 85)

Where a knowledge of how students might be assisted is lacking, the natural recourse is to rely upon the many study skills guides and manuals which college and university bookshops routinely stock. Typically, such guides have tended to recommend specific techniques or methods of studying which students should master and adhere to. Yet the study techniques advocated are often of limited value and may sometimes be misleading or even harmful (see Gibbs, 1981, for a fuller discussion). Only seldom do such guides respond to the issues which have just been raised above: the demanding particularities of individual learning tasks, the critical and distinctive influence of the specific discipline and course setting, and the wider perspectives which individual students bring to their everyday learning. A strategy for reading, for example, may be recommended without consideration of whether to read in search of essay material is equivalent to reading an article which will be the focus of an extended seminar discussion; or whether a metallurgy textbook, a research monograph on social psychology, or the collected poems of Goethe might vary in the demands they place on the reader, or whether the inner logic of the strategy suggested might be at odds with students notions of what learning means as an activity. No less importantly, and almost without exception, study manuals are not grounded in an informed understanding of students' experience of learning. Their advice is idealised and often unrealistic (Gibbs, 1981).

Nonetheless, side by side with a growing questioning of conventional guidance in 'study skills', there has been an increasing number of attempts to develop more appropriate 'learning-to-learn' strategies (Hounsell, 1979). The change in terminology is deliberate. While the former tends to stress the acquisition of skills and is concerned with means or techniques, the latter emphasises an awareness of purpose and is concerned with ends and the individual's relationship to those ends.

Consider, for example, the following extract from one of the newer generation of guides to studying :

> This book focuses on you — who you are and what you bring to your learning. Throughout the book you are encouraged to examine your purposes and what you want to learn. You are also encouraged to look at how you learn informally, and to build on this self-knowledge in your formal learning. Implicit in this approach are the beliefs that there is no one way of learning which suits everyone and that it is your right and responsibility to shape your own learning ... Within each chapter you'll find questions and ideas about you as a learner. These are intended to centre the book on you and to help you discover your own purposes and methods for learning. Because the questions are based on the premise that only you can answer them, we don't prescribe one 'best' way of learning, but instead suggest alternative study techniques. We give reasons for these techniques so you can decide how useful they are for your purposes, and we encourage you to try them as you actually learn and study to find those which suit you ... (Marshall and Rowland, 1983, pp. x—xi)

The tenor of this passage contrasts sharply with the directiveness and rigidity of traditional study skills manuals. Indeed what the book as a whole evinces is a concern with students as individuals, a recognition of diversity in purposes and strategies, and a sensitivity to subject differences. Advice on reading, for example, is focused around the very different purposes which students may bring to reading a book: for entertainment; to gain an overall impression of its contents; to locate a specific idea or discussion; to familiarise oneself with its central concept or theme; and to understand the whole book in detail.

This pronounced shift in the nature and direction of guidance on learning and studying has increasingly been echoed in other publications. A guide to essay-writing by Clanchy and Ballard (1983) is explicitly geared to the social sciences student and starts from a discussion of what lecturers generally expect from essays. Pirie (1985) represents a similar example for students of literature. Similarly, Marland and others (1981) have shown how a framework of 'question-steps' can help raise pupils' and teachers' awareness of what is entailed in assignments involving information-handling, while for Northedge (1990), advice on how an academic task might be tackled is set firmly in the context not only of a range of credible subject-specific examples, but also of explanations of what particular tasks are seeking to achieve .

One of the most tangible aspects of this shift, however, has been in terms of approaches to group-based activities (see for example Hills, 1979). A thoroughgoing and pioneering example is provided by Gibbs (1981) who maps out procedures for a series of workshop exercises and articulates the rationale from which they stem. Rather than inculcating rigid techniques, Gibbs' aim is to promote in students a questioning, self-analytic attitude to studying. Students are encouraged to articulate their own perceptions of study demands and to pool knowledge of the strategies they have developed in their everyday studying. Above all, the emphasis is on clarifying and exploring intentions and purposes — key determinants of students' approaches to learning, as the present book clearly shows.

Learning-to-learn activities of the kind Gibbs has developed are of course adaptable to different subject and course settings — indeed, they are most likely to have a real impact on students when they are focused in this way. Their impact is also likely to be stronger when they form part of a wider series of measures to embed learning-to-learn within everyday curricula. One outstanding example of such an initiative is represented by the work of Eizenberg (1986, 1988), who has discussed what he calls 'an orchestrated set of interventions in teaching and assessment', explicitly rooted in recent research findings on student learning. The context for these interventions was the development of a new programme of anatomy for first- and second-year medical students at the University of Melbourne. Since students studying anatomy and similar pre-clinical programmes encounter a large volume of factual information, such programmes, Eizenberg suggests, are particularly prone to inducing surface or atomistic approaches to learning.

Eizenberg's intervention strategy was therefore a two-fold one which took into account both the referential ('what') and the structural ('how') aspects of learning. The referential component, summarised in Figure 15.1, sought to convey to students the importance of quality of understanding rather than quantity of information. Departmental handbooks which each set out a syllabus and the detailed set of objectives which underpinned it played a key role in this component of the strategy. As far as the structural component was concerned, on the other hand, a fundamental reorganisation of the teaching programme was called for:

A conventional and sequential course of instruction (which had by its very structure inadvertently promoted the accumulation of isolated facts) was converted to a programme that enabled the body to be viewed as an integrated whole. Patterns were revealed where the specifics could be seen in relation to the general principles, with multiple opportunities for overview and review. (Eizenberg, 1988, p. 186)

TABLE 15.1

Interventions in Curriculum, Teaching and Assessment

(from Eizenberg, 1986, p. 186)

Action taken	Rationale from research findings
Curriculum	
• linking curriculum to faculty goals	*displaying to students and teachers*
• matching curriculum, teaching and assessment	*to clarify goals and standards*
• incorporating professional applications	*to increase vocational relevance*
• defining 'essential' information	*to rationalise workload*
• selecting appropriate textbooks	*which encourage understanding*
Teaching	
• analysing the derivation of new terms	*rather than encouraging memorisation*
• emphasising principles and concepts	*rather than accumulation of details*
• creating opportunities for 'good' teaching	*rather than 'covering the syllabus'*
• actively engaging students	*by learning from problem solving*
Assessment	
• providing adequate feedback	*to monitor progress and minimise anxiety*
• constructing assessments	*which encourage understanding*
• marking strategies	*to recognise and reward understanding*

Encouraging though such initiatives are, this still leaves untouched the issue of individual guidance. Our research findings have prompted questions — about the quality of current procedures for monitoring student learning and providing individually directed guidance — which can only be briefly raised rather than treated thoroughly here. Essays, reports and other forms of coursework assignment represent an arena of learning where feedback is likely to be at its fullest and most penetrating, yet as Chapter 7 indicated, some students may fail to grasp the import of their tutor's comments, even in a course setting where such comments are more than usually attentive. Indeed, it appears as though tutors' comments often amount to summary judgements rather than specific diagnoses, alluding to an academic form of discourse which is largely tacit and thus invisible to students who have not already perceived its distinctive features (Hounsell, 1987). Thus a student may be informed that an essay is "poorly structured", or that "you fail to make your points as clearly and as tellingly as you ought", but not be shown in what respects the essay content lacks structure or cogency, nor understand why careful attention to these aspects might be thought essential in an academic essay. Similarly, a student may be urged to "make a plan before you commit your thoughts to paper", but the more fundamental issue, of precisely what it is the student should be planning (Hounsell, 1984a) is not addressed. At the core of the problem is what Bruner (1966, p. 151) has described elsewhere as *telling* out of context rather than *showing* in context. Yet even where well-documented comments have made the diagnosis readily comprehensible, the gulf which lies between diagnosis and remedy may remain unbridged and, for some students, unbridgeable without sustained support.

To conclude this section of the chapter, a major challenge for lecturers is to seek ways of more firmly integrating guidance on learning into everyday teaching. That is not to argue that study counsellors and specialist advisers have no role to play. But the chief responsibility for teaching students to learn the fundamentals of what Raaheim (1981) has called academic discourse should lie with tutors themselves. For they are the subject specialists, who know best the complexities of their discipline, its characteristic modes of analysis and discourse, and the special demands it makes of its practitioners. Learning-to-learn is not merely redemptive (Roueche and Snow, 1977), an optional adjunct for the weaker student, but something from which all students can benefit. As Chapter 13 showed, perceived good teaching — and particularly, help with studying — is strongly associated with an orientation by students towards meaning and understanding. As a fully integrated part of an undergraduate course, learning-to-learn can contribute to the quality of student learning.

Creating a Context for Learning

Skill in learning, as Lennart Svensson reminded us in Chapter 4, is not equivalent to skill in studying. In coming to a full understanding of the experience of learning, it is also necessary to consider the course and institutional contexts in which learning takes place.

The contextual dimension of learning has been the third of the threads which weave together the fabric of this book. A knowledge of students' perceptions of course setting was an important backcloth to understanding learning in lectures and in essay-writing, while in problem-solving, as we saw in Chapter 8, students' approaches were almost wholly governed by their responses to the task in its educational setting. But it was Chapter 13 which dealt directly with the theme of context, disclosing its pervasive influences upon students' experience of learning. The chapter drew attention to critical differences between subject areas in the weight given to contrasting learning styles and in the varying guises which deep and surface approaches typically assumed. It provided evidence of strong associations, across a spectrum of disciplines, between students' orientations to studying and their perceptions of assessment, of workload, of the quality of teaching and of the degree of choice over content and method of study. It also demonstrated how students' approaches to a specific task could be frustrated or facilitated by interest and prior knowledge, and how overloaded syllabuses and inappropriate forms of assessment could push students towards rote-learning and reproduction.

This searching analysis of the context of learning has several important implications for an experiential conception of the teaching-learning process. In the first instance, as is noted in Chapter 13 itself, it indicates that the strength of students' commitment to pursuing understanding may be just as much a function of their experiences in a particular course setting as of any individual qualities which they bring to their academic studies. It is therefore misleading and unjust to attribute poor academic achievement to inherently 'weak' or 'unmotivated' students. Interest, commitment and approach are products of the interaction between student and situation. Second, to view the 'impact' or 'effectiveness' of teaching solely in terms of teaching methods or the quality of their execution by lecturers, as countless studies of undergraduate teaching have tried to do, is narrow and inadequate. Student learning is subject to a dynamic and richly complex array of influences which are both direct and indirect, intentional and unintended. This web of influences spans assessment procedures and course content and structure as well as teaching, and it takes in lecturers' perceived commitment to teaching and their readiness to help with study difficulties as well as their degree of mastery of teaching methods.

It follows too, as Paul Ramsden made clear in Chapter 13, that initiatives which flow from an understanding of context must proceed along a combination of paths and recognise that lecturers' perceptions are not necessarily the perceptions of students:

> It is useless, for example, simply to tell students that verbatim reproduction of information in an examination is wrong, to expect this warning to discourage surface approaches, and to blame the students when it does not. If students feel that there is insufficient time to study the examined topics properly (perhaps because of the demands of other courses), or if they have experienced inadequate teaching, or if they are given high marks for reproducing lecture notes, or if their previous knowledge within the area is insufficiently developed, then they will feel constrained to use surface approaches.

Lecturers can try to provide greater freedom in learning, exercised within a defined and supportive framework that does not grant the anxious student too much autonomy too suddenly. When they plan their courses, devise assignments or set examination questions, lecturers can make strenuous efforts to avoid seeming to demand surface approaches or to reward students who adopt them. And lecturers can do more to help students improve their approaches to learning, in ways indicated earlier in the present chapter.

Nonetheless, if it is students' contextual perceptions which are paramount, how are lecturers to determine what these are? In part at least, like student-centred teaching (Bligh, 1982, p. 19), a sensitivity to context springs from an attitude of mind, but a student perspective cannot simply be guessed at or predicted. Positive efforts need to be made to engage in dialogue with students.

We noted earlier that coming to know students as individuals is widely valued in contemporary higher education, and there are no necessary barriers to an equivalent emphasis on open discussion of course perceptions and learning experiences, or to course feedback questionnaires which invite students to share their perceptions rather than simply rating their 'satisfaction' on predetermined items. Course demands and assessment expectations have often been tacit for fear of 'spoon-feeding' students or leading them to devote too much of their time to assessed work. Yet paradoxically, a lack of openness and a reluctance to clarify or patiently explain may have precisely the opposite effect to that intended: mechanical or reproductive strategies, born of student uncertainty, anxiety or disenchantment.

Teaching as a Holistic Strategy

Thus far we have considered teaching-learning process under three broad headings: teaching for understanding; teaching students how to learn; and creating a context for learning. But though convenient for the purposes of discussion, this risks fragmenting what should be seen interconnectedly. The three headings are representative less of distinct areas than of complementary and interrelated aspects of teaching in higher education. Indeed, to seek to view teaching in the round, conjunctively and holistically, is perhaps the most important element in an experiential conception. This might seem a very obvious point to make, but obvious or not, it has been at odds with many aspects of contemporary practice. Just as it has been commonplace to consider lecturers and teaching in isolation from students and learning, so have there been long-established but unwarranted boundaries which separate discussion of curriculum from discussion of assessment and discussion of teaching. This compartmentalisation is apparent not only in the literature of education, but also in the procedures which many colleges and universities have followed in designing and administering courses.

Marking and assessment schemes may be devised or modified without reference to the possible consequences for what or how students learn, or without regard to any ensuing tensions between assessment as feedback and assessment as evaluation of student achievement — or indeed without an alertness to what is called in Chapter 9 the 'bifurcation of attention' during revision between understanding the content and preparing to answer exam questions on it. How many academics, it might reasonably be asked, genuinely share Lewis Elton's view that "the overriding purpose of assessment is that it should encourage learning in consonance with my declared student learning aims" Elton (1982, p. 107)? Where conflicts do arise between assessment and teaching strategies, a holistic view can help to resolve them, as an Australian study suggests (Newble and Jaeger, 1983). In the School of Medicine at Adelaide University, final-year assessment was revised so as to give greater weight to clinical competence. But the effect of the reform was in precisely the opposite direction. Once it became apparent to students that the risk of failing the new ward-based clinical assessment was low, they began to spend little time in the wards and made studying for the much more hazardous theoretical component of final assessment a priority. Only when the faculty responded to this "selective negligence" (Snyder, 1971) by introducing a more demanding and innovative form of clinical assessment did a more balanced set of priorities emerge. A consideration of the situation in the round therefore made it possible to restore equilibrium without abandoning the desire to innovate which had prompted the earlier reforms.

Another form of compartmentalisation occurs when institutional norms are established for 'course contact hours' or 'appropriate' ratios of large-group lectures to small-group discussions, but in isolation from consideration of specific course content, students' workloads or the level and incidence of one-to-one guidance which may be essential if students are to achieve genuine understanding. When students then press for more individual help, tutors may be driven to plead, and with justification, that their formal teaching load and their marking commitments make this impractical. A more unified view, weighing the respective needs and perspectives of lecturers and students, could provide the basis for a more balanced strategy. A parallel problem may arise because, especially following the widespread introduction of modular schemes of study, only students themselves may fully perceive what a particular selection of course units implies for their workload. In fact, few academics are probably well-informed about the basics of students' working life. One small-scale study (Hounsell and Ramsden, 1978) has suggested that lecturers not only lack, as we might expect, knowledge of ways in which students tackle the learning tasks assigned them, but that they are uncertain even of how much time students spend on such tasks. A survey of coursework assignments in a range of disciplines (Roe, 1974) revealed similar shortcomings. Students' advance estimates of the percentage of their study time an assignment would take to complete were double the figures suggested by their tutors, while the proportion of their time the students actually spent on those assignments turned out to be nearly three times the tutors' original estimates. Such disparities suggest that tutors' expectations of what students might reasonably accomplish have little grounding in reality. Yet such expectations, based on largely unquestioned yardsticks, critically determine the decisions taken on teaching methods, study activities, syllabus content and assessment.

It is also desirable that in a holistic view, learning and teaching are seen developmentally. Courses in higher education already reflect this in some respects. Many curricula, for example, are designed to offer steadily greater opportunity for choice and specialisation, building from a broad and secure foundation of subject-matter in the first or second years of the course. The curriculum of the Medical School of the University of Newcastle, New South Wales, shows how that same structured and gradualist approach can be taken to how students learn. In setting out its overall objectives,

> The Faculty wished to place emphasis not only on the content to be mastered by its students, but also on the process by which students should be assisted towards the stipulated goals. (Engel and Clarke, 1979, p. 17)

TABLE 15. 2

Skills required for independent learning

(from the School of Medicine, University of Newcastle, NSW)

Students will be able and willing to:
- recognise their assets and limitations
- identify what aspects of knowledge, understanding, skills and attitudes they need to acquire
- locate the information and experiences they require for this learning
- examine critically the evidence on which scientific information is based
- organise their learning activities in a pattern that will be both effective and efficient for them
- monitor their progress in the acquisition of new competence
- monitor their performance as future physicians
- evaluate their educational experiences

An aim which the school was particularly keen to stress was that students should become self-reliant in their learning. One step which was therefore taken was to identify the skills required for independent learning (see Figure 15.2), while another was to abandon lectures as a method of teaching. But it was also seen as crucial to plan a curricular and teaching strategy which systematically fostered the growth of independent learning:

> From the first day of the first term students are encouraged to identify what they need to learn in order to solve and manage problems. The main thrust of this approach is centred, but by no means exclusively, on problem-based learning. Here the students are helped to ask themselves questions in a logical order, so that the resultant sequence of learning will lead to the answers that can be applied to the problem in hand. This approach is reflected in the way in which each first problem-solving group meeting is organized and the way in which the related learning material is planned. (Engel and Clarke, 1979, p. 24)

Initially students are helped to plan their learning and locate the necessary information through the provision of course materials which include detailed lists of objectives, resource sheets and 'learning units'. The materials are very specific during the early part of the undergraduate course to enable students to become accustomed to the new way of organising their studies, and there is close monitoring of achievement and strong tutorial support. As the student's studies progress, however,

> Such guidance will become less and less detailed until the mere presentation of a patient-centred problem will enable students to define their own objectives, seek out the necessary information and apply it to the solution or management of the problem. (Engel and Clarke, p. 24)

Teaching Reflectively

One of the conclusions of a project on small-group teaching in universities was as follows:

> It did not seem common for teachers to combine in tutorials, or to visit each other's, or to have much discussion about the rationale of the various administrative arrangements ... Often participants in our discussions had not had other opportunities of discussing their teaching with colleagues, and only in a very few cases had teachers discussed their intentions or methods with their students. (Abercrombie and Terry, 1978, p. 148)

Similar observations could be made about all forms of teaching in higher education, and an underlying aim of this chapter has been to show the need for more considered and systematic reflection about the teaching-learning process. More specifically, we have tried to demonstrate how academics can ally their own experiences and perspectives to an understanding of those of their students, and thus learn from an experiential conception of teaching. We have indicated directions which fresh initiatives might follow, but without prescribing fixed routes forward, for every teaching-learning situation is in its own way unique and calls for strategies which are sensitively tailored to the particularities of curriculum purposes, to the nature of the discipline concerned and to characteristics of the course, departmental and institutional setting. Reflective teaching and the quality of learning go hand in hand.

Acknowledgements

The author would like to express his sincere thanks to the Swedish Institute and to the Department of Education, University of Gothenburg. Their generous support made the preparation of this chapter possible. For the examples described in the section entitled 'Building from existing conceptions', I am indebted to Graham Gibbs and Lennart Svensson.

Notes

1. Of the many examples now to be found of books focusing on teaching in higher education generally, those which might be singled out include the seminal work of Beard (1972), later revised by Beard and Hartley (1984) and the handbooks of Hall and Cannon (1975), McKeachie (1978), Brown and Atkins (1988) and Gibbs and Habeshaw (1989). Discussions of specific teaching-learning methods are now legion, but those which can justly claim a ground-breaking role include Bligh (1972) and Brown (1978) on the lecture and Abercrombie (Abercrombie, 1980; Abercrombie and Terry, 1978) and Rudduck (1978) on small-group teaching. An early illustration of the advocacy of a fresh approach is the work of Keller and Sherman (1974) on individualised instruction, while more contemporary examples would be represented by, *inter alia*, Denicolo, Entwistle and Hounsell (1992) and Gibbs (1994b).

2. Unit 5. Modern Britain: The Economic Base. In: *Understanding Society* (D102). Milton Keynes: The Open University. p. 46.

Bibliographic References

Abercrombie, M.L.J. *The anatomy of judgement.* London: Hutchinson, 1960.
— *Aims and techniques of group teaching.* Rev. edn. Guildford: SRHE, 1980.
Abercrombie, M. L. J. and Terry, P. M. *Talking to learn: improving teaching and learning in small groups.* Guildford: SRHE, 1978.
Anderson, C. *Learning to discuss, discussing to learn: a study of tutorial groups in a faculty of social sciences.* Unpublished Ph.D. thesis, University of Edinburgh, 1995.
— A study of discussion classes. I — The perceptions of students. *Higher Education* (in press).
— A study of discussion classes. II — The practice of tutoring. *Higher Education* (in press).
Ashby, E. The structure of higher education: a world view. *Higher Education,* 1973, *2,* 142–151.
Ausubel, D. P., Novak, J. S., and Hanesian, H. *Educational psychology: a cognitive view.* New York: Holt, Rinehart & Winston, 1978.
Bantock, G. H. Educational research: a criticism. *Harvard Educational Review,* 1961, *31,* 264–280.
Bartlett, F. C. *Remembering: a study in experimental and social psychology.* London: Cambridge University Press, 1932.
— The bearing of experimental psychology upon human skilled performance. *Journal of Industrial Medicine,* 1951, *8,* 209.
— *Thinking.* New York: Basic Books, 1958.
Baumgart, N. L. and Johnstone, J. N. Some implications of continuous assessment as an evaluation practice. *The Australian University,* 1974, *12* , 103–124.
Beard, R. and Hartley, J. *Teaching and learning in higher education.* Rev. edn. London: Harper & Row, 1984.
Beaty, E. and Morgan, A. Developing skill in learning. *Open Learning,* 1992, *7* (3), 3–11.
Becher, T. Editorial. *Studies in Higher Education,* 1978, *3* , 1–3.
Becker, H. S., Geer, B. and Hughes, E. C. *Making the grade: the academic side of college life.* New York: Wiley, 1968.
Belenky, M.F., Clinchy, B.M., Goldberg, N.R. and Tarule, J. M. *Women's ways of knowing.* New York: Basic Books, 1986.
Bennett, R. (Ed.), *First class answers in History.* London: Weidenfeld &Nicholson, 1974.
Berger, J. *Pig earth.* London: Writers' and Readers' Publishing Cooperative, 1979.
Biggs, J. B. Faculty patterns in study behaviour. *Australian Journal of Psychology,* 1970, *22,* 161–174.
— Individual and group differences in study processes. *British Journal of Educational Psychology,* 1978, *48,* 266–279.
— What do inventories of students' learning processes really measure? A theoretical review and clarification, *British Journal of Educational Psychology,* 1993, *63,* 3–19.

√Biggs, J. B. and Collis, K. F. *Evaluating the quality of learning.* New York and Sydney: Academic Press, 1982.

Bligh, D. A. *What's the use of lectures?* 3rd edn. Harmondsworth: Penguin, 1972.

— Recommendations for learning. In D.A. Bligh (Ed.), *Professionalism and flexibility in learning.* (Leverhulme Programme of Study into the Future of Higher Education, vol. 6). Guildford: SRHE, 1982, 11–30.

Bliss, J. and Ogborn, J. *Student reactions to undergraduate science.* London: Heinemann, 1977.

Bloom, B. S. Thought processes in lectures and discussions. *Journal of General Education,* 1953, *3* , 160–167.

— *Taxonomy of educational objectives. Handbook 1: Cognitive domain.* New York: Longmans Green, 1956.

Boden, M. A. *Purposive explanation in psychology.* Sussex: Harvester Press, 1978.

\ Boud, D. (Ed.), *Developing student autonomy in learning.* London: Kogan Page, 1981.

Branthwaite, A., Trueman, M. and Hartley, J. Writing essays: the actions and strategies of students . In J. Hartley (Ed.), *The psychology of written communication.* London: Kogan Page, 1980, 98–109.

Brennan, J. L. and Percy, K. A. What do students want? An analysis of staff and student perceptions in British higher education. In A. Bonboir (Ed.), *Instructional design in higher education.* Louvain: European Association for Research and Development in Higher Education, 1977.

Britton, J., Burgess, T., Martin, N., McLeod, A. and Rosen, H. *The development of writing abilities, 11–18.* London: Macmillan Education, 1975.

Brown, G. *Lecturing and explaining.* London: Methuen, 1978.

Brown, G. and Atkins, M. *Effective teaching in higher education.* London: Methuen, 1988.

Brown, W. F. and Holtzman, W. H. *Manual of the survey of study habits and attitudes.* New York: Psychological Corporation, 1966.

Brumby, M. N. *Students' perceptions and learning styles associated with the concept of evolution by natural selection.* Unpublished Ph.D. thesis, University of Surrey, 1979.

Bruner, J. S. *Toward a theory of instruction.* Cambridge, Mass.: Harvard University Press, 1966.

⌐ Bruner J., Goodenough J. and Austin J. *A study of thinking.* New York: Wiley, 1956.

Butler, J. A. Use of teaching methods within the lecture format. *Medical Teacher,* 1992, *14,* 11–25.

Byrne, C. Tutor-marked assignments at the Open University: a question of reliability. *Assessment in Higher Education,* 1980, *5* , 150–167.

Centra, J. A. *Student ratings of instruction and their relationship to student learning.* Princeton, N.J.: Educational Testing Service, 1976.

Choppin, B. H. L. *et al. The prediction of academic success.* Slough: National Foundation for Educational Research, 1973.

Clanchy, J. and Ballard, B. *How to write essays: a practical guide for students.* Melbourne: Longman Cheshire, 1983 . (Orig. publ. as *Essay writing for students,* 1981).

Clark, B. R. and Trow, M. The organizational context. In T. M. Newcombe and E. K. Wilson (Eds.), *College peer groups.* Chicago: Aldine, 1966.

Coats, W. D., Swierengal, B. and Wickert, J. Student perceptions of teachers: a factor analytic study. *Journal of Education Research,* 1972, *65,* 357–360.

Cohen, A. M., Trent, W. and Rose, C. Evaluation of teaching. In R. M. W. Travers (Ed.), *Handbook of research on education.* Chicago: Rand McNally, 1973.

Collier, K. G. Teaching methods in higher education: the changing scene with special reference to small-group work. *Higher Education Research and Development,* 1985, *4,* 3–27.

Collis, K. F. *A study of concrete and formal operations in school mathematics. A Piagetian viewpoint.* Melbourne: Australian Council for Educational Research, 1975.

Cowell, M. D. and Entwistle, N. J. Personality, study attitudes and academic performance in a technical college. *British Journal of Educational Psychology,* 1971, *41,* 85–89.

Craik, F. M. and Lockhart, R. S. Levels of processing: a framework for memory research. *Journal of Verbal Learning and Verbal Behavior,* 1972, *11,* 671–684.

Crick, P. and Ralph, T. Towards an analysis of language in the further education classroom. *Journal of Further and Higher Education,* 1980, *4,* 42–50.

Dahlgren, L. O. *Qualitative differences in learning as a function of content oriented guidance.* Gothenburg: Acta Universitatis Gothoburgensis, 1975.

— Effects of university education on the conception of reality. (Paper presented at the 4th International Conference on Improving University Teaching. Aachen, F.R. Germany, July 26–29, 1978.) *Reports from the Department of Education, University of Gothenburg,* 1978, 65.

Dahlgren, L. O. and Marton, F. Students' conceptions of subject matter: an aspect of learning and teaching in higher education. *Studies in Higher Education,* 1978, *3,* 25–35.

Dahlgren, L. O. and Pramling, I. Hogskolestudier och omvarldsuppfattning. (Undergraduate studies and conceptions of reality.) *Reports from the Department of Education, University of Gothenburg,* 1982.

Dahllöf, U. Nya fakta om de fria fakulteterna. (New facts about the open faculties.) *Dagens Nyheter,* Sept. 10, 1968.

Dale, R. Phenomenological perspectives and the sociology of the school. *Educational Review,* 1973, *25,* 175–189.

Denicolo, P. , Entwistle, N. J. and Hounsell, D. *What is active learning?* (Effective learning and teaching in higher education, Module 1). Sheffield: CVCP Universities' Staff Development and Training Unit, 1992.

Dewey, J. *Democracy and education.* New York: Macmillan, 1916.

Douglas, J. *Understanding everyday life.* London: Routledge & Kegan Paul, 1971.

Dubin, R. and Taveggia, T. *The teaching-learning paradox.* Eugene: University of Oregon Press, 1969.

Duffy, T., Lowyck, J. and Jonasson, D. (Eds.), *Designing environments for constructive learning.* Berlin: Springer-Verlag, 1993.

Durbridge, N. Whose dream? A case study of educational multimedia design and Art explorer. PLUM Paper No. 53. Milton Keynes: Institute of Educational Technology, Open University, 1995.

Ebbinghaus, H. *Memory. A contribution to experimental psychology.* New York: Dover, 1964. (Originally publ. 1885.)

Edfelt, A. A general model for the reading process. *Research Bulletins from the Institute of Education,* University of Stockholm, 1981, *9* (3).

Eizenberg, N. Applying student learning research to practice. In J.A. Bowden (Ed.), *Student learning: research into practice.* Parkville: Centre for the Study of Higher Education, University of Melbourne, 1986, 21–60.

— Approaches to learning anatomy: developing a programme for preclinical medical students. In P. Ramsden (Ed.), *Improving learning: new perspectives* . London: Kogan Page, 1988, 178–198.

Elton, L. Assessment for learning. In D.A. Bligh (Ed.), *Professionalism and flexibility in learning.* (Leverhulme Programme of Study into the Future of Higher Education.) Guildford: SRHE, 1982, 106–135.

— Enterprise in higher education: an agent for change. In P. Knight (Ed.), *Staff development and institutional change.* SEDA Paper No. 83. Birmingham: Staff Education and Development Association, 1994.

Elton, L. R. B. and Laurillard, D. M. Trends in research on student learning. *Studies in Higher Education,* 1979, *4,* 87–102.

Engel, C. E. and Clarke, M. R. Medical education with a difference. *Programmed Learning and Educational Technology,* 1979, *16,* 70–87.

Entwistle, A. C. and Entwistle, N. J. Experiences of understanding in revising for degree examinations. *Learning and Instruction,* 1992,2, 1–22.

Entwistle, N. J. Complementary paradigms for research and development work in higher education. In W. A. Verreck (Ed.), *Methodological problems in research and development in higher education.* Amsterdam: Swets & Zeitlinger, 1974, 75–88.

— How students learn: information processing, intellectual development and confrontation. *Higher Education Bulletin,* 1975, *3,* 129–148.

— The verb 'to learn' takes the accusative. *British Journal of Educational Psychology,* 1976, *46,* 1–3.

— Stages, levels, styles or strategies: dilemmas in the description of thinking. *Educational Review,* 1979, *31,* 123–132.

— Motivation to learn: conceptualisations and practicalities. *British Journal of Educational Studies,* 1987, *XXV,* 129–148.

— Motivational factors in students' approaches to learning. In R.R. Schmeck (Ed.), *Learning strategies and learning styles.* New York: Plenum, 1988a.

— *Styles of learning and teaching.* London: David Fulton, 1988b.

— Frameworks for understanding as experienced in essay writing and in preparing for examinations. *Educational Psychologist ,* 1995a, *30,* 47–54.

— The nature of academic understanding. In G. Kaufmann, T. Helstrup, K.H. Teigen (Eds.) *Problem solving and cognitive processes.* Bergen: Fagbokforlaget, 1995b, 347–368.

— Approaches to learning and forms of understanding. In B. Dart and G. Boulton-Lewis (Eds.), *Teaching and learning in higher education: from theory to practice.* Hawthorn, Vic.: Australian Council for Educational Research (in press).

Entwistle, N. J. and Brennan, T. The academic performance of students II — Types of successful students. *British Journal of Educational Psychology,* 1971, *41,* 268–276.

Entwistle, N. J. and Entwistle, A.C. Contrasting forms of understanding for degree examinations: the student experience and its implications. *Higher Education,* 1991, *22*, 205–227.

Entwistle, N. J., Hanley, M. and Ratcliffe, G. Approaches to learning and levels of understanding. *British Journal of Educational Psychology,* 1979a, *5*, 99–114.

Entwistle, N. J., Hanley, M. and Hounsell, D. J. Identifying distinctive approaches to studying. *Higher Education,* 1979b, *8*, 365–380.

Entwistle, N. J. and Marton, F. Knowledge objects: understandings constituted through intensive academic study. *British Journal of Educational Psychology,* 1994, *64*, 161–178.

Entwistle, N. J. and Percy, K. A. Educational objectives and student performance within the binary system. In *Research into higher education, 1970.* London: SRHE, 1971.

— Critical thinking or conformity? An investigation of the aims and outcomes of higher education. In *Research into higher education, 1973.* London: SRHE, 1974.

Entwistle, N. J., Percy, K. A. and Nisbet, J. B. *Educational objectives and academic performance in higher education.* (Vol. 2). Unpublished research report, Department of Educational Research, University of Lancaster, 1971.

Entwistle, N. J. and Ramsden, P. *Understanding student learning.* London: Croom Helm, 1983.

Entwistle, N.J. and Tait, H. Approaches to learning, evaluations of teaching, and preferences for contrasting academic environments. *Higher Education,* 1990, *19*, 169–194.

Entwistle, N. J. and Wilson, J. D. *Degrees of excellence: the academic achievement game.* London: Hodder & Stoughton, 1977.

Eraut, M., MacKenzie, N. and Papps, I. The mythology of educational development: reflections on a three-year study of economics teaching. *British Journal of Educational Technology,* 1975, *6* (3), 20–34.

Fearn-Wannan, H. Students' perceptions of lecturers as determinants of academic performance in first-year chemistry. In D. Billing (Ed.), *Course design and student learning.* Guildford: SRHE, 1980.

Finger, J. A. and Schlesser, G. E. Non-intellective predictors of academic success in school and college. *School Review,* 1965, *73*, 14–29.

Fransson, A. On qualitative differences in learning. IV—Effects of motivation and test anxiety on process and outcome. *British Journal of Educational Psychology,* 1977, *47*, 244–257.

Frederick, J. *et al. Learning skills: a review of needs and services to university students.* Melbourne: University of Melbourne, Centre for the Study of Higher Education, 1981.

Gaff, J. G., Crombag, H. F. M. and Chang, T. M. Environments for learning in a Dutch university. *Higher Education,* 1976, *5*, 285–299.

Gagné, R. M. *The conditions of learning.* 3rd edn. New York: Holt, Rinehart & Winston, 1977.

Gardner, H. *Frames of mind.* London: Heinemann, 1984.

Geertz, C. *The interpretation of culture.* New York: Basic Books, 1973.

Gibbs, G. *Teaching students to learn: a student-centred approach.* Milton Keynes: Open University Press, 1981.

— *Improving the quality of student learning*. Bristol: Technical & Educational Services, 1992.

— *Improving student learning: theory and practice*. Headington, Oxford: Oxford Centre for Staff Development, Oxford Brookes University, 1994a.

— *Course design for resource-based learning*. Oxford: Oxford Centre for Staff Development,Oxford Brookes University, 1994b.

Gibbs, G. and Habeshaw, T. *Preparing to teach: an introduction to effective teaching in higher education*. Bristol: Technical & Educational Services, 1989.

Gibson, E. and Levin, H. *The psychology of reading*. Cambridge, Mass.: MIT Press, 1975.

Glaser, B. G. and Strauss, A. L. *The discovery of grounded theory. Strategies for qualitative research*. New York: Aldine, 1967.

Goodman, N. *Ways of worldmaking*. Sussex: Harvester Press, 1978.

Grieve, C. Knowledge increment assessed for three methodologies of teaching physiology. *Medical Teacher,* 1992, *14,* 27–32

Hall, W. C. and Cannon, R. *University teaching*. Adelaide: Advisory Centre for University Education, University of Adelaide, 1975.

Hartley, J. (Ed.), *The psychology of written communication*. London: Kogan Page, 1980.

Hasselgren, B. *Ways of apprehending children at play*. Gothenburg: Acta Universitatis Gothoburgensis, 1982.

Havelock, E. A. *Preface to Plato*. Cambridge, Mass.: Harvard University Press, 1963.

Heywood, J. *Assessment of undergraduate performance*. (Background paper, Universities' Conference, Mar. 27, 1969). London: CVCP, 1969.

Hildebrand, M. The character and skills of the effective professor. *Journal of Higher Education,* 1973, *44,* 41– 60.

Hilgard, E. R. and Bower, G. H. *Theories of learning*. 3rd edn. New Jersey: Prentice-Hall, 1981.

Hills, P. J. (Ed.), *Study courses and counselling*. London: SRHE, 1979.

Hirst, P. What is teaching? *Journal of Curriculum Studies,* 1971, *3* , 5–18.

Hounsell, D. Learning to learn: research and development in student learning. *Higher Education,* 1979, *8* , 453– 469.

— Essay planning and essay writing. *Higher Education Research and Development,* (Australia), 1984a , *3* (1), 13–31.

— *Students' conceptions of essay-writing*. Unpublished Ph. D. thesis, University of Lancaster, 1984b.

— Essay writing and the quality of feedback. In J. T. E. Richardson *et al* . (Eds.), *Student learning: research in education and cognitive psychology.* Milton Keynes: SRHE & Open University Press, 1987, 109 – 119.

— Towards an anatomy of academic discourse: meaning and context in the undergraduate essay. In R. Säljö (Ed.), *The written world: studies in literate thought and action*. Berlin: Springer-Verlag, 1988, 161 – 177.

Hounsell, D. and Ramsden, P. Roads to learning: an empirical study of students' approaches to coursework and assessment. In D. Billing (Ed.), *Course design and student learning*. Guildford: SRHE, 1978, 132–139.

Hughes-Jones, H. A. Students' perception of the reasons for academic success and failure. In D. Billing (Ed.), *Indicators of performance*. (Papers presented at the 15th Annual Conference of the Society for Research into Higher Education.) Guildford: SRHE, 1980, 151–154.

Hunter, I. M. L. An exceptional memory. *British Journal of Psychology,* 1977, *68,* 155–164.

Johansson, B. Krafter vid rorelse. Teknologers uppfattningar av nagra grundlag gande fenomen inom mekaniken. (Forces in motion. Technological students' conceptions of some basic phenomena in Mechanics.) *Reports from the Department of Education, University of Gothenburg,* 1981, 14.

Johnson, H. C., Rhodes, D. M. and Rummery, R. G. The assessment of teaching in higher education. Part 1: a critical retrospect. *Higher Education,* 1975, *4,* 173–199.

Kalmus, H. The seeds of modern genetics. *Times Higher Education Supplement,* Feb. 10, 1984, 15.

Katona, G. *Organizing and memorizing.* New York: Columbia University Press, 1940.

Keller, F. S. and Sherman, J. G. *The Keller Plan handbook.* Menlo Park, California: W. A. Benjamin, 1974.

Kozeki, B. Motives and motivational styles in education. In N.J. Entwistle (Ed.), *New directions in educational psychology: learning and teaching.* Brighton: Falmer Press, 1984.

Laurillard, D. M. *A study of the relationship between some of the cognitive and contextual factors in student learning.* Unpublished Ph.D. thesis, University of Surrey, 1978.

— The processes of student learning. *Higher Education,* 1979, *8,* 395– 409.

— The different forms of learning in psychology and education. In J.H.E. Richardson, M.W. Eysenck and D. Warren-Piper (Eds.), *Student learning.* London: SRHE & Open University Press, 1987.

— The pedagogical limitations of generative student models. *Instructional Science,* 1988, *17,* 235– 250.

— *Rethinking university teaching: a framework for the effective use of educational technology.* London: Routledge, 1993.

Layton, D. (Ed.), *University teaching in transition.* Edinburgh: Oliver & Boyd, 1968.

Lindsay, P. H. and Norman, D. A. *Human information processing.* New York: Academic Press, 1972.

Luker, P. A. *Academic staff development in universities with specific reference to small group teaching.* Unpublished Ph.D. thesis, University of Nottingham, 1989.

Luria, A. R. *The mind of a mnemonist.* London: Cape, 1969.

McCracken, J. and Laurillard, D. A study of conceptions in visual representations: a phenomenographic investigation of learning about geological maps. Paper presented at the Ed-Media 94 World Conference in Educational Multimedia and Hypermedia, Vancouver, Canada, June, 1994.

McKeachie, W. J. *Teaching tips: a guidebook for the beginning college teacher.* 7th edn. Lexington, Mass.: D. C. Heath, 1978.

MacKenzie, K. Some thoughts on tutoring by written correspondence in the Open University. *Teaching at a Distance,* 1974, *1,* 45–51.

Marland, M. *et al. Information skills in the secondary curriculum.* London: Methuen Schools Council, 1981.

Marris, D. *The experience of higher education.* London: Routledge & Kegan Paul, 1964.

Marshall, L. A. and Rowland, F. *A guide to learning independently.* Milton Keynes: Open University Press, 1983. (Orig. publ. Melbourne: Longman Cheshire, 1981.)

Marton, F. *Structural dynamics of learning.* Stockholm: Almqvist & Wiksell, 1970.

— Inlarning och studiefardighet. (Learning and study skill.) *Reports from the Department of Education, University of Gothenburg,* 1974, 121.

— What does it take to learn? In N. J. Entwistle and D. Hounsell (Eds.), *How Students Learn.* Lancaster: Institute for Post-Compulsory Education, 1975a, 125–138. (Reprinted in N.J. Entwistle (Ed.), *Strategies for research and development in higher education.* Amsterdam: Swets & Zeitlinger/Council of Europe, 1976).

— On non-verbatim learning. I. Level of processing and level of outcome. *Scandinavian Journal of Psychology,* 1975b, *16,* 273–279.

— On non-verbatim learning. II. The erosion of a task-induced learning algorithm. *Scandinavian Journal of Psychology,* 1976a, *17,* 41–48.

— Omvarldsuppfattning hos vuxna — enprojektbeskrivning. (Conceptions of reality in adults — a description of a research project.) *Reports from the Department of Education, University of Gothenburg,* 1976b, *144.*

— Describing conceptions of the world around us. *Reports from the Department of Education, University of Gothenburg,* 1978, *66.*

— Phenomenography — Describing conceptions of the world around us. *Instructional Science,* 1981, *10, 177*–200.

— Towards a phenomenography of learning. III. Experience and conceptualization. *Reports from the Department of Education, University of Gothenburg,* 1982, *8.*

— Phenomenography. In T.Husen and N. Postlethwaite (Eds.), *International encyclopaedia of education .* Oxford: Pergamon, 1994, 4424–4429.

— Discontinuities and continuities in the experience of learning: an interview study with high-school students in Hong Kong. (Paper presented at the 6th EARLI Conference, Nijmegen, Aug. 1995.)

Marton, F., Beaty, E. and Dall'Alba, G. Conceptions of learning, *International Journal of Educational Research,* 1993, *19,* 277–300.

Marton, F. and Dahlgren, L. O. On non-verbal learning. III. The outcome space of some basic concepts in economics. *Scandinavian Journal of Psychology,* 1976, *17,* 49–55.

Marton, F., Dahlgren, L. O., Svensson, L. and Saljö, R. *Inlarning och omvarldsuppfattning.* (Learning and conceptions of reality.) Stockholm: Almqvist & Wiksell, 1977.

Marton, F. and Säljö, R. On qualitative differences in learning. I. Outcome and process. *British Journal of Educational Psychology,* 1976a, *46,* 4–11.

— On qualitative differences in learning. II. Outcome as a function of the learner's conception of the task. *British Journal of Educational Psychology,* 1976b, *46,* 115–127.

Marton, F. and Svensson, L. Conceptions of research in student learning. *Higher Education,* 1979, *8,* 471–486.

Meyer, J.H.F. Study orchestration: the manifestation, interpretation and consequences of contextualised approaches to studying. *Higher Education*, 1991, *22*, 297–316.

Miller, C. M. L. and Parlett, M. Up to the mark: a study of the examination game. London: SRHE, 1974.

Miller, G. The magical number seven, plus or minus two: some limits on our capacity for processing information. *Psychological Review*, 1956, *63*, 81–96.

Morgan, A.R. What shall we do about independent learning? *Teaching at a Distance*, 1985, *26*, 38–45.

— *Improving your students' learning: reflections on the experience of study.* London: Kogan Page, 1993.

Morgan, A. R., Gibbs, G. and Taylor, E. The work of the Study Methods Group. *Study Methods Group Report No. 1.* Open University, Institute of Educational Technology, 1980, (ERIC Document Reproduction Service No. ED 190561).

Morgan, A. R., Taylor, E. and Gibbs, G. Variations in students' approaches to studying. *British Journal of Educational Technology*, 1982, *13*, 107 – 113.

Neisser, U. *Cognition and reality.* San Francisco: W. H. Freeman, 1976.

Newble, D. I. and Jaeger, K. The effect of assessments and examinations on the learning of medical students. *Medical Education*, 1983, *17*, 25–31.

Newell, A. and Simon, H.A. *Human problem solving.* Englewood Cliffs, NJ: Prentice-Hall, 1972.

Newman, J. H. *On the scope and nature of university education.* London: Dent, 1852.

Newman, S. E. Student vs. instructor design of study method. *Journal of Educational Psychology*, 1957, *48*, 328–333.

Nias, J. (Ed.), *The human nature of learning: selections from the work of M.L.J. Abercrombie.* Buckingham: SRHE & Open University Press, 1993.

Nimmo, D. B. The undergraduate essay: a case of neglect? *Studies in Higher Education*, 1977, *2*, 183–189.

Nisbet, J. D. and Welsh, J. Predicting student performance. *Universities Quarterly*, 1966, *20*, 468–481.

Northedge, A. *The good study guide.* Milton Keynes: Open University Press, 1990.

Olson, D. From utterance to text: the bias of language in speech and writing. *Harvard Educational Review*, 1977, *47*, 257–281.

Parlett, M.R. Motivation and study skills in context. In *Proceedings of the 6th International Conference on Improving University Teaching*, University of Maryland & Ecole Polytechnique de Lausanne, 1980.

Parlett, M. R. and Hamilton, D. *Evaluation as illumination: a new approach to the study of innovatory programs.* Unpublished report, 1972. (Reprinted in D. Hamilton *et al. Beyond the numbers game.* Basingstoke: Macmillan, 1977).

Parlett, M. R. and Simons, H. *Learning from learners.* London: Nuffield Foundation, Group for Research and Innovation in Higher Education, 1977.

Pask, G. Learning strategies and individual competence. *International Journal of Man-machine Studies*, 1972, *4*, 217–253.

— Styles and strategies of learning. *British Journal of Educational Psychology*, 1976, *46*, 4–11.

Pattison, M. Philosophy of Oxford. *Mind*, 1876, *1*, 84–97.

Perkins, D. Technology meets constructivism: do they make a marriage? In T. Duffy and D. Jonassen (Eds.), *Constructivism and the technology of instruction.* Hillsdale, N.J.: Lawrence Erlbaum, 1992, 45–56.

Perkins, D. and Blythe, T. Putting understanding up front. *Educational Leadership,* 1994, *51 (5),* 4–7.

Perry, W. G. *Forms of intellectual and ethical development in the college years: a scheme.* New York: Holt, Rinehart & Winston, 1970.

— Studying and the student. *Higher Education Bulletin,* 1977, *5* , 119–157.

— Cognitive and ethical growth: the making of meaning. In A. Chickering (Ed.), *The modern American college.* San Francisco: Jossey Bass, 1981.

Pervin, L. A. *Personality: theory, assessment, and research.* 2nd edn. New York: Wiley, 1975.

Peters, R. S. *The concept of motivation.* London: Routledge, 1958.

Pirie, D.B. *How to write critical essays.* London and New York: Methuen, 1985.

Pollitt, A.B., De Luca, C., Hutchinson, C. and Entwistle, N.J. *What Makes Exam Questions Difficult ?* Edinburgh: Scottish Academic Press, 1985.

Pond, L. A study of high achieving and low achieving freshmen. *Australian Journal of Higher Education,* 1964, *2,* 73–78.

Popper, K. R. *Objective knowledge. An evolutionary approach.* Oxford: Oxford University Press, 1972.

Powell, J. L. *Selection for university in Scotland.* Edinburgh: SCRE, 1973.

Raaheim, K. The first examinations at university. In K. Raaheim and J. Wankowski, *Helping students to learn at university.* Bergen: Sigma Forlag, 1981, 83–100.

Raaheim, K. and Wankowski, J. *Helping students to learn at university.* Bergen: Sigma Forlag, 1981.

Ramsden, P. Student learning and perceptions of the academic environment. *Higher Education,* 1979, *8,* 411–428.

— *A study of the relationship between student learning and its academic context.* Unpublished Ph.D. thesis, University of Lancaster, 1981.

Ramsden, P. and Entwistle, N. J. Effects of academic departments on students' approaches to studying. *British Journal of Educational Psychology,* 1981, *51,* 368–383.

Reichenbach, H. *Experience and prediction.* Chicago: University of Chicago Press, 1938.

Roe, E. *Assignments.* (Report on a study of assignment work in the university.) Brisbane: University of Queensland, Tertiary Education Institute, 1974.

Rogers, C. R. *Freedom to learn.* Columbus, Ohio: Merrill, 1969.

Rommetveit, R. *On message structure.* London: Wiley, 1974.

— In search of a truly inter-disciplinary semantics. A sermon on hopes of salvation from hereditary sins. In C. Svensson, *Om kommunikation, 1.* (On Communication.) Department of Communication Studies, University of Linkoping, SIC 3. Also in *Journal of Semantics,* 1983, *2,* 1–28.

Roueche, J. E. and Snow, J. J. *Overcoming learning problems: a guide to developmental education in college.* San Francisco: Jossey Bass, 1977.

Rowntree, D. *Assessing students: how shall we know them?* London: Harper & Row, 1977.

Rudduck, J. *Learning through small-group discussion: a study of seminar work in higher education.* Guildford: SRHE, 1978.

Säljö, R. *Qualitative differences in learning as a function of the learner's conception of the task.* Gothenburg: Acta Universitatis Gothoburgensis, 1975.

— *Learning in the learner's perspective. I. Some common-sense conceptions.* Reports from the Department of Education, University of Goteborg, 1979, 76.

— *Learning and understanding: a study of differences in constructing meaning from a text.* Gothenburg: Acta Universitatis Gothoburgensis, 1982.

Samuelson, P. A. *Economics.* 9th edn. Tokyo: McGraw-Hill Kogakusha, 1973.

Scannell, D. P. Prediction of college success from elementary and secondary school performance. *Journal of Educational Psychology,* 1960, *51,* 130–134.

Schon, D. *The reflective practitioner: how professionals think in action.* London: Temple Smith, 1983.

Shaughnessy, M. P. *Errors and expectations: a guide for the teacher of basic writing.* New York: Oxford University Press, 1977.

Sheffield, E. F. *Teaching in the universities: no one way.* Montreal: McGill Queen's University Press, 1974.

Sherman, T. M. Trick or trait: a look at student evaluation of instruction. *Educational Technology,* 1976,*16,* 38–40.

Shore, B. M., Pinker, S. and Bates, M. Research as a model for university teaching. *Higher Education,* 1990, *19,* 21–35.

Shotter, J. Vygotsky: the social negotiation of semiotic mediation. *New Ideas in Psychology,* 1993a, *11,* 1, 61–75.

— Bakhtin and Vygotsky: internalization as a boundary phenomenon. *New Ideas in Psychology,* 1993b, *11,* 3, 379–390.

— *Conversational realities: constructing life through language.* London: SAGE, 1993c.

Singleton, W. T. (Ed.), *The study of real skills: Volume 1. The analysis of practical skills.* Lancaster: MTP Press Ltd., 1978.

Snyder, B. R. *The hidden curriculum.* New York: Knopf, 1971.

Svensson, L. *Study skill and learning.* Gothenburg: Acta Universitatis Gothoburgensis, 1976.

— On qualitative differences in learning: III. Study skill and learning. *British Journal of Educational Psychology,* 1977, *47,* 233–243.

— *The concept of study skill(s).* Reports from the Department of Education, University of Gothenburg, 1981,*1.*

— The conceptualization of cases of physical motion. *European Journal of Psychology of Education,* 1989, *4,* 529–545.

Svensson, L. and Theman, J. *The relationship between categories of description and an interview protocol in a case of phenomenographic research.* Reports from the Department of Education, University of Gothenburg, 1983, 2.

Tait, H. and Entwistle, N.J. Identifying students at risk through ineffective study strategies.
Higher Education, 1996. (in press)

Tate, A. Quality in teaching and the encouragement of enterprise. In R. Ellis (Ed.), *Quality Assurance for University Teaching.* Buckingham: SHRE & Open University Press, 1993, 285–300.

Taylor, E. *Orientations to study: a longitudinal interview investigation of students on two human studies degree courses at Surrey University.* Unpublished Ph.D. thesis, University of Surrey, 1983.

Taylor, E., Morgan, A. R. and Gibbs, G. The orientations of Open University students to their studies. *Teaching at a Distance,* 1981, *20,* 3–12.

— *Students' perceptions of gains from studying D101, the Social Science Foundation Course.* Study Methods Group Report No. 11. Open University, Institute of Educational Technology, 1982, (ERIC Document Reproduction Service No. 221142).

Taylor, J. Analysing novices analysing Prolog: what stories do novices tell themselves about Prolog? *Instructional Science,* 1990, *19,* 283–309.

Thomas, P. R. and Bain, J. D. Contextual dependence of learning approaches: the effects of assessments. *Human Learning,* 1984, *3,* 227–240.

Thorndike, P. W. Cognitive structures in comprehension and memory for narrative discourse. *Cognitive Psychology,* 1977, *9,* 77–110.

Tulving, E . Subjective organization in free recall of "unrelated" words. *Psychological Review,* 1962, *69 ,* 344–354.

— Organized retention and cued recall. *Journal of Experimental Education,* 1968, *37,* 3–13.

Van Rossum, E.J., Diejkers, R. and Hamer, R. Students' learning conceptions and their interpretation of significant educational concepts. *Higher Education,* 1985, *14,* 617–641.

Van Rossum, E. J. and Schenk, S. M. The relationship between learning conception, study strategy and learning outcome. *British Journal of Educational Psychology,* 1984, *54,* 73–83.

Veblen, T. *The higher learning in America.* New York: Hill & Wang, 1957. (Orig.publ. 1918).

Wade, B. *Anxiety and achievement motivation in relation to the cognitive attainment and behaviour of pupils in formal and informal classrooms.* Unpublished Ph. D. thesis, University of Lancaster, 1979.

Walkerdine, V. *The mastery of reason.* London and New York: Routledge, 1988.

Ware, J. E. and Williams, R. G. The Dr Fox effect: a study of lecturer effectiveness and ratings of instruction. *Journal of Medical Education,* 1975, *50,* 149–156.

Watkins, D. Depth of processing and the quality of learning outcomes. *Instructional Science,* 1983, *12,* 49–58.

Wenestam, C.-G. *Qualitative differences in retention.* Gothenburg: Acta Universitatis Gothoburgensis, 1980.

Wenger, E. *Artificial intelligence and tutoring systems.* Los Altos, Ca: Morgan Kaufman Publishers Inc., 1987.

Wertheimer, M. *Productive thinking.* London: Associated Book Publishers, 1959.

Whitehead, A. N. *The aims of education and other essays.* London: Benn, 1950. (Orig. publ. 1932).

Williams, E. Student attitudes towards approaches to learning and assessment. *Assessment and Evaluation in Higher Education,* 1992, *17,* 45–58.

Wimberley, R. C., Faulkner, G. L. and Moxley, R. L. Dimensions of teacher effectiveness. *Teaching Sociology,* 1978, *6 ,* 7–20.

Wood, D., Bruner, J. and Ross, G. The role of tutoring in problem-solving.
  Journal of Child Psychology and Psychiatry, 1976, *17,* 89–100.
Zelby, L. W. Student-faculty evaluation. *Science,* 1974, *183,* 126–127.

Index